CW01455867

Systems Thinking and Modelling – Understanding Change and Complexity

Kambiz E. Maani

Robert Y. Cavana

Prentice Hall

an imprint of **PEARSON EDUCATION**

Dedication

We dedicate this book to our families:

Sholeh, Jason, Neda
and
Carolyn, Emily, Elisabeth and Oliver

Acknowledgements

The run-time version of *ithink*, the tutorial models and the service model on the CD that accompanies this book and the service model in Chapter 6 are the copyright material of:
High Performance Systems, Inc.
45 Lyme Road, Suite 300
Hanover, New Hampshire 03755
USA (http://www.hps-inc.com)

Cartoons by Jock Macneish

Your comments on this book are welcome at
feedback@pearsoned.co.nz

Pearson Education New Zealand Limited
46 Hillside Road, Auckland 10
New Zealand

Associated companies throughout the world

© Pearson Education New Zealand Limited 2000

ISBN 1 877258 00 8

Produced by Pearson Education New Zealand Limited
Printed in Malaysia, KVP

We use **paper from sustainable forestry**

Contents

PART II Case studies

Foreword

Whenever a new text in a young field appears, it is a cause for celebration, for it signals a growth and dynamism rewarding the work of the field's pioneers and current practitioners. When the new text grows from work geographically remote from the original works in the field, even today in this age of instantaneous global communication it suggests a healthy spread of the tools, techniques, and perspectives of the field.

Here, in this work by Kambiz Maani and Bob Cavana, we see the ideas that first shimmered at MIT in Cambridge, Massachusetts, around 1960 now spread halfway around the world, about as geographically distant as one can get from Cambridge. The spread does involve some translation and alteration — in style, examples, and applications with a decided New Zealand flavor. That development is all to the benefit of the system dynamics community and the wider private sector, government, and academic communities we seek to serve and support.

This text is the most recent in a line of works tracing directly back to Jay W. Forrester's classic *Industrial Dynamics* (1961). That book is still remarkable for the completeness of the vision and approach it laid out. In the forty years since its publication, the field has grown too big for its original industrial name and purview — not industrial dynamics, or R&D dynamics, or urban dynamics, or even business dynamics, but 'any system' dynamics. It is worth noting here that the word 'system' in the name causes some confusion in identifying the methodological and philosophical ancestry of the field. The name 'system dynamics' comes not from systems analysis or general systems theory — as the misnomer 'systems dynamics' might suggest. Rather, the four grandparents of the field, as described by Forrester enduringly in 1958, are computer technology, computer simulation, strategic decision making, and feedback thinking. It was a fortuitous mix, for the engineer's notion of feedback connects seamlessly with the circular causal complexity that strategic thinkers encounter. And the interconnected, interdependent worlds that strategy and feedback complexity imply confound mental simulations. Today, every system dynamics application, even the qualitative, reflects this fourfold ancestry: practitioners strive to use computer technology to trace reliably through simulated time the dynamic implications of strategic decisions in complex feedback systems.

Here in these pages the reader will find a very modern overview of the main elements of the system dynamics approach. It is within the last ten years that bridges have been built between system dynamics practitioners, scenario planners, and the soft systems modeling and soft operations research communities. This is one of the first texts to make these bridges available to people new to system dynamics, to enhance the conceptual phases of system dynamics modeling with the incorporation of helpful problem-structuring approaches taken from SSM (soft systems methodology) and soft OR (operations research).

Here also will the reader begin to experience the power of the system dynamicist's continuous perspective on the behavior of complex systems. Although a discrete view, focusing on separate events and decisions, is entirely compatible with the field's characteristic endogenous feedback perspective, the system dynamics approach emphasizes a continuous view. The continuous view strives to look beyond events to see the dynamic patterns underlying them. Moreover, the continuous view focuses not on discrete decisions but on the policy structure underlying decisions. Events and decisions are seen as surface phenomena that ride on an underlying tide of system structure and behavior. It is that underlying tide of policy structure and continuous behavior that is the system dynamicist's focus and the source of strategic policy insights.

There is thus a distancing inherent in the system dynamics approach which the careful reader will observe in these pages — not so close as to be confused by discrete decisions and myriad operational details, but not so far away as to miss the critical elements of policy structure and behavior. Events are deliberately blurred into dynamic behavior. Decisions are deliberately blurred into perceived policy structures. Insights into the connections between system structure and dynamic behavior, which are the goal of the system dynamics approach, come from this particular distance of perspective.

What are the kinds of insights one can hope to find from this perspective? First and foremost, identifying the stock-and-flow/feedback structure at the heart of a complex dynamic problem can reveal the endogenous 'within system' sources causing or exacerbating that problem. Dynamics are, at least partially, a consequence of endogenous system structure. Uncovering those endogenous sources of behavior in any given system is empowering, for it enables actors in the system to focus on effective policies within their own control. Second, the feedback perspective provides powerful understandings of the frequently observed phenomenon that complex systems are 'policy resistant.' Well-intentioned policy initiatives frequently are found to be either ineffective or even counterproductive. The system dynamics approach reveals that complex systems have myriad adjustment mechanisms, usually embedded in negative (balancing) feedback loops that naturally counteract and compensate for well-intentioned policy initiatives, just like a car's cruise control naturally compensates when the car encounters a hill. Policy resistance becomes a natural and expected phenomenon in complex, interdependent systems, a phenomenon that can be understood and dealt with. A third kind of insight is related: We often find in complex social or environmental problems that what works in the short run usually fails to provide long run benefits and may even make things eventually worse. 'Worse before better' behavior can be understood in feedback terms, and those understandings can lead to more robust policies that yield more lasting benefit.

It is these sorts of understandings and insights that one strives for as one approaches a difficult problem using the tools and perspectives presented here. The going will not be easy, partly because the problems we hope to solve are far from easy and for any one of them there are many perspectives to meld, and partly because the arts of building insightful models that really help people think are difficult to acquire and to practice. I commend to you the journey Kambiz Maani and Bob Cavana have begun for you.

George P. Richardson
The Rockefeller College of Public Affairs and Policy
University at Albany - State University of New York
October, 1999

Preface

The objective of this book is to make systems thinking and modelling accessible to people in a range of academic disciplines and from a variety of professional backgrounds. The book aims to demystify systems thinking, explain its concepts, and demonstrate its applications.

Experience has taught us that often 'simple' problems evade simple solutions, that human factors underlie most technical and organisational challenges. We have also found that the idea of 'divide and conquer', as a management and social paradigm, is false and counterproductive. This has led each of us to the field of systems thinking and modelling as a way of understanding and dealing with change and complexity - two interacting and permanent features of the techno-social life as we enter the third millennium. Understanding the dynamics underlying change and complexity is crucial to all decision making.

While several excellent publications exist on the subject, *Systems Thinking and Modelling - Understanding Change and Complexity* provides a unique blend of theory, practice and case studies in one volume.

As a practical learning tool, a CD-ROM containing the simulation models and one of the learning labs outlined in the book is provided. We are grateful to High Performance Systems Inc., USA for permission to reproduce the run-time version of *ithink*, its Tutorial Model and its Service Model. We would also like to thank Dr Paul Martin from Victoria University of Wellington for his assistance in producing the master copy of the CD-ROM.

The book would not be complete if we did not acknowledge those who have contributed to its development in special ways. Foremost are our families, who have provided encouragement and support. The inspiration for the book came from several individuals who have laid the intellectual foundation of the field. First of all is Professor Jay Forrester from the Massachusetts Institute of Technology, USA who established the field of system dynamics. The continuation of this work by Dr Peter Senge and others at MIT's Organisational Learning Centre has made systems thinking a 'household' name in managerial science. Many others have advanced the field in its theoretical foundation, technical rigour and scope of application. Professor Geoff Coyle (formerly with the Universities of Bradford and Cranfield, UK) and Professor George Richardson (State University of New York, Albany, USA), in particular, deserve special mention and thanks in relation to this book.

The contributions of graduate students and professional colleagues are acknowledged where they appear in the text. However, we would like to take this opportunity of thanking them. These people include: Campbell Benton, John Chester, Jeremy Cooper, Philip Davies, David Dinesh, Jeremy Howcroft, Robert Hughes, David Rees, Rachel Robson, David Todd, Keith Wallace, Ken Wilson, and Alex Yeoh. We also acknowledge Professor Rolf Clark (George Washington University, USA) for the use of the beer distribution model. Grants from the University of Auckland's School of Business and its Research Committee, and assistance from the School of Business and Public Management at the Victoria University of Wellington are gratefully acknowledged.

We thank Jock Macneish for his excellent cartoons illustrating our ideas from each chapter and case. Finally, we express our gratitude to our publisher, Bronwen Nicholson, and our editor, Dina Cloete, for their patience and professionalism throughout this project.

Kambiz Maani and Bob Cavana
November, 1999

PART

I

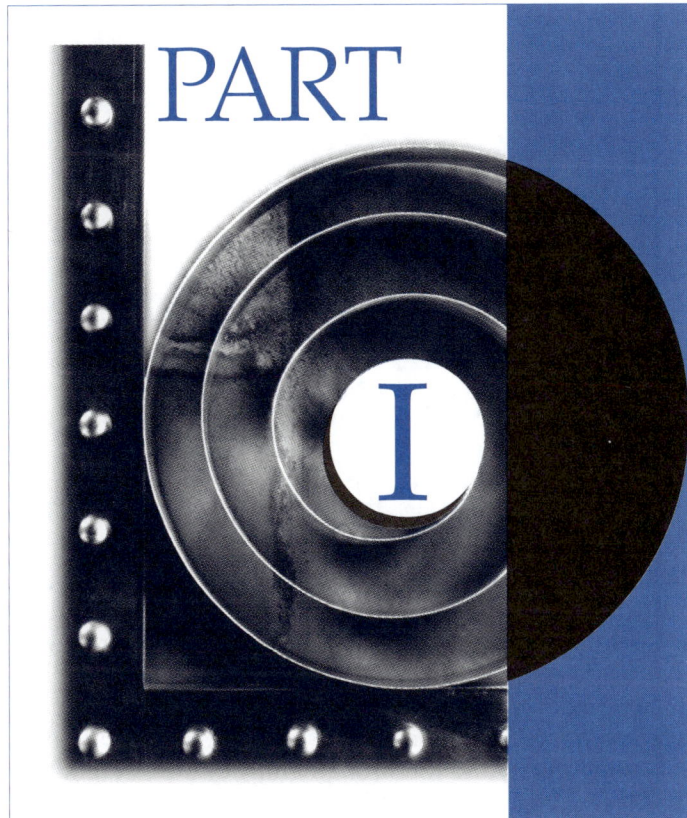

Theory and practice

Chapter **1**

Introducing systems thinking

Why this book?

For well over a century we have subscribed to ways of thinking based on division and analysis. This 'divide and conquer' approach has served us well. It has made efficient mass production of goods and services possible. It has brought a new social and economic order, which has produced unprecedented wealth and a high standard of living in the industrialised world.

Now as we approach the end of the 20th century, this way of thinking is showing its age. The signs of division and fracture are increasing daily, begging for fresh approaches to stubborn and chronic problems. In the business and management field, which is the focus of this book, this way of thinking has resulted in fragmentation of functions and has created complexity and cross-purposes within organisations. Today, the accelerated interconnectedness and interdependence of businesses, organisations, industries, economies, and nations is evident and inevitable. This sense of 'globalisation' has resulted in a growing number of unions, alliances and joint ventures in recent years. At the political and trade levels, we see the emergence of the EU (European Union) and APEC (Asia-Pacific Economic Co-operation) and the strengthening of the UN (United Nations), NATO (North Atlantic Treaty Organisation), and GATT (General Agreement on Tariffs and Trade). At the industry level, we observe the global alliances of airlines such as STAR Alliance and One World as well as numerous partnerships and shared activities. In the health sector, the implementation of integrated care which attempts to link and co-ordinate the disjointed primary, secondary and tertiary segments is becoming an international trend. In business and commerce, the fast emergence of cross-boundary and integrative models of management such as TQM (Total Quality Management), BPR (Business Process Re-engineering), supply-chain management, enterprise resource planning (ERP) and electronic commerce are manifestations of this growing interdependence.

Systems thinking offers a new way of thinking based on the primacy of the 'whole' and of relationships. It deals with hidden complexity, ambiguity and mental models. It provides tools and techniques to unravel complexity and to create lasting interventions for chronic problems. In the words of Peter Senge:

> 'Systems Thinking. A cloud masses, the sky darkens, leaves twist upward, and we know that it will rain. We also know that after the storm, the runoff will feed into groundwater miles away, and the sky will grow by

tomorrow. All these events are distant in time and space, and yet they all connected within the same pattern. Each has an influence on the rest, an influence that is usually hidden from view. You can only understand the system of a rainstorm by contemplating the whole, not any individual part of the pattern.

Business and other human endeavours are also systems. They, too, are bound by invisible fabrics of interrelated actions, which often take years to fully play out their effects on each other. Since we are part of that lacework ourselves, it's doubly hard to see the whole pattern of change. Instead, we tend to focus on snapshots of isolated parts of the system, and wonder why our deepest problems never seem to get solved. Systems thinking is a conceptual framework, a body of knowledge and tools that has been developed over the past fifty years, to make the full patterns clearer, and to help us see how to change them effectively.'

(Senge, 1990: 6–7)

The purpose of this book is to provide a comprehensive treatment of the field of systems management (i.e. systems thinking and modelling). Like computers, which used to be the domain of specialists, 'systems' was considered to be a technical subject requiring proficiency in mathematics and computer modelling. This book intends to demystify systems thinking and make it accessible to a wide range of audiences. It aims to help the reader gain a deeper understanding of the concepts and theories of systems thinking and modelling and enable him/her to apply its tools. To this end, the relevance and application of systems thinking to current business and organisational problems and challenges will be demonstrated throughout the book.

A brief history of management thought

Despite our most impressive advances in sciences and technology, our prevailing worldview and the way we work, at the close of the 20th century, is deeply influenced by thinking that originated in the seventeenth century. This thinking is rooted in the sciences as they were then understood, and in particular in Newtonian physics. Newton viewed the world as a machine that was created to serve its master – God (Ackoff, 1993). The machine metaphor has persisted since then and still occupies our thinking and vocabulary. Expressions like 'a cog in the wheel', 'the wheels of government', 'the machinery of state' (Zohar and Marshal, 1994: 25) are but a few examples. This mechanistic view of the world was developed during the Renaissance and was based on three fundamental beliefs (Ackoff, 1993), namely that:

- complete understanding of the universe is possible;
- the world can be understood through analysis (breaking wholes into pieces), and
- all relationships can be described through a simple cause-and-effect model.

Oxford physicist Danah Zohar says in this regard 'The power and simplicity of Newton's ... mechanical laws of motion, and the force of the new empirical method, drew nearly every influential social, political, and economic thinker of the seventeenth, eighteenth, and nineteenth centuries to use them as model' (Zohar and Marshal, 1994: 24). These laws have served us well in the past and will continue to be valid in the future. They helped humans to walk on the moon and their machines to reach planetary stars. They have made our daily physical chores much simpler and somewhat trivial.

However, beyond scientific and mechanical devices, the philosophical extension of the mechanical laws to social and political domains have outlived their useful purpose. Futurist Alvin Toffler, cited by Zohar, puts this idea succinctly: 'the Age of the Machine is screeching to a halt' (Zohar and Marshal, 1994: 28). Zohar explains the nature and implications of these laws to society: 'The basic building blocks of Newton's physical world were isolated atoms that bounce around in space and collide with one another like billiard balls ... Political thinkers of the time compared these colliding atoms and their interacting forces to the behaviour and interactions of individuals in society as they confront each other in pursuit of their self-interest ... Still today, economists and sociologists who follow "Rational Choice" theory argue that individuals will always choose to act in pursuit of their own self-interest' (Zohar and Marshal, 1994: 25). Zohar demonstrates (Zohar and Marshal, 1994: 26–28) how the atomistic/mechanistic view stresses:

- the hierarchy;
- stability, certainty, and the absolute;
- isolated, separate and interchangeable parts;
- relationships based on conflict and confrontation;
- a single point of view;
- the specialist expertise.

The major industrial breakthroughs that followed the Renaissance and became the bedrock of our modern society, including division of labour, free-market economics, mass production, and scientific management, all embody the above characteristics. The mechanistic view of the enterprise became less tenable in the twentieth century, due in part to the emergence of the corporation and the increasing prominence of human relation issues at work. At the turn of the century, as the need for growth capital increased, major companies became publicly owned (corporatised). The human relation movements that became popular between the 1940s and 1970s, in particular, the hierarchy-of-needs model, the two-factor model, Theory X, Theory Y and Theory Z,[1] made organisations more benevolent.

But it was not until the 1980s that the management practices of the West came under serious scrutiny. This was precipitated by the oil crisis of the early 1970s that awakened the mighty US auto industry to its problems. This crisis shifted the focus of attention from the West to the East – the rising star of Japan. Underlying this shift was a new management paradigm that became known as Total Quality Management (TQM). TQM became the single most important 'thought revolution' (Shiba et al., 1994) of the eighties. The basic tenets of TQM, namely, customer focus, continuous improvement, and total participation, challenged the 'Fordism' and 'Taylorism'[2] concepts of the time. Quality management principles have now permeated the business and management practices of many organisations.

The late 1980s saw another development in management thinking, known as Business Process Re-engineering (BPR). Although not new fundamentally, BPR added another dimension to TQM by focusing the attention on *radical* process-oriented changes in work and organisational design.

In the early 1990s, the work of the Massachusetts Institute of Technology's systems dynamics group became known internationally through the book by Peter Senge, *The Fifth Discipline – The Art and Practice of the Learning Organization*. That made 'learning organisation' the buzzword of the nineties. According to this book, systems thinking is the fifth (and final) discipline or core capability of learning organisations (a learning organisation is an organisation that learns, as an entity). Both Deming[3] and Senge agree that quality management and organisational learning have much in common. Senge identifies three stages or 'waves' of quality management: (1) workers' learning through their own problem solving and decision making; (2) middle management's learning to empower (sharing of power and decision making), and (3) institutionalised learning where learning permeates the entire enterprise and becomes an organisational asset (Senge, 1992). He asserts that Western management is going through the first and second waves of quality movement and that it will be some time before it reaches the third wave.

Summary: Why do we need systems thinking?

- Increasing complexity in our lives.
- Growing interdependence of the world.
- Revolutions in management theories and practice.
- Increasing 'global' consciousness and yet 'local' decision making.
- Increasing recognition of learning as a key organisational capability.

Origins of systems thinking

In the early part of the twentieth century, a new breed of (quantum) physicists began to challenge Newtonian precepts. Foremost amongst these was Werner Heisenberg, whose questioning of the Newtonian 'truth' led to his formulating the 'uncertainty principle' in 1923. Later, in 1947, Norbert Weiner developed cybernetics, which is the science of human–machine relationships. Another milestone in systems science was set by Von Bertalanffy's book *General Systems Theory*, published in 1954. Later, Jay Forrester of the Massachusetts Institute of Technology (MIT), in an 1958 *Harvard Business Review* article, introduced and demonstrated the applications of feedback control theory in simulation models of organisations (Forrester, 1958). Forrester's seminal work marks the birth of the professional field known as 'system dynamics', which is the application of systems theory to economics and organisations. Senge and others, also of MIT, extended the concepts of system dynamics into five disciplines for organisational learning, of which systems thinking is the last discipline.[4]

Another major contributor to the field of system dynamics over the last 30 years has been Geoff Coyle, formerly with the University of Bradford Management Centre. Geoff Coyle received the first lifetime achievement award of the International System Dynamics Society (see Coyle, 1998). For an excellent history of the field of system dynamics, see the recent book by Juan Rego (1999).

In the early 1980s, a different approach to systems thinking was developed in the UK. The hallmark of this approach is known as soft systems methodology (SSM). Developed by Peter Checkland (1981) of the University of Lancaster, this approach, sometimes referred to as the 'British' approach or soft OR (operations research) is distinctly different from the MIT approach, which is based on system dynamics. Later, other methods such as cognitive mapping and strategic options development and analysis (SODA) (Eden, 1989) were introduced. These developments are also considered under the banner of systems thinking.

The approach and methodology used in this book are based on systems thinking and modelling developed at MIT. However, soft systems methodology and cognitive mapping/ SODA are briefly discussed in Chapter 2.

What is a system?

The word *system* evokes different images in our minds: something that is a collection of other things that form a group or entity. Words such as 'whole' and 'interconnected' often come to mind in relation to systems. Daily, we use, influence, and are influenced by systems. These systems can be biological, social, mechanical, and natural. In the morning, our biological clock tells us it is time to get up. A host of mechanical systems – a shower, a toaster, a refrigerator, a garage door opener, a car, a computer – help us to perform routine functions. Our work itself is a system comprising many subsystems: human, technical, legal and social. The weather system influences our daily life plans and lifestyle. Our lifestyles, in turn, influence the weather system.

So, what do these systems have in common? A system is a collection of parts that interact with one another to function as a *whole*. However, a system is more than the sum of its parts – it is the product of their *interactions* (Ackoff, 1993). A system subsumes its parts and can itself be part of a larger system.

Examples of systems

- solar systems
- mechanical systems (thermostat, cruise control, float valve, guided missile, etc.)
- biological systems (digestive system, body temperature, thirst/hunger, balance, etc.)
- ecological systems (population/food, predator/prey, etc.)
- social-economic systems (judicial, political, management, production, inflation, etc.)

(Kauffman, 1980: 11–12)

What is systems thinking?

Systems thinking (ST) is an emerging discipline for understanding complexity and change. This complexity underlies business, economic, scientific and social systems. ST has three dimensions: paradigm, language, and methodology, and these dimensions are described below.

Paradigm

Systems thinking is a way of thinking about and describing dynamic relationships that influence the behaviour of systems. It consists of three types of thinking (Richmond, 1997):

- dynamic thinking – recognising that the world is not static and that things change constantly;
- operational thinking – understanding the 'physics' of operations and how things *really* work;
- closed-loop thinking – recognising that cause and effect are not linear and that often the end (effect) can influence the means (cause).

Language

As a language, systems thinking provides a tool for understanding complexity and dynamic decision making. Systems thinking language (Anderson and Johnson, 1997: 20–21):

- is visual and diagrammatic;
- has a set of precise rules;
- translates perceptions into explicit pictures;
- emphasises closed interdependencies (it is a 'circular' language).

Methodology

A set of modelling and learning technologies is used in systems thinking. The modelling tools can be used to understand the structure of a system, the interconnection between its components, and how changes in any area will affect the whole system and its constituent parts over time. Hence these models can be used to measure and predict the behaviour of systems, as well as to facilitate and accelerate group learning. These tools are the following:

- causal loop diagrams (CLD);
- microworlds (computer simulation);
- stock and flow (S&F) diagrams;
- learning laboratory (LLab).

Systems thinking in daily language

Several expressions that we use in our daily language reflect systems thinking. Some of these are listed below, and many other such expressions and idioms can be found both in English and in other languages and cultures.

- What goes around comes around.
- Cyclical pattern.
- We're in this together.
- Fluctuating pattern.
- Vicious/virtuous cycle.
- Domino effect.
- He/she is on a roll.
- Ripple effect.
- Chronic behaviour.
- Downward/upward spiral.
- Self-fulfilling prophecy.
- Closing the loop.
- Snowballing.

Principles of systems thinking

Systems thinking embodies a number of 'universal' principles that collectively provide a framework for its theory and practice. These principles are explained below (Anderson and Johnson, 1997: 18–20).

1 The Big Picture

This principle teaches the art of seeing the forest *and* the trees (Senge, 1990), namely that whatever situation we are in or whatever problem we are experiencing can be related to a larger system.

2 Short and long term

This principle states that while habitual short-term 'solutions' can impede long-term outcomes, one cannot ignore short-term measures. A child who is facing a dangerous situation must be saved, even if doing so calls for an immediate harsh action that may hurt the child in the process. In this case, the aim is survival. Organisations sometimes face 'life-threatening' situations. A drastic short-term intervention may well be justified in these circumstances. However, if 'crisis management' attitudes and interventions persist and become the normal mode of operation, their side effects can jeopardise the very life of the organisation in the long term. In fact, a significant number of organisations 'die' every year – the average 'life span' of a Western organisation is just over half that of the average human being (De Geus, 1995).

3 Soft indicators

This principle indicates that there is more to a problem than what we can 'see'. The popular performance indicators, including the widely known KPI (key performance indicator) and CSF (critical success factor) and even the balanced score card, can only reveal part of the story. Invariably, a host of other, more subtle, 'invisible', and potentially more powerful factors are at play and these influence the behaviour and performance of organisations. We call these 'soft' measures. They include such things as morale, burnout, commitment, loyalty, confidence, care for customers and learning capacity, and can be regarded as the 'measures' of the *internal* health and vitality of an organisation. They can determine the 'pulse' of the organisation well before the 'hard' performance indicators do.

4 System as a cause

This principle states that we contribute to our own problems not only because of the unintended consequences of our decisions and actions but also because of our mental models (assumptions, beliefs, values, etc.). However, many individuals as well as organisations view themselves as 'victims' rather than the cause of their own problems.

5 Time and space

This principle teaches that cause and effect are often not close in time and space and that time delays and the chain effects of actions often mask the connection between cause and effect. By extension, many of today's problems are related to and often the consequence of yesterday's solutions (Senge, 1990).

6 System versus symptom

This principle states that a problem cannot be solved without understanding the system that generates that problem. This principle also underlies the continuous improvement philosophy of quality management, which holds that root causes of a 'problem' have to be identified (using a cause-and-effect diagram, also known as an Ishikawa or fishbone diagram) before a lasting solution can be found.

7 'And' versus 'or'

This principle states that there are often several causes for a given problem or situation (multiple causality). This is in contrast to the 'single-cause' or 'either-or' thinking that is prevalent in society in general and in management practice in particular.

Linear versus systems thinking

Let's do a simple exercise. Write down your answer to the following question:[5]

What makes organisations successful?

Now examine your answer. *How* did you write your answer? Chances are that you wrote a *list* of items or factors. Surprising? Hardly! This is the way we are conditioned to think. We call this linear thinking. Implicit in linear thinking are the following assumptions:

1 that factors are independent;
2 that causality runs one way (from cause to effect);
3 that factors are equally important.

This highlights the weakness of performance indicators such as critical success factors (CSFs) that implicitly assume the above. By contrast, closed-loop or systems thinking maintains that factors are not independent, and that causality is 'circular' (e.g. if A affects B and C, then it is very likely that B and C affect A as well as each other, and so on). For example, one of the success factors that you listed might well have been 'investment in training'; such a factor will surely affect the organisation's overall capability and, down the line, its financial position. The firm's financial strength will increase its ability to invest in further training, and so on. Over time, this becomes a self-reinforcing process. This means that as a firm invests in training, its performance and financial position will improve – and this increases the likelihood that the firm will invest in yet more training.

The structure of this book

In Chapter 2 we provide an overview of the systems thinking and modelling methodology used in this book. Chapter 3 will introduce causal loop modelling, the conceptual and graphical tool of systems thinking. Chapter 4 will introduce dynamic modelling and its relationships to causal loop modelling. In Chapter 5 we present scenario planning and demonstrate applications of causal loop and dynamic modelling to scenario analysis. Chapter 6 will extend the applications of modelling to learning laboratories and organisational learning. In Chapter 7, we discuss the introduction and implementation of systems thinking in the organisation. In Part II we provide five extensive case studies of systems thinking and modelling to reinforce the concepts and tools presented in Part I.

Notes

1 These models are attributed to Maslow, Herzberg, McGregor, and Ouchi respectively.

2 This refers to Henry Ford's concept of mass production and Frederick Taylor's scientific management.

3 Edward W. Deming, American statistician known as the father of modern quality management.

4 Among the members of the Systems Dynamics Group are Michael Goodman, Jennifer Kemeny, Ernst Diehl, Christian Kampmann, John Sterman, Daniel Kim and Jack Nevison.

5 This exercise is adapted from one presented at a High Performance Systems workshop at Systems in Action Thinking Conference, Boston 1995.

REFERENCES

Anderson, V. and Johnson, L. (1997) *Systems Thinking Basics*. Pegasus Communications, Cambridge, MA.

Checkland, P. (1981) *Systems Thinking, Systems Practice*. John Wiley, Chichester, UK.

Coyle, R.G. (1998) The practice of system dynamics: milestones, lessons and ideas from 30 years' experience. *System Dynamics Review*, 14(4).

De Geus, A. (1995) Systems Thinking in Action Conference, Boston.

Eden, C.L. (1989) Using cognitive mapping for strategic options development and analysis (SODA). In Rosenhead, J.V. (ed.). *Rational Analysis for a Problematic World*. John Wiley, Chichester.

Forrester, J. (1958) Industrial Dynamics – A Major Breakthrough for Decision Makers. *Harvard Business Review*, 36(4): 37–66.

Kauffman, D.L. (1980) *Systems One, An Introduction to Systems Thinking*. (The Innovative Learning Series). Future Systems, Minneapolis, MN.

Rego, J.C. (1999) *System Dynamics: An Ever-Present Vision*. OIKOS, Buenos Aires.

Richmond, B. (1997) The 'Thinking' in Systems Thinking; How can we make it easier to master? *The Systems Thinker*, 8(2), March.

Senge, P.M. (1990) *The Fifth Discipline: The Art and Practice of the Learning Organization*. Doubleday/Currency, New York.

Senge, P. (1992) The Real Message of the Quality Movement: Building Learning Organizations. *Journal of Training and Participation*, March.

Shiba, S., Graham, A. and Walden, D. (1993) *A New American TQM – Four Practical Revolutions in Management*. Productivity Press, Portland, Oregon.

Zohar, D. and Marshal, I. (1994) *The Quantum Society*. Morrow Press, New York.

Chapter **2**

Systems methodology

OVERVIEW

This chapter provides an overview of the field of systems management and its major components. A discussion of the four levels of thinking and their implications for organisations and management is followed by the core of the chapter which introduces the five phases of systems thinking and modelling (ST&M) methodology and their associated steps. These phases are presented as the structured process that forms the foundation of this book. Some general and specific applications of systems thinking are then discussed and hard and soft modelling approaches are compared and contrasted. Finally, two other popular approaches to systems thinking, namely soft systems methodology (SSM) and cognitive mapping and strategic options development and analysis (SODA) are briefly discussed.

Four levels of thinking

Daily, we are exposed to information from a multitude of sources: the news media, newspapers, radio, TV, and the Internet. Generally this kind of information reports events – what happened, where, when, how, who was involved, etc. This is a snapshot view of the world because this level of information is very shallow; the reports only touch the surface of what actually happened. For example, the stock market information that is reported daily gives a snapshot of the day's activities. It tells us whether stocks, on average, went up or down (often the index goes both up and down within one day) and by how much. We also get information on the volume of shares traded, the dollar value of stocks traded (capital turnover) and much more. All of this information is at event level.

" I HAVE A PROBLEM USING HIERARCHICAL MODELS TO UNDERSTAND SYSTEMIC THINKING..."

Sometimes there is commentary about a news item or an issue, and this allows one to look back and examine the trends and patterns of events and data. This provides a richer picture of reality and gives more insight into the 'story'. In the stock market example, this means looking at the trends over past months or years, observing the fluctuations and trying to explain what caused 'pulses' in the system – for example, news of a merger, a quarterly economic report or a political scandal.

However, it is rare to see a study of *how* such trends and patterns relate to and affect *one another*. This represents a much deeper level of thinking that can show how the interplay of different factors brings about the outcomes that we observe. In the stock market example, this would mean trying to relate a host of factors that *systemically* cause the fluctuating patterns. These factors could be economic, social, political or structural. The critical thing at this level of thinking is to understand how these factors interact.

Furthermore, there is yet another, much deeper level of thinking that hardly ever comes to the surface. This represents the 'mental models' of individuals and organisations that influence *why* things should/do or should not/do not work. Mental models are based on the beliefs, values, and assumptions that we (privately) hold, and underlie our reasons for doing things the way we do them. Harvard educationalist Chris Argyris (1990: 25–27) calls these the 'undiscussables'.

The four levels of thinking described above are depicted in Figure 2.1. This figure uses the analogy of an iceberg, where the event level of thinking is represented by the tip and yet most of us are satisfied with this level.

Figure 2.1 Four levels of thinking

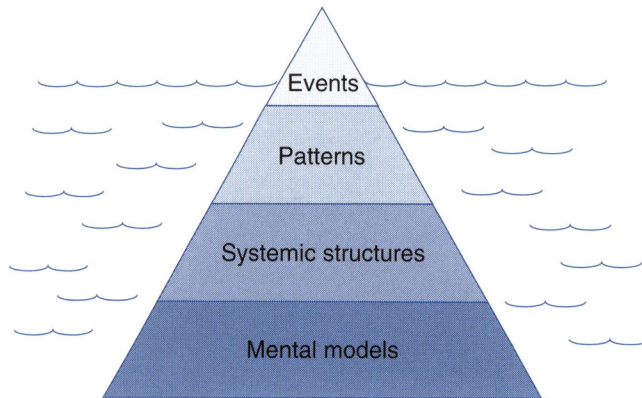

Systems methodology

Systems methodology or the systems approach refers to a set of conceptual and analytical methods used for systems thinking and modelling. The general methodological approach towards systems thinking and modelling used in this book is based on the system dynamics method. The field of system dynamics was developed by Jay Forrester and others at the Massachusetts Institute of Technology in the late 1950s, based on developments following World War II in:

- the theory of information feedback systems;
- the understanding of decision-making processes;
- the use of mathematical models to simulate complex systems; and
- the development of high-speed electronic digital computers as a means of simulating mathematical models.

There are several definitions of the system dynamics methodology, but the one recently provided by Eric Wolstenholme (1997) is most appropriate. Wolstenholme's description of the scope of system dynamics is set out below.

What: A rigorous way to help thinking, visualising, sharing, and communication of the future evolution of complex organisations and issues over time;

Why: for the purpose of solving problems and creating more robust designs, which minimise the likelihood of unpleasant surprises and unintended consequences;

> **How:** by creating operational maps and simulation models which externalise mental models and capture the interrelationships of physical and behavioural processes, organisational boundaries, policies, information feedback and time delays; and by using these architectures to test the holistic outcomes of alternative plans and ideas;
>
> **Within:** a framework which respects and fosters the needs and values of awareness, openness, responsibility and equality of individuals and teams.
>
> (Wolstenholme, 1997)

The development of a systems thinking and modelling (ST&M) intervention involves five major phases:

1 problem structuring;
2 causal loop modelling;
3 dynamic modelling;
4 scenario planning and modelling;
5 implementation and organisational learning (learning lab).

These phases follow a process, each involving a number of steps, as outlined in Table 2.1. However, it must be emphasised that a ST&M intervention does not require all phases to be undertaken, nor does each phase require all the steps listed in Table 2.1, on the following page. Rather, these phases and steps are presented as guidelines, and which phases and steps are included in a particular ST&M intervention depends on the issues or problems that have generated the systems enquiry and the degree of effort that the organisation is prepared to commit to the intervention.

Figure 2.2 shows the progression of the phases. As mentioned earlier, although these phases can be used individually, their cumulative use adds more value and power to the investigation. These phases are described below.

Figure 2.2 Phases of the systems thinking and modelling methodology

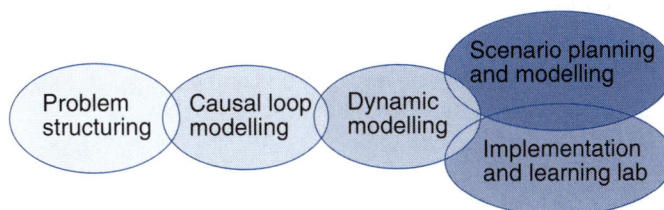

Table 2.1 Systems thinking and modelling process

Phases	Steps
1 Problem structuring	1 Identify problems or issues of concern to management 2 Collect preliminary information and data
2 Causal loop modelling	1 Identify main variables 2 Prepare behaviour over time graphs (reference mode) 3 Develop causal loop diagram (influence diagram) 4 Analyse loop behaviour over time 5 Identify system archetypes 6 Identify key leverage points 7 Develop intervention strategies
3 Dynamic modelling	1 Develop a systems map or rich picture 2 Define variable types and construct stock-flow diagrams 3 Collect detailed information and data 4 Develop a simulation model 5 Simulate steady-state/stability conditions 6 Reproduce reference mode behaviour (base case) 7 Validate the model 8 Perform sensitivity analysis 9 Design and analyse policies 10 Develop and test strategies
4 Scenario planning and modelling	1 Plan general scope of scenarios 2 Identify key drivers of change and keynote uncertainties 3 Construct forced and learning scenarios 4 Simulate scenarios with the model 5 Evaluate robustness of the policies and strategies
5 Implementation and organisational learning	1 Prepare a report and presentation to management team 2 Communicate results and insights of proposed intervention to stakeholders 3 Develop a microworld and learning lab based on the simulation model 4 Use learning lab to examine mental models and facilitate learning in the organisation

Problem structuring

In this phase, the situation or issue at hand is defined and the scope and boundaries of the study are identified. This is the common first step in most problem-solving approaches. The problem structuring phase consists of the following steps.

1 Identification of the problem area or policy issues of concern to management. This step requires that we clearly establish the objectives, taking into account multiple stakeholders and perspectives.

2 Collection of preliminary information and data including media reports, historical and statistical records, policy documents, previous studies, and stakeholder interviews.

Causal loop modelling

During this phase, conceptual models of the problem, known as causal loop diagrams (CLDs) will be created. This is a major component and the most commonly used part of the systems thinking approach. The following steps are used in causal modelling, and these steps are discussed in detail in Chapter 3.

1 Identify main (key) variables.

2 Draw behaviour over time charts (or reference modes) for the main variables.

3 Develop causal loop diagrams (influence diagrams) to illustrate the relationships among the variables.

4 Discuss behaviour over time of the dynamics implied by the causal loop diagrams.

5 Identify system archetypes that would describe high-level causal patterns.

6 Identify key leverage points.

7 Develop intervention strategies.

Dynamic modelling

This phase follows the causal modelling phase. Although it is possible to go into this phase directly after problem structuring, performing the causal modelling phase first will enhance the conceptual rigour and learning power of the systems approach. The completeness and wider insights of systems thinking is generally absent from other simulation modelling approaches, where causal modelling does not play a part. The following steps are generally followed in the dynamic modelling phase. Chapter 4 is devoted to this topic.

1 Develop a high-level map or systems diagram showing the main sectors of a potential simulation model, or a 'rich picture' of the main variables and issues involved in the system of interest.

2 Define variable types (e.g. stocks, flows, converters, etc.) and construct stock flow diagrams for different sectors of the model.

3 Collect detailed, relevant data including media reports, historical and statistical records, policy documents, previous studies, and stakeholder interviews.

4 Construct a computer simulation model based on the causal loop diagrams or stock-flow diagrams. Identify the initial values for the stocks (levels), parameter values for the relationships, and the structural relationships between the variables using constants, graphical relationships and mathematical functions where appropriate. This stage involves using specialised computer packages like STELLA, *ithink*, POWERSIM, DYNAMO, DYSMAP, COSMIC or VENSIM.

5 Simulate the model over time. Select the initial value for the beginning of the simulation run, specify the unit of time for the simulation (e.g. hour, day, week, month, year, etc.). Select the simulation interval (DT) (e.g. 0.25, 0.5, 1.0) and the time horizon for the simulation run (i.e. the length of the simulation). Simulate model stability by generating steady state conditions.

6 Produce graphical and tabular output for the base case of the model. This can be produced using any of the computer packages mentioned above. Compare model behaviour with historical trends or hypothesised reference modes (behaviour over time charts).

7 Verify model equations, parameters and boundaries, and validate the model's behaviour over time. Carefully inspect the graphical and tabular output generated by the model.

8 Perform sensitivity tests to gauge the sensitivity of model parameters and initial values. Identify areas of greatest improvement (key leverage points) in the system.

9 Design and test policies with the model, to address the issues of concern to management and to look for system improvement.

10 Develop and test strategies (i.e. combinations of functional policies, for example operations, marketing, finance, human resources, etc.).

Scenario planning and modelling

In this phase, various policies and strategies are postulated and tested. Here 'policy' refers to changes to a single internal variable such as hiring, quality, or price. Strategy is the combination of a set of polices and as such deals with *internal* or *controllable* changes. When these strategies are tested under varying *external* conditions, this is referred to as scenario modelling. Chapter 5 deals with scenario planning and modelling.

1 Develop general scope, time frame and boundaries of external environment for scenarios. Prepare stories of possible futures or theme scenarios.

2 Identify key drivers of change, uncertainties and factors that could have a significant impact on the decisions, policies and strategies being evaluated. Determine ranges for external parameters and graphs.

3 Construct forced scenarios by placing all the positive outcomes in an optimistic scenario and all the negative scenarios in a pessimistic scenario. Check the forced scenarios for internal consistency. Modify these scenarios as learning scenarios.[1]

4 Simulate the scenarios (either the individual scenarios varying the key uncertainties or the learning scenarios) with the model. Redesign scenarios if necessary.

5 Evaluate the performance of the policies and strategies with the model for each scenario. Assess the performance against a range of relevant performance measures for overall robustness. Select the policies or strategies that meet management's objectives for the investigation.

Implementation and organisational learning

One of the most beneficial and enduring outcomes of systems thinking and modelling is organisational and team learning. Once simulation models have been developed, they can be enhanced by extending them into a microworld. Microworlds (also known as management flight simulators) provide an interactive and user-friendly interface for managers to experiment with the model. The learning laboratory uses microworlds in a structured process, akin to a scientific environment, to test hypotheses and mental models designed to create individual and group learning. Chapter 6 will discuss microworlds and learning labs. The following steps summarise this phase

1 Prepare a report and presentation to the management team and other stakeholders. This should document the background and development of the systems thinking project, the challenges faced and lessons learned.

2 Communicate results and insights of the study and the reasons for the proposed intervention to all stakeholders.

3 Develop a microworld and design a learning lab for the simulation model. This involves adding necessary features (i.e. from computer software) to convert the simulation model into an interactive and user-friendly microworld. Then design a learning lab process for the microworld.

4 Use the learning lab process to diffuse and facilitate learning in the organisation.

Systems thinking applications

Systems thinking has a wide range of general and specific applications. The general applications are:

- design of new systems;
- re-engineering or improvement of existing systems;
- prediction of behaviour of complex systems under varying conditions;
- understanding the interaction of component sub-systems;
- strategy development and testing;
- scenario modelling and testing;
- group and organisational learning.

The specific applications of systems thinking cover both strategic and functional aspects of business and organisations. Some of these are outlined below.

Strategy and policy

Systems thinking is widely used for strategy formulation and testing. This occurs at the level of government and industry (e.g. health care, communication, regulation, etc.) as well as at the organisational level (e.g. marketing, production, human resources, finance and their interfaces). Systems thinking highlights the following areas of strategy, which are often ignored or missed by other methodologies:

- internal contradictions in a strategy;
- hidden strategic opportunities;
- untapped strategic leverages.

Operations and design

Systems thinking also has widespread applications in operations and design. Traditionally, manufacturing systems have been a prominent area of application. Service industries such as health care, communications and logistics are the upcoming areas that readily lend themselves to the application of systems thinking and modelling. Some of the specific applications are:

- new product and service development;
- supply-chain management;
- enterprise resource planning (ERP);
- network design and management.

Functional modelling

In addition to the areas mentioned above, systems thinking methodology can be used to model functional areas such as finance, marketing, information technology and human resource management. In the following chapters we discuss these applications and illustrate how to integrate them using systems models.

Hard and soft modelling

As the terms *model* and *modelling* are used frequently in this book, it is important to clarify their meaning in this context. *Model* is defined as being a representation of the real world. Models can take on different forms, physical, analog, digital (computer), mathematical, and so on. This sense of the word *model* is the more traditional one and is sometimes referred to as quantitative or 'hard'. More recently, the concept of *soft modelling* has been developed by Checkland[2] and others. *Soft modelling* refers to conceptual and contextual approaches that tend to be more realistic, pluralistic and holistic than 'hard' models. Hard and soft models are sometimes referred to as 'quantitative' and 'qualitative', respectively. The differences between the hard and soft approaches are summarised in Table 2.2.

Table 2.2   Hard versus soft approaches

	Hard approaches	Soft approaches
Model definition	A representation of the real world	A way of generating debate and insight about the real world
Problem definition	Clear and single dimensional (single objective)	Ambiguous and multi-dimensional (multiple objectives)
People and organisation	Not taken into account	Are integral parts of the model
Data	Quantitative	Qualitative
Goal	Solution and optimisation	Insight and learning
Outcome	Product or recommendation	Progress through group learning

(Adapted from Pidd, 1996: 121)

The methodologies presented in this book cover both hard and soft approaches, because we regard these approaches as complementary and mutually reinforcing. Systems thinking tends to fall in the category of soft approaches, while dynamic modelling gravitates toward the category of hard modelling.

In the following sections, two other approaches to 'systems thinking' are outlined. These are soft systems methodology and cognitive mapping. While these approaches are most useful in the problem-structuring phase of systems methodology, their potential use is much wider.

Soft systems methodology (SSM)

Another approach to systems thinking, known as soft systems methodology (SSM), originated in the UK (Checkland, 1981). Soft systems methodology is based on the notion that human and organisational factors cannot be separated from problem solving and decision making. Thus SSM takes a systems view of the organisation (Pidd, 1996: 122).

Soft systems methodology consists of seven interrelated stages. These stages are listed below and shown in Figure 2.3 (Pidd, 1996: 132).

1 The problem situation is unstructured.
2 The problem situation is expressed.
3 Root definitions of relevant systems are identified.
4 Conceptual models are developed.

5 The problem situation (stage 2) and the conceptual models (stage 4) are compared.

6 Feasible and desirable changes are considered.

7 Action is taken to improve the problem.

These stages are conceptually similar to the seven-step method or the plan-do-check-act (PDCA) process of quality management (Shiba et al., 1994). The focus of SSM on root definition is also analogous to the PDCA model's root cause analysis (i.e. the cause-and-effect or 'fishbone' diagram). In essence, like quality management methods, SSM provides a powerful learning process for individuals as well as for groups and organisations.

Figure 2.3   Soft systems methodology (adapted from Checkland, 1981)

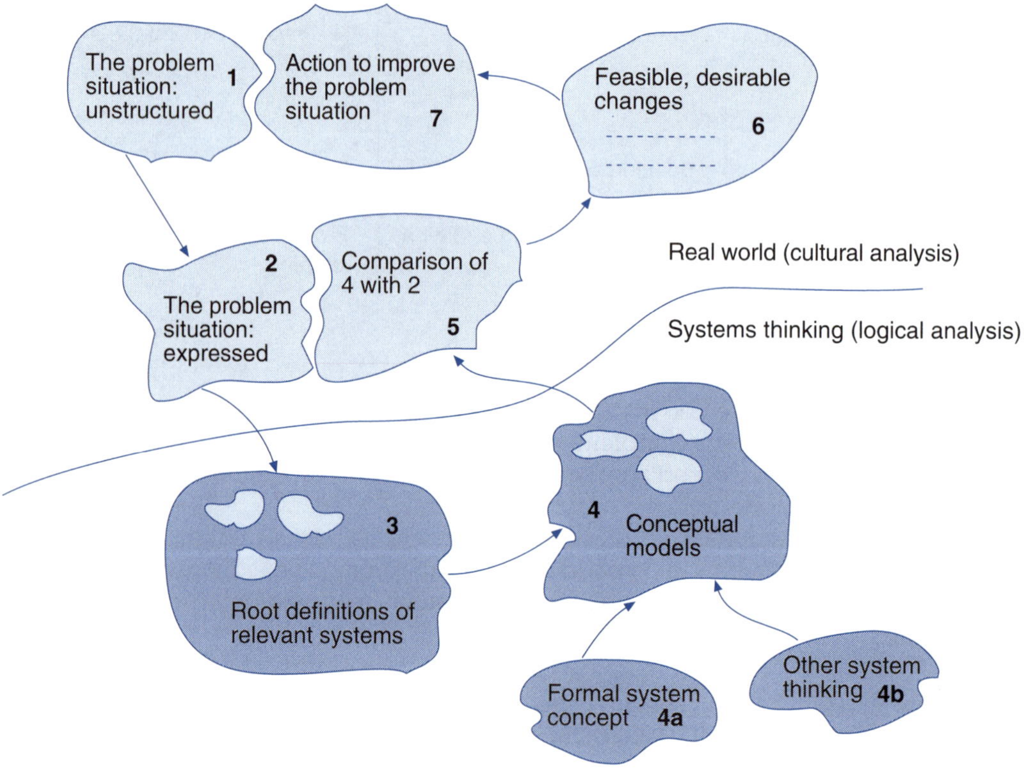

Cognitive mapping and SODA

Cognitive mapping and strategic options development and analysis (SODA) were developed by Eden and his colleagues (Eden, 1989; Eden et al., 1983). This approach focuses on how individuals view their world and how they behave within the organisation (Pidd, 1996: 122), thus it is more individualistic than the SSM approach.

The main premise of Eden's approach is that desirable outcomes are the product of both *content* and *process* (i.e. the end and the means). This means that, in organisations, the effectiveness of policies and strategic plans, for example, depends not only on the plan itself or the apparent results, but also on *how* the plans are arrived at, because this determines people's *commitment* to organisational plans and decisions.

Cognitive maps are tools for thinking and problem solving. They are intended for unravelling mental models and mapping how people think about a certain issue or problem. The main building blocks of cognitive maps are called 'concepts'. The concepts are generated during an interview process using the words used by the interviewee (Pidd, 1996: 152). These concepts or ideas are then linked together by arrows to form a cognitive map, as shown in Figure 2.4.

Figure 2.4   A cognitive map model (Pidd, 1996)

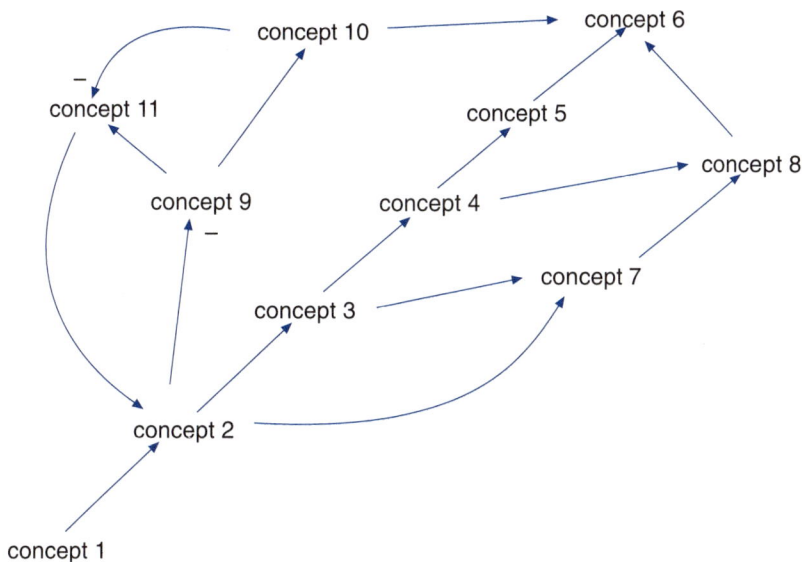

Although cognitive maps and causal loop diagrams – one of the main types of tool in this book – are somewhat similar visually, they are distinctly different both conceptually and methodologically (Richardson, 1999: 448). In the first place, the 'concepts' used in cognitive mapping are phrases that often contain comparative adjectives (e.g. better, bigger, fewer, less). On the other hand, the 'variables' used in causal loops are nouns which have 'quantities' associated with them (e.g. demand, supply, quality, motivation, etc.). In the second place, the linkages in cognitive maps are not 'closed' and hence loops tend not to arise in cognitive maps. In causal loop diagrams however, loops are the mainstay of the method, indicating dynamic and recurring patterns. Causal loop modelling will be covered in detail in Chapter 3.

When more than one individual is involved, the SODA methodology is used to create group commitment, especially with a focus on action. This is based on the premise that in order for people to work as a team and create a shared understanding, it is essential that they should be jointly involved in problem definition and the search for ways in which to solve problems (i.e. strategy formulation). SODA methodology moves people through a process of debate and negotiation towards a joint commitment to action (Pidd, 1996: 157).

While there are differences between SSM and cognitive mapping, 'neither assumes that an organisation is a machine, which grinds on its way regardless of the people who compose it' (Pidd, 1996: 122).

Notes

1   This step is based on the method outlined by P.J.H. Schoemaker (1995).
2   Peter B. Checkland (1981) *Systems Thinking, Systems Practice*. John Wiley.

REFERENCES

Argyris, C. (1990) *Overcoming Organizational Defenses – Facilitating Organizational Learning.* Allyn and Bacon, Boston.

Eden, C.L. (1989) Using cognitive mapping for strategic options development and analysis (SODA). In Rosenhead, J.V. (ed.). *Rational Analysis for a Problematic World*. John Wiley, Chichester.

Eden, C.L., Jones, S. and Sims, D. (1983) *Messing About in Problems*. Pergamon Press, Oxford.

Forrester, J. (1961) *Industrial Dynamics.* MIT Press, Cambridge, MA.

Pidd, M. (1996) *Tools for Thinking, Modelling in Management Science*. Wiley, Chichester.

Richardson, G.P. (1999) Reflections for the future of system dynamics. *Journal of the Operational Research Society, Special Issue: System Dynamics for Policy, Strategy, and Management Education.* 50(4) (April).

Schoemaker, P.J.H. (1995) Scenario planning: a tool for strategic thinking. *Sloan Management Review*, Winter.

Shiba, S., Graham, A. and Walden, D. (1994) *A New American TQM – Four Practical Revolutions in Management.* Productivity Press, Portland, Oregon.

Wolstenholme, E. (1997, 24 October) System dynamics in the elevator (SD1163), e-mail communication, system-dynamics@world.std.com

Chapter 3

Causal loop modelling

'No theory, no learning'

W.E. Deming

OVERVIEW

In this chapter we introduce causal loop modelling and illustrate how it can be used in the areas of operational and strategic decision making. The chapter begins by presenting the basic elements of the causal loop diagrams (CLD), namely variables and links and showing how to construct causal loops from these elements. The two types of feedback process are discussed next, followed by a demonstration of the use of related tools such as behaviour over time (BOT) diagrams and hexagons for developing variables. We then introduce systems archetypes or generic systems structures and use several examples to describe their applications. Finally, we bring these tools and concepts together in a learning activity and a case study of a real organisation, Hanover Insurance.

Causal loop diagrams

Causal loop diagrams provide '... a framework for seeing interrelationships rather than things, for seeing patterns of change rather than static snapshots'.

(Senge, 1990: 68)

A causal loop diagram (CLD) is a tool for revealing the causal relationships among a set of variables (or factors) operating in a system. The basic elements of CLDs are **variables** (factors) and **arrows** (links). A 'variable' is a condition, situation, action, or decision which can influence, and can be influenced by, other variables. A variable can be quantitative (measurable) such as profit, productivity, or absenteeism, or it can be qualitative (soft).

Examples of soft variables are motivation, trust, morale, burnout, reputation and so on. Qualitative variables do not generally lend themselves to direct measurement. One of the strengths of causal loop methodology is its ability to incorporate qualitative variables in the systems thinking approach.

The second element of causal loop diagrams is an arrow, or link. An arrow indicates a causal association between two variables, or a change in the state of these variables. For example, advertising increases demand and a higher price can cause a fall in demand. In general, if variable X directly affects variable Y (or influences, has an impact on, or causes change to, variable Y), then the various relationships of this type can be shown graphically as follows:

Figure 3.1   Causal links between pairs of variables

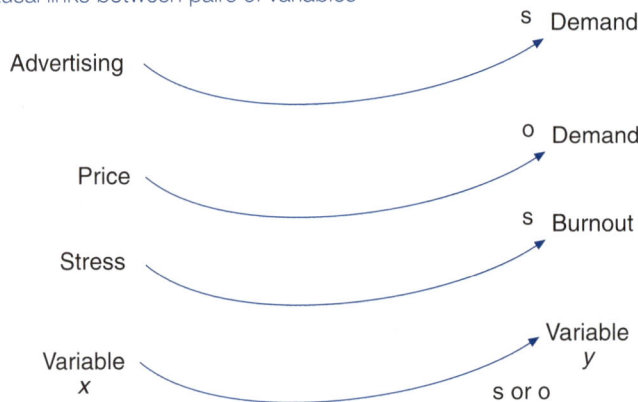

Once we have established that such a causal relationship exists, it is necessary to know *how* the variables are related. In general there are two possibilities:

1 the two variables can move in the **same** (s) direction, or

2 they can move in **opposite** (o) directions.

In other words, if an *increase* (or *decrease*) in variable X at the tail of an arrow causes a corresponding *increase* (or *decrease*) in variable Y at the head of the arrow, then this is a change or movement in the *same* direction (denoted by 's' near the head of arrow). That is, the two variables move up and down together. Examples are changes in advertising and demand, motivation and effort, or stress and burnout, which move in the same direction.

The second possibility is that the two variables move in opposite directions. In this case, an *increase* (*decrease*) in one variable will cause a *decrease* (*increase*) in the other variable. In other words, as one variable moves up, the other will move down and vice versa. This is a change in the *opposite* direction and is denoted by 'o' on the head of arrow – for example, price and demand, or discouragement and performance, generally move in opposite directions.

It is important to note that the direction of relationship between two variables is not always fixed and can change under different assumptions or circumstances or within a different range of the variables. For example, it is generally accepted that, as a result of process improvement, higher quality can lead to lower costs (an opposite change). Yet improving product quality through the use of higher grade components or ingredients will increase cost (change in same direction). Likewise, dieting and weight loss are often

associated: i.e., harder dieting, more weight loss. However, sometimes more intense dieting does not lead to greater weight loss because body metabolism sets a 'limit' to this loss which can then only be increased by exercise.

In some systems thinking literature, causal relationships are indicated by '+' or '-' signs, where '+' means a positive correlation or movement in the same direction, while '-' indicates negative correlation or movement in the opposite direction. These conventions are summarised in Figure 3.2. Since '+' and '-' intuitively (and colloquially) convey the potentially confusing notions of 'more' and 'less', we adopt the 's' and 'o' convention in this book to avoid this misconception.

Figure 3.2 Determining types of causal relationship

If X adds to Y, or if a change in X causes a change in Y in the same direction,

then use 's' or '+'

If X subtracts from Y, or if a change in X causes a change in Y in the opposite direction,

then use 'o' or '-'

(Based on Richardson, 1997: 249)

It should be noted that causal loop diagrams use one symbol for two ideas: an arrow can represent a 'causal influence' and an arrow can represent an addition to or subtraction from an accumulation.

Causal loops

A causal loop is a conceptual tool which reveals a dynamic process in which the chain effect(s) of a cause is/are traced, through a set of related variables, back to the original cause (effect). Once a group of variables has been linked together in a connected path, this forms a causal loop. A 'loop' need not be circular, but it must form a closed path from the starting variable back to itself. Theoretically, any variable can be a starting variable. However, key actions or conditions make the best candidates for starting variables.

Every causal loop tells a story. The story shows how the effects eventually catch up with the cause, or how the end meets the means. The colloquial expression *closing the loop* refers to this process. Figure 3.3 is an example of a causal loop diagram showing the chain effects of quality improvements on a firm's reputation, market share, revenues and profit, which increases the firm's capacity for training and further improvement in quality. Here, the 'lead' or starting variable is *quality* as the loop illustrates the circular chain effect of quality and profitability.

Figure 3.3   Causal loop diagram for quality improvement

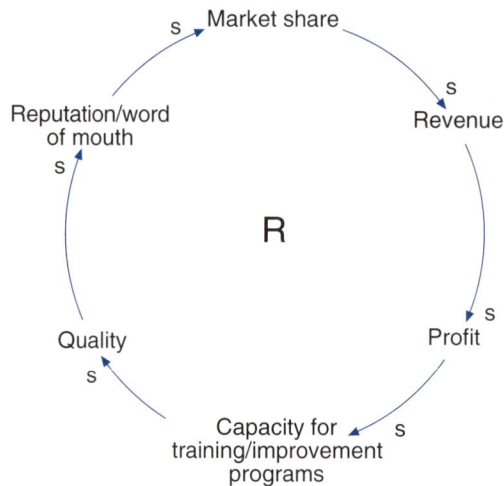

Feedback processes

In general, there are two types of causal loop. These are **R**einforcing (R) or positive feedback, and **B**alancing (B) or negative feedback (also known as counteracting or self-regulating) loops. These represent the generic feedback processes for all causal loops. The origins of these processes can be found in feedback theory, which has been widely used by scientists and engineers for many decades. Feedback processes also abound in nature, in society, and in human-made devices. The human body, for example, contains an amazing array of feedback systems. Our eating mechanisms are far more complex than the most sophisticated guided missile. While eating we can move our head and mouth (the 'target' of the spoon or fork) freely and yet our hands hardly ever miss the target. Far from being a trivial process, our feeding system embodies combinations of hundreds of feedback signals that guide our hand to our mouth with perfect accuracy. Other biological systems and functions such as breathing, sweating, healing, blinking, blood pressure, body temperature, body balance, hunger and sleep are further examples of feedback processes. 'Blood alone contains hundreds of chemicals – oxygen, carbon dioxide, water, salts, sugars, enzymes, fats, minerals, hormones, etc. – each of which is regulated by one or more loops … Other natural and social systems depend on negative feedback just as much for their survival' (Kauffman, 1980: 12).

Household appliances and devices that we use daily possess numerous feedback mechanisms. The timing of a toaster, the temperature of a shower, the stoppage device of a toilet flush, the automatic frequency control on FM radios are but a few examples.

In ecology, the relationships between predator and prey, population and disease, plants and CO_2 balance demonstrate similar feedback cycles (Kauffman, 1980: 11).

Our social systems provide further examples. The reciprocal relationships between crime and punishment, poverty and wealth, education and income, investment and revenue, economic boom and bust, over- and undersupply of graduates, all represent cyclical patterns governed by feedback processes. At the level of the firm, feedback patterns are evident in the ripple effects of management's policies and actions on staff motivation, morale, and the subsequent performance of the firm.

Reinforcing feedback

Reinforcing loops are positive feedback systems. They can represent growing *or* declining actions. Funds in a savings account accumulate interest, which increases the current balance. A larger account balance will, in turn, attract more interest, which will compound into an even greater balance, and so on. This is a reinforcing process with *growing* effect. In contrast, under-investment in a firm's service capacity (e.g. training and quality programmes) will undermine its financial viability, which will reduce its ability to invest, thereby further inhibiting the company's financial position. This is a reinforcing process of *declining* nature. In lay terms, a reinforcing pattern can be either a *vicious* or *virtuous* cycle, depending on the situation and choice of variable names. In general, negative feedback loops 'negate' or dampen change to create stability, while positive or reinforcing loops amplify or add to change. For example, the relationship between birth rate and population is a reinforcing process whereas the death rate and population represent a negative feedback loop. Here 'positive' and 'negative' should not be confused with 'good' and 'bad'. 'Just remember that whether feedback is considered positive or negative depends on what it does to *changes* in the system' (Kauffman, 1980:24). Examples of reinforcing loops are discussed below. (The letter '**R**' inside a loop indicates a reinforcing process.)

• Growing action

Figure 3.4 on the following page illustrates a reinforcing pattern between team building and team spirit. As a group engages in team building, the team spirit (co-operation, communication, and shared goals) improves. When there is a heightened team spirit, members are more likely to engage further in team building. Over time, this results in an increasing growth pattern. One can imagine similar reinforcing patterns between skill and performance, interest and account balance, exercise and health, systems thinking and learning, and so on. Of course, these dynamics create growth to certain points, beyond which growth will be constrained by other forces.

Figure 3.4 Example of a growing action

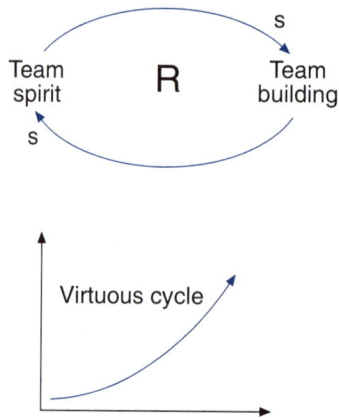

● Declining action

Declining action represents another type of reinforcing process. It is important to remember that in this context, 'decline' refers to a downward process and does not necessarily indicate an adverse phenomenon. For example, manufacturing defects or crime rate could be on the decline and the process could be driven by underlying reinforcing processes such as training or investment in technology.

An example of a declining action is provided in Figure 3.5. In this example, quality is 'trapped' in a vicious cycle, creating a downward spiral.

Figure 3.5 Example of a declining action – downward spiral of quality

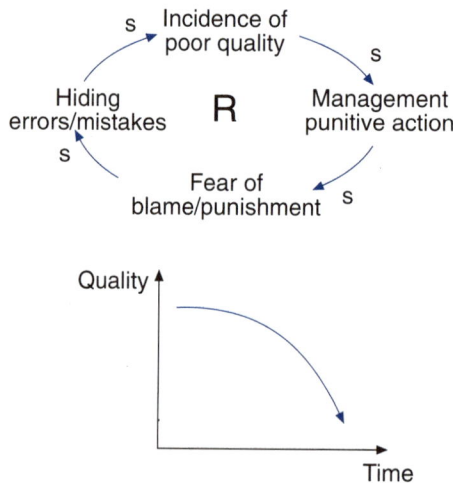

Balancing feedback

Unlike a reinforcing loop, a balancing loop seeks stability or return to control, or aims for a specified target. As mentioned earlier, there are numerous balancing mechanisms all around us: in our bodies, at home, in our workplace, in society and in ecological systems. For example, a budgeting cycle represents a 'return to control' balancing loop while a thermostat provides an example of a goal-seeking process. Balancing loops are also referred to as counteracting or negative feedback loops. (The letter '**B**' inside the loop denotes a balancing loop.)

The following causal loop diagram (Figure 3.6) shows the feedback system of a thermostat. Here the difference between the desired and the actual room temperature creates a gap ('creative tension') which triggers an adjusting action by the thermostat. This action, after some delay, results in a change (increase or decrease) in the actual room temperature, hence reducing the gap. This cycle repeats itself until the gap is closed or the target is reached. The effect of delay in the balancing process is significant. In general, the longer the delay, the larger the oscillations and the longer the time it takes to reach stability.

Figure 3.6   Feedback process of a thermostat

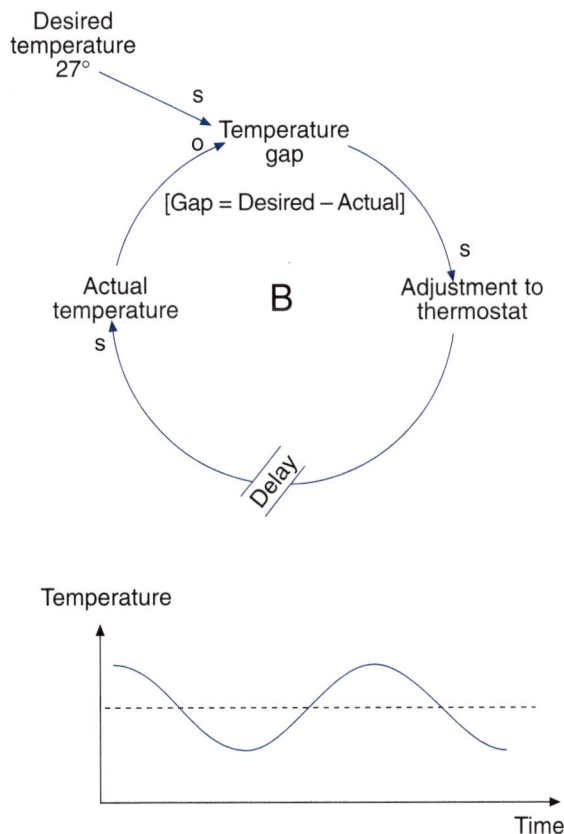

Telling the 'B' from the 'R'

One of the common pitfalls in learning and understanding causal loop modelling is the correct identification of the loop type, as it is not often intuitively apparent which loop is being dealt with. We offer three methods for identifying whether a loop is a balancing or a reinforcing loop.

1 The first method uses logic or intuition to identify the nature of the loop. This method reviews the story to see whether the loop represents a growing or declining action (a reinforcing loop), or a goal-seeking or counteracting process (a balancing loop). For example, in the quality spiral case (Figure 3.5), one can intuitively see that punitive actions by management will have adverse effects on workers and their attitude towards quality, which can only increase the incidence of poor quality, hence *reinforcing* the very actions that precipitated the effect in the first place. In contrast, in the thermostat example, the temperature gap induces an adjusting action in the system, which will seek to reduce the gap. Therefore, this is a goal-seeking balancing action. Using this method inculcates systems thinking ability in the individual. We recommend this as the preferred method because its use will, in time, ensure that systems thinking becomes an intuitive way of thinking for the individual.

2 The second method involves tracing the loop step by step (variable by variable) and recounting the effect of each variable on the following variable until the loop is covered.
  This method follows the following process: start with any variable by stating 'an *increase* in this variable will increase (or decrease) the (level of the) following variable', and so on, until you return to the starting variable. If your tracing ends with the *same* verb, '*increase*' or '*decrease*', that you started with, then you have a reinforcing loop. This is because the phenomenon under study is feeding into itself. If the starting verb is not the same as the ending one, then you have a balancing loop because the end result creates an action opposite to the one with which we started. Alternatively, you can start the trace with the word 'decrease' instead of 'increase'. To sum up, the rule goes as follows: if you end up with the same verb (increase or decrease) as you started with, the loop is reinforcing. Otherwise, i.e. if you finish with the opposite verb to the one with which you started, then the loop is balancing. You can also use pairs of contrasting adjectives, such as 'more' and 'less', or 'higher' and 'lower'.
  Alternatively, you may use a small 'up' or 'down' arrow (↑ or ↓) instead of using words. At the end of the loop, if you finish with the same arrow type (up or down) that you started with, then the loop is reinforcing, otherwise it is balancing. The pairs of relationships in the thermostat model (Figure 3.6) are depicted below, using this technique and assuming an increase in desired temperature.

- Desired temperature $\longrightarrow$ (↑) Temperature gap
- Temperature gap $\longrightarrow$ (↑) Adjustment to thermostat
- Adjustment to thermostat $\xrightarrow{\text{delay}}\!\!\!/\!\!/$ (↑) Actual temperature
- Actual temperature $\longrightarrow$ (↓) Temperature gap

3   The third method is a shortcut developed by Michael Goodman of the Innovations Associates. In this method, you count the number of o's (or '-' signs) in the loop. If this number is zero or an even number, then the loop is reinforcing. If there is an odd number of o's, the loop is balancing. This method should be used mainly as a check in conjunction with other methods and not as the primary technique, as it can slow down the intuitive systems thinking learning process.

System delays

Delays are inherent in most systems. In systems thinking, delay means the time lapse between a cause and its effects. In business systems, delays occur because of information or physical transfers, or are imbedded in business and production processes such as set-up or change-over functions in a production line. However, the most insidious delays are 'strategic' delays. These are the effects of policies or strategies that occur much later than the causing actions and often in unsuspected places. The problem with such delays is that the underlying cause-and-effect relationships are masked over time and space. Some strategic delays have serious and sometimes disastrous consequences. For example, it has been suggested that the seeds of World War II were sown at the end of World War I. How might the leaders of the time have 'seen' this consequence and averted it by systemic thinking?

Other systems delays are not as dramatic as the example above but if ignored could nonetheless be very harmful. Systems thinking acknowledges the existence of such delays and identifies them in the modelling process. In causal loop diagrams, the notation || on the arrow is used to denote delay in the cause-and-effect relationship. In dynamic modelling, discussed in Chapter 4, delay is modelled as a mathematical function. The effect of delays is especially powerful in balancing loops. As was noted in the example of the thermostat, the longer the delay the greater the oscillations and the longer it takes for the system to reach its target or to find stability. Lack of awareness of systems delays causes managers to make erroneous decisions or to intervene unnecessarily and harmfully. This point is amply illustrated in the so-called 'beer game' (Senge, 1990: 27) where retail, wholesale and factory managers in a supply chain create damaging fluctuations in stocks by over- or under-ordering during shipment and production delays. This case is discussed in detail in Part II, Case 4.

Choosing variable names

Choosing variable names for a causal loop model is not an intuitive skill. The correct use of variable names has a significant bearing on the accuracy, ease of construction and validity of a CLD. In some situations, especially when cross-functional members or diverse stakeholders are involved, deciding on a set of common variables that are relevant and important to all parties requires brainstorming, discussion and sometimes compromise. There are a number of techniques that can be used to facilitate this process. These tools are particularly useful in the early conceptualisation stage of modelling. Below, we briefly outline a generic methodology known as 'affinity diagrams' and a tool known as 'hexagons'.

● Affinity diagrams

The affinity diagram method, also known as KJ,[1] is a process of mapping creative group thoughts and ideas. The aim of this process is to allow new thought patterns and breakthroughs to emerge naturally from a large pool of 'raw' ideas. The affinity technique has three main applications:

- formulation of vague problems;
- synthesis of non-numerical data (also called semantic or language data);
- teamwork and consensus building.

There are seven steps in constructing an affinity diagram (Brassard, 1989:20). They are:

1 assemble the right team;
2 phrase issues to be considered;
3 generate and record ideas (each on a separate card);
4 randomly lay out completed cards;
5 sort cards into related groupings;
6 create header (or label) cards for each grouping (cluster);
7 construct the affinity diagram by placing the header and sub-header (on top of the whiteboard or flip chart page) with all the other cards beneath them. This should mean that a column is formed for each cluster or grouping.

   Each of the header (or label) cards generated in Step 6 can be condensed into a single noun or short phrase and be used as a variable in a causal loop diagram.

● Hexagons

The hexagons (Hodgson, 1994) process is conceptually similar to the affinity diagram method. Instead of cards, the hexagon technique uses hexagon-shaped labels, which make it convenient to form clusters of ideas. The hexagon process is also further simplified since causal loops can be generated directly from the 'cluster' labels. This process is outlined below (Kreutzer, 1995):

1 generate a hexagon for each issue, problem or challenge;
2 group the hexagons into 'similar' clusters;
3 identify a small number of variables for each cluster;
4 use arrows to connect related pairs of variables (this provides a first cut or initial CLD);
5 refine the CLD and identify reinforcing and balancing loops.

The use of hexagons by a group to generate variables is illustrated in Part II, Case 3.

Tips on choosing variable names

- Use nouns rather than verbs/participles for variable names. For example, use 'production' rather than 'producing'.
- Do not include adjectives or descriptors such as 'increased', 'decreased', 'more', 'less', 'lower', and 'higher' in variable names.
- Do not use a variable name more than once in any loop.
- Use the positive sense of a variable. For example, use 'encouragement', not 'discouragement'; 'investment' rather than 'divestment'.

Pitfalls in interpreting causal loop diagrams

Sometimes one can run into 'logical' pitfalls when interpreting causal loop diagrams. We will use the simple population dynamics model shown in Figure 3.7 to illustrate this point (Vennix, 1996:66).

Figure 3.7   Pitfalls of interpreting causal loop diagrams

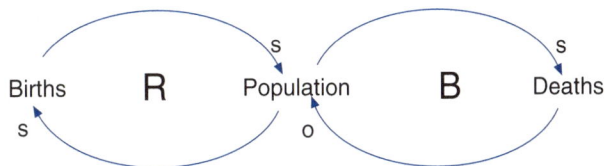

Assuming momentarily that the death rate is zero (or less than the birth rate), the reinforcing loop indicates that *more* births will increase population. However, if we reverse the sentence by starting with *'less* (or decreasing) births', we see that the logic does not hold any more, since less births will still *increase* the population. Some system dynamics experts view this as a weakness of causal loop models (Vennix, 1996).

Also Richardson (1997) sees this type of problem as a weakness of the 's' and 'o' notation in word-and-arrow diagrams (as compared with the more traditional '+' and '-' notation). However, we suggest that this problem can be overcome by using the alternative definition of 's' and 'o' outlined on page 27. For example, the 's' on the link between Births and Population in Figure 3.7, also means that Births 'add to' Population (even if Births are decreasing compared with a previous time period). Similarly, the 'o' on the link between Deaths and Population also means Deaths 'subtract from' Population. Knowing when to use the appropriate definition for 's' and 'o', depends on an understanding of the stocks and flows within the system. This is covered on pages 62–64 in Chapter 4.

Behaviour over time (BOT)

One of the tools of systems thinking is behaviour over time (BOT), which is also referred to as 'reference mode behaviour'. BOT shows the pattern of a variable over an extended period, typically several months to several years. This pattern can indicate the variations and trends in the variable of interest – for example growth, decline, oscillations or a combination thereof. In BOT graphs, the horizontal axis represents time and the vertical axis represents the performance measure of interest. The important elements of BOT are the overall directions and variations, not the numerical value of the variable. Therefore, BOT graphs are usually drawn in a 'rough' sense without exact numerical values attached. Therefore, several variables can be shown on the same diagram, as demonstrated in the BOT in Figure 3.8.

Figure 3.8   Behaviour over time examples

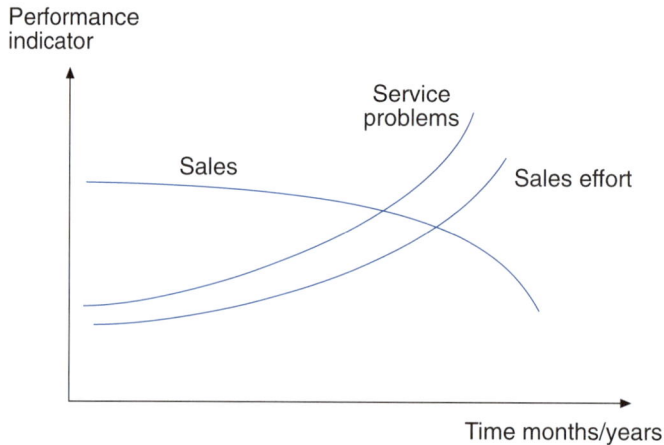

BOTs can provide significant insights into underlying dynamics present in a system. For example, in Figure 3.8, the pattern of sales is stable for a considerable period before it 'suddenly' begins to drop. This information by itself cannot reveal the full story. In fact, looking at a single picture or trend can be misleading, as the underlying or influential variables can often not be 'seen' easily. However, taking the pattern of service problems into consideration can shed additional light here. As we can see, service problems and a corresponding increase in sales efforts started long before sales began to decline. But why was this pattern allowed to continue for a long period by management without any intervention? In reality, in most organisations these patterns are 'seen' only by people responsible for the individual functions, and therefore their interdependencies are not recognised.

This brings to mind W. Edward Deming's famous statement that everyone doing his (or her) best is not good enough! Examining the sales effort BOT is a useful thing to do in this case, as an increase in sales effort is an indication of growing customer resistance or tighter competition, or both. In practice, the patterns of service problems and sales effort individually and collectively can provide timely signals for management that could make it possible to foresee and avert the downturn in sales.

Leverage versus solution

Unlike that of most management science methodologies, the focus in systems thinking is not on 'solving' problems. Problem solving methods assume that the problem is well defined and well understood, and that an 'optimal' solution can be found. This implies that the 'problem' can be neatly isolated from its environment and external factors. As a result, conventional problem solving does not explicitly consider the *context* of the problem. Systems thinking, in contrast, acknowledges the *messiness* of the world and views a problem in the context of its environment. This is one reason why qualitative variables play an important role in systems thinking, as these variables represent conditions or phenomena that cannot be measured or accounted for in strictly quantitative approaches.

Leverage

In systems thinking, *leverage* refers to actions or interventions that can have a lasting impact on the system in terms of reversing a trend or breaking a vicious cycle. This has much deeper implications than merely finding a solution to a problem, as leverage often requires fundamental and long-term changes to the system, as opposed to removing the symptoms of a problem. In health care, for example, we can attempt to 'solve' the surgical waiting list in public hospitals by applying the sophisticated queuing theory and creating computer models to minimise waiting times. However, a key cause of a growing waiting list could be rooted, partly, in the lack of co-operation and co-ordination amongst health providers, which leads to poor capacity management and resource utilisation across the system. The latter requires systemic thinking and consideration of multifaceted structural changes. Systems thinking and modelling make it easier to see these leverage points in order to create relevant intervention strategies. Cases 1 to 3 in Part II describe in detail the process of causal loop modelling in the context of different policy issues and demonstrate the use of leverage points in creating intervention strategies. Table 3.1 summarises the differences between solution and leverage.

Table 3.1   Solution vs leverage

Solution	Leverage
short term	long term
local	global
optimal	fundamental
neat	realistic
content	content and context
symptom	cause

Systems archetypes[2]

'… reveal an elegant simplicity underlying the complexity of management issues … [they] recondition our perceptions, so as to be more able to *see* structures at play and to see the leverage in those structures.'

(Senge, 1990: 94–95)

Systems archetypes are generic systems models or templates that represent a wide range of situations. Systems archetypes provide a high-level map of dynamic processes. Using the analogy of language to illustrate systems thinking, we can say that while *variables* are 'words' (building blocks) and pairs of variables (and the connecting arrows) are sentences, causal loops are stories, and *systems archetypes* are common phrases.

Systems archetypes have been developed by the System Dynamics Group at MIT. There are eight systems archetypes that are commonly used, and we refer to these archetypes by the names used by their originators.

Fixes that fail

'Today's problems come from yesterday's "solutions".'

(Senge, 1990: 57)

The 'fixes-that-fail' archetype represents situations in which unintended and often harmful consequences follow well-intentioned actions. Often, these side effects undermine the impact of the intervention and the system reverts to its original conditions after some delay. A generic fixes that fail archetype and its BOT are shown in Figure 3.9.

Figure 3.9   Fixes that fail archetype

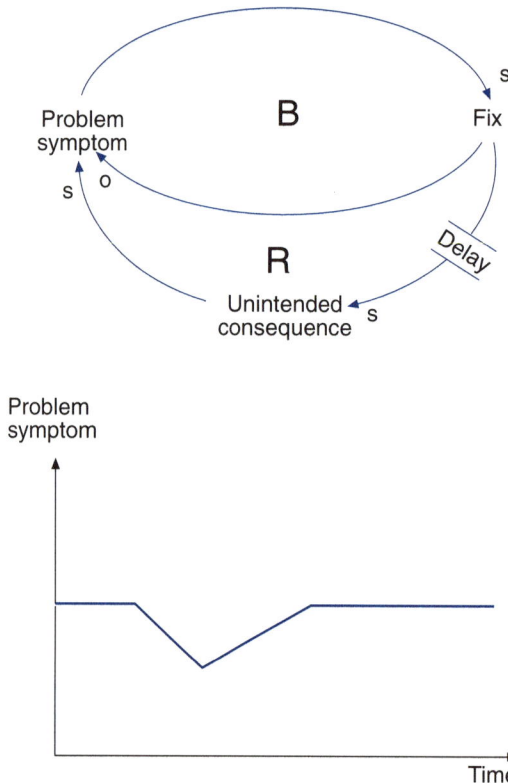

In the fixes-that-fail archetype, the story goes like this: a problem symptom manifests itself and demands attention from the authority in charge (e.g. the manager, the parent, or the government). The response is usually a quick-fix or a short-term solution. The result is that the problem symptom is temporarily removed – leading to a sense of relief – only to appear again and often with greater intensity.

Why are quick-fix actions so predominant and so popular? There are two obvious reasons: they are faster and *initially* they are less costly. Unfortunately, such solutions often have undesirable consequences in the long term. An example is the practice of expediting customer orders. In response to customer complaints regarding late deliveries, managers often expedite late orders by interrupting other customers' orders. This will provide relief for the manager for the moment, as the problem has temporarily been 'solved'. However, the unintended consequences, namely production disruptions and delays to other customers' orders, exacerbate the original problem and result in growing customer dissatisfaction – a reinforcing pattern – as shown in Figure 3.10.

Figure 3.10   Unintended consequences of expediting

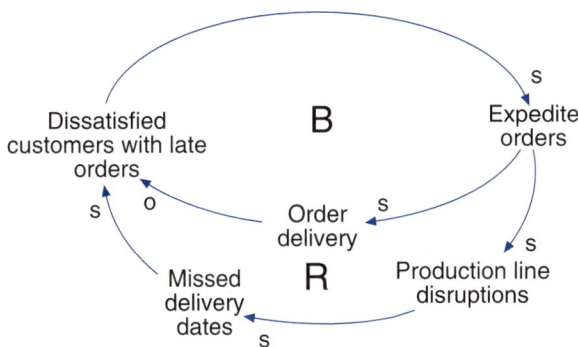

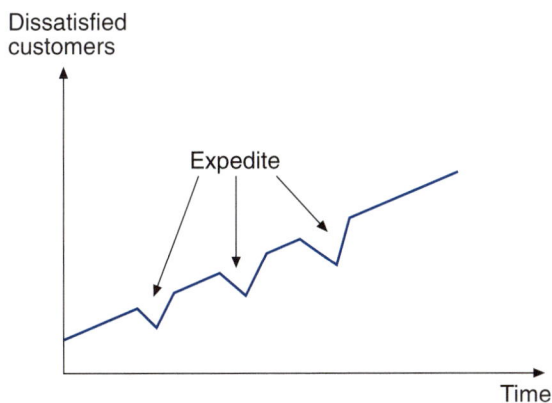

A more serious example of this archetype can be found in the so-called Y2K (Year 2000) bug. Back in the 1970s and early 1980s, system programmers found a short-sighted solution to the problem of insufficient computer memory, by setting aside only two digits to represent the year – for example '99' for 1999. The 'Y2K bug' is expected to rear its head as computer clocks all over the world 'tick' over to '2000'. It is possible – some say probable – that the mathematics of program coding will 'go haywire', causing unpredictable malfunctions and chaos in every area of life, from grocery shopping and banking to air travel. Considering the potential economic and social costs should this happen, this could by far become the most costly and far-reaching industrial 'accident' in history.[3]

Shifting the burden

The 'shifting-the-burden' archetype represents a prevalent mentality and a common pattern of behaviour which people adopt in their roles as individuals, parents, workers, managers, politicians, etc. It represents a human tendency to deal with the easy, the obvious and the urgent before one is forced into dealing with the difficult, the ambiguous, and the important. 'Procrastination' is one term used to describe this behaviour; that is, putting off difficult decisions or actions, probably in the hope that they will go away. Using mind-numbing substances such as alcohol and drugs to relieve personal difficulties or depression is another example of 'shifting-the-burden' behaviour.

Figure 3.11   Shifting the burden archetype and BOTs

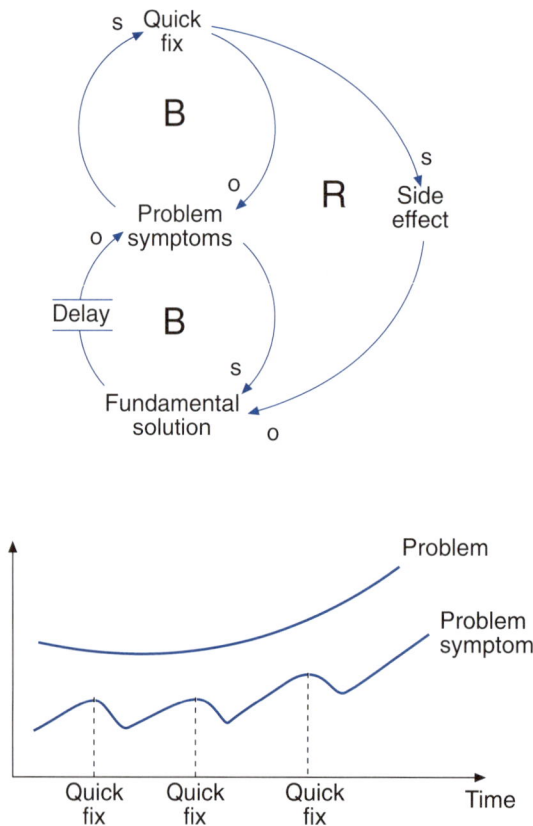

A generic shifting the burden archetype is shown in Figure 3.11. As in the case of the fixes that fail archetype, a problem symptom manifests itself and demands attention. Again, a common tendency is to apply a quick fix to get rid of the problem. This is shown by the top balancing loop in the figure. The quick fix usually works and that is why it can be so harmful in the long run: the apparent 'success' of the quick fix encourages and reinforces such short-term behaviour, which then becomes addictive. That is, it becomes more difficult to tackle fundamental issues and hence 'quick fix seeking' becomes an addictive behaviour. This is shown by the reinforcing loop in Figure 3.11. This loop begins with a quick fix which creates the side effect and delays the achievement of a fundamental solution. In turn, the delay exacerbates problem symptoms and increases the need for further quick fixes, resulting in a reinforcing (vicious) cycle.

This archetype has also been referred to as the 'Helen Keller archetype' (Kim, 1995). Can you see the relationship? At the age of two Helen Keller lost her sight and hearing and was therefore also unable to speak. In her early years, her parents gave her all the attention and love that is expected of a 'good' parent by doing everything possible for her. For years there was no progress in Helen's condition; she remained completely dependent. Then Helen's parents hired a nanny and teacher, Anne Sullivan, to look after her. The nanny, unlike the parents, began to teach Helen to do things for herself, and also to speak and read – an extremely challenging and tedious task. Slowly, Helen responded and gradually she became an independent person. She went on to complete a university degree at Radcliffe, with honours. What is the moral of the story? Can you relate it to the shifting the burden archetype? Figure 3.12 shows the 'Helen Keller archetype'. This archetype represents Helen's growing inability and dependence on her parents before the cycle was broken by Anne Sullivan's intervention.

Figure 3.12   The 'Helen Keller' archetype

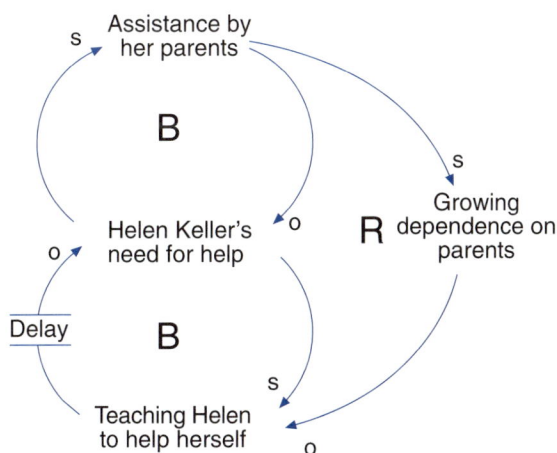

We can also see this pattern of behaviour in workplaces, in the relationship between workers (i.e. Helen) and managers (i.e. the parents). The side effects of such a relationship are growing dependence on the manager and a delay in training and empowerment of the workers.

◆ Limits to success (growth)

This archetype consists of a reinforcing and balancing loop, as illustrated in Figure 3.13. The reinforcing loop symbolises the desirable effect of motivation and hard work on one's performance which, in turn, further motivates one toward an even greater exertion, and so on. The balancing loop, on the other hand, acknowledges the fact that there are 'other' (limiting) forces such as fatigue and burnout that, if unchecked, can slow and even reverse the prospects of success. This same pattern can be observed in fluctuating company or stock market performance or personal fortunes; the rise and fall of civilisations; population growth, and numerous other phenomena.

The key leverage point is to recognise this pattern and find ways to remove or relax the constraints that limit progress. To return to a previous example, it is a well-known fact that dieting will result in weight loss. But as dieting is intensified, the body's ability to lose weight decreases. This is because of 'limits' in body metabolism that reduce calorie burn rate. If this continues beyond a certain point, repeated periods of dieting will actually result in weight *gain* – the opposite of the desired outcome! How can one break this cycle? In the dieting example, the leverage lies in increasing body metabolism through exercise.

Figure 3.13 Limits to success archetype

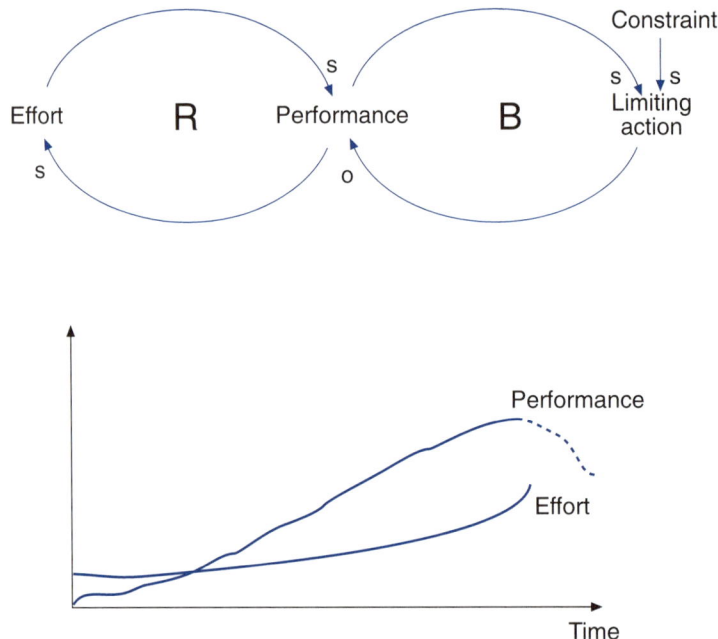

A compelling example of the 'limit-to-success' archetype is the story of People Express Airline. Founded in 1980, People Express, a new airline, became the fastest growing company in the history of the industry. The company was founded by Don Burr, a visionary manager with inspirational leadership skills and a cadre of motivated and well-trained staff. The phenomenal success of the airline was, however, due largely to rock-bottom fares that the company was able to offer because of its 'no frill' services. Despite this fairy-tale beginning and substantial growth in its first few years, the airline went on to become grounded (bankrupt) within six years of its takeoff. The causal loop diagram in Figure 3.14, representing a limit to success archetype, shows the dynamics that brought People Express down.

Figure 3.14   People Express story

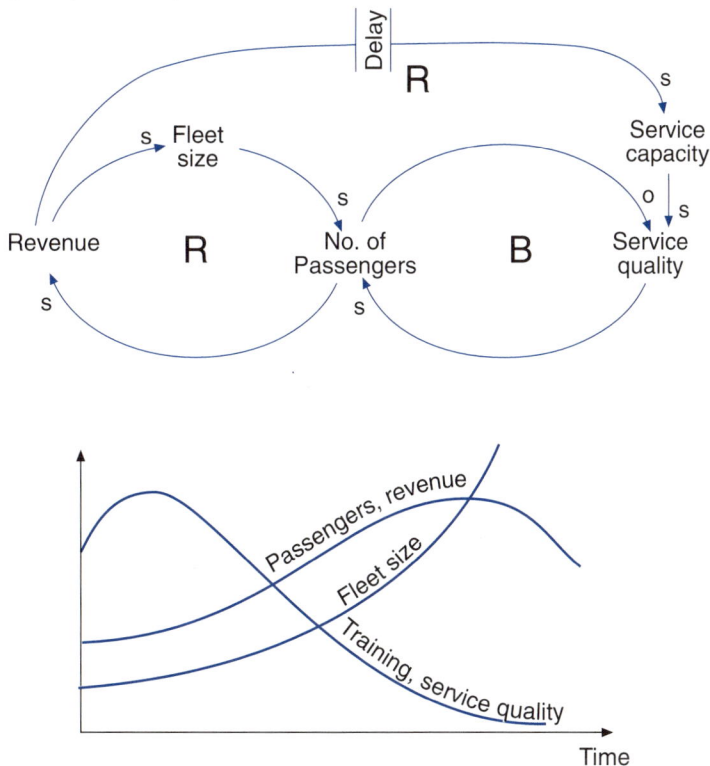

Tragedy of the commons

This archetype reveals that 'common-sense' behaviour can lead to destructive consequences over time. Hardin coined the phrase 'tragedy of the commons' to describe a pattern of behaviour in which a common resource is over-exploited (Hardin, 1968). A desirable activity or situation is the object of an ever-increasing demand, which could lead to undesirable and sometimes disastrous outcomes for all concerned. The activity or situation or item could be a natural resource, an attractive city, a good investment, a popular profession, etc. The environment provides us with telling stories in this regard: excessive and unregulated use (i.e. abuse) of natural resources by one generation can leave the next generation deprived of such resources. Water and air pollution, global warming, ozone layer depletion, and rain forest destruction are but a few examples. Figure 3.15 shows the generic tragedy of the commons archetype.

Figure 3.15 The tragedy of the commons archetype

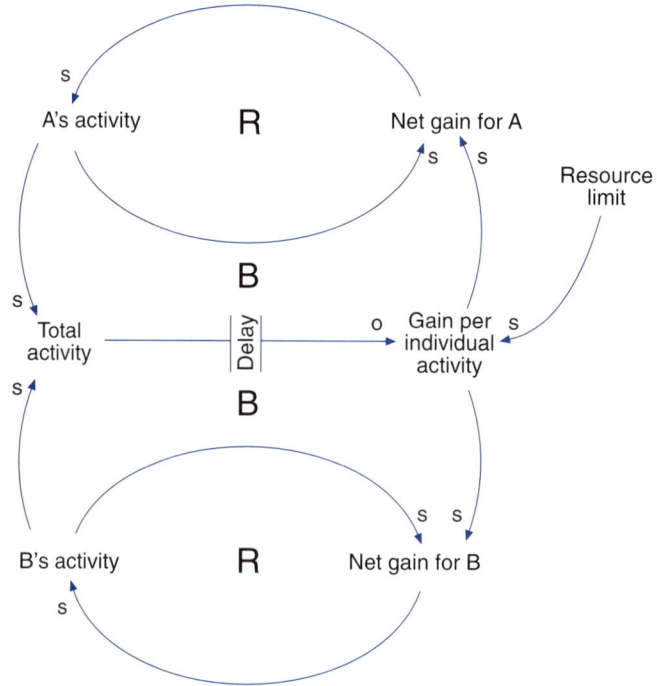

Figure 3.16 Traffic growth dynamics

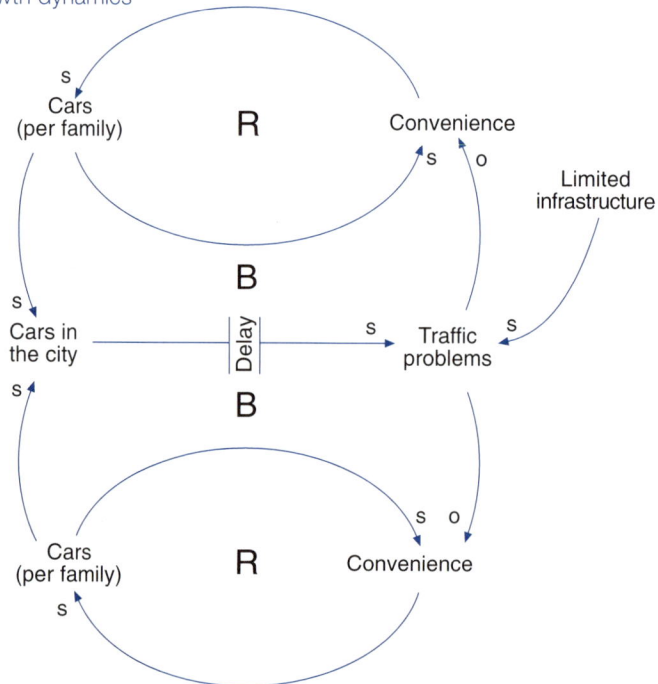

An example closer to home is shown in Figure 3.16. Here, the use of personal cars brings more convenience to an individual or family. Naturally, since everyone wants to maximise convenience, more cars are acquired. Before long, this will increase the number of cars in the street, the neighbourhood and the city. As infrastructures (i.e. roads and public transport) are limited and do not expand as rapidly as the increase in car numbers (or perhaps do not expand at all), the large number of cars will soon become an inconvenience for all. Many of the world's large cities have experienced such a 'tragedy of the commons' archetype, where their attractiveness has become their enemy.

Eaves provides an example of the tragedy of the commons archetype in information systems development in terms of trade-offs between productivity (i.e. rapid systems development) and quality: 'The cyclical and probably universal patterns of periods of high productivity with low quality are interspersed with other periods of the reverse. Some of the periods of high productivity will result in systems that simply do not work. The frequency of failure is not trivial. Estimates of the proportions of such failures of major projects range from a minimum of 25% to a maximum of 82% of dollar investment in the US federal public service' (Eaves, 1992: 2). This phenomenon is illustrated in Figure 3.17.

Figure 3.17 Productivity and quality in systems development

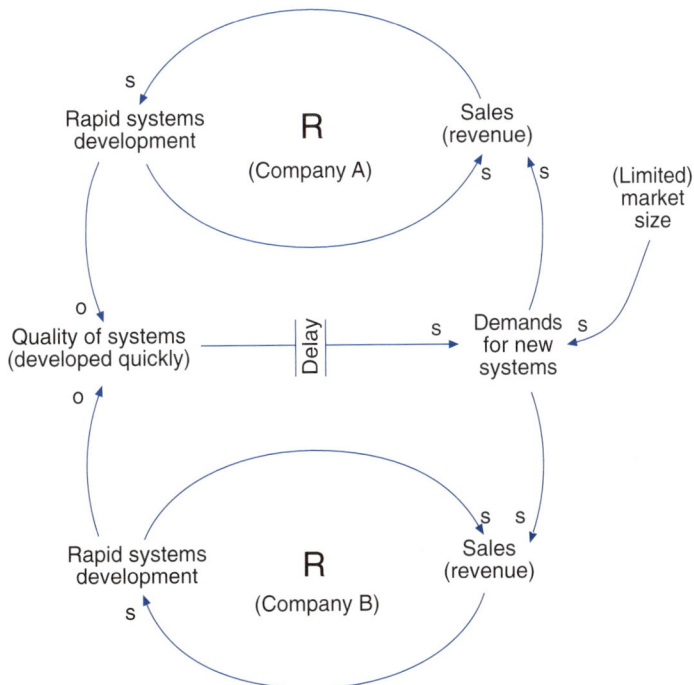

Learning activity

Dynamics of price wars[4]

Price wars are a reality of today's competitive business environment. Often well-established companies find themselves threatened by new players who aggressively undercut prices to gain market share. This is particularly challenging for niche market players who differentiate themselves on quality and service and can therefore command higher prices. Below is the story of one such company.

Corporate Couriers has operated in the parcel and package delivery market for over three decades. Its scrupulous management and customer-focused philosophy have earned it a reputation for quality unrivalled in the market place. In the last few years, however, an increasing number of new and aggressive companies have flooded the courier market with cheaper and 'cut-throat' rates. This has brought mounting pressure to bear on Corporate Couriers by its long-standing customers, who want it to lower its rates and to match competitor's prices. Some competitors, however, bid for contracts at prices well below their cost. This has put Corporate's management in a very difficult position. If it cuts its prices, it would lose the ability to maintain its high service level. This means it would have to reduce or downgrade its rigorous staff training programme and customer service personnel. It also means that the company will be less likely to invest in a new database and bar-code technology. If, on the other hand, it does not bid for low-price contracts, it runs the risk of losing market visibility and some of its major clients. Corporate's management hopes that if it decides to engage in price war, this would be for a short time only until the competitors with weaker financial resources retreat or withdraw from the market. The following graphs (BOTs) depict the probable effect of a price war on Corporate Couriers' financial position.

- ### Questions
- Construct a CLD that shows the key dynamics at play here.
- Do you see any systems archetypes?
- What strategy would you recommend?

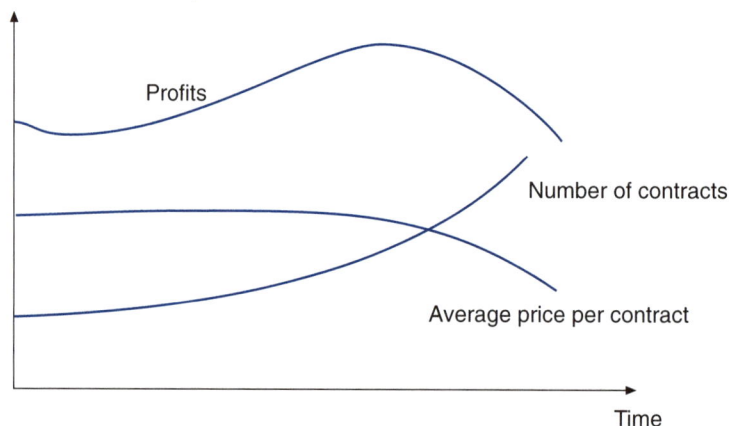

Discussion

As the above BOT graphs suggest, Corporate's profit would drop as the average price per contract declines over time. This could force the company to accept a greater number of low-priced contracts. The continuous upward and downward trends of these graphs suggest the presence of reinforcing loops. In particular, two reinforcing loops that can explain the above dynamics can be envisaged. First, the competitive pressure could result in a price war. This will lead to lower average prices, which will increase the percentage of low-priced contracts and will reduce the overall profit. The second reinforcing loop results from the weaker financial position that could ensue from the price war. One of the critical effects of a price war is the impact on service quality, which could result from reduced training efforts and other quality programmes. Lower service quality weakens companies' negotiating ability, and will amplify the pressure to accept lower-priced contracts which will put further pressure on profits and exacerbate competitive pressure. These reinforcing loops are shown in Figure 3.18.

Figure 3.18   Dynamics of the price war

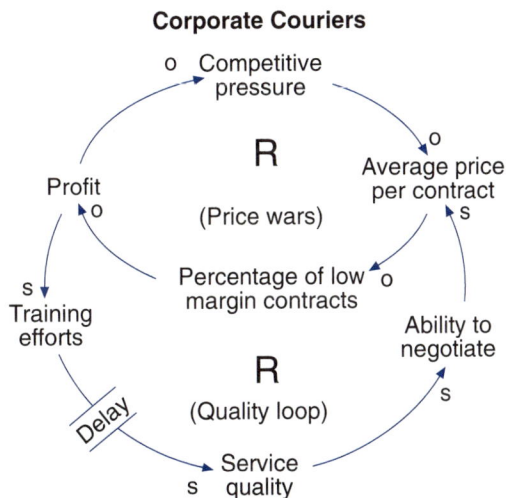

The CLD in Figure 3.18 suggests that once the company is engaged in a price war, it would be very difficult to retreat from it. In the meantime, the damage to the company's market position and its strategic direction could force the company out of business. It is instructive to examine the probable effect of a price war on new competitors with a weaker financial position than Corporate Couriers. This can be shown by the following 'limit to success' archetype. The archetype indicates the vulnerability of weaker competitors who are engaged in the price war. As operating costs tend to remain constant (or even go higher), the price war will result in lower profit margins. This will put pressure on the service quality of companies involved and make them more vulnerable, thus forcing them to accept further contracts at lower prices – which amplifies the price war.

Figure 3.19 Competitor's limit to success

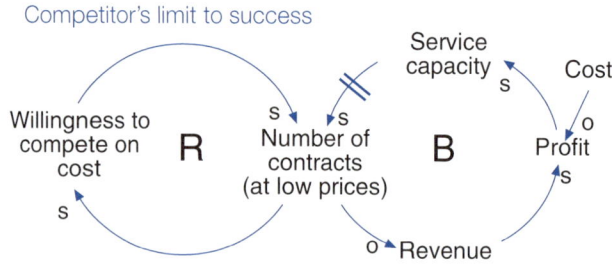

Figure 3.19 and the discussion above demonstrate the pitfalls of continued price wars when the company is operating in a niche market and differentiating on quality and service. However, some niche companies deal with persistent competitive prices by setting up a 'parallel' company that differentiates on cost and volume and competes in the 'low end' of the market. However, this approach is a strategic decision and not an option for a temporary wait-and-see tactic.

Case

Hanover Insurance Company[5]

This case tells the story of Hanover, an insurance company based on the east coast of the USA. Hanover was founded in 1852. In the late 1960s it was at the bottom of the industry, but by the mid-1980s, Hanover had emerged as an industry leader. During this period it grew 50% faster than the rest of the industry.

The insurance business is a large sector in the US, accounting for about 2.5% of the GNP. Starting in the early 1980s, the US insurance industry began to experience significant changes. Automobile insurance premiums, for instance, doubled from 1983 to 1988. At the same time, the average size of insurance court claims increased fivefold.

What caused the insurance 'crisis' of the eighties? Most companies believed that greedy lawyers, biased juries and dishonest policy holders were responsible for the skyrocketing insurance cost. Hanover, however, decided that blaming outside forces prevented the company from finding its own weaknesses and hence being able to improve the company. As a result, it began to look inwards. Hanover decided to start with claims management, as claims operation was responsible for more than 67% of total company expenses. With the rapid growth of the company, it had experienced more claims and also more complex claims, requiring litigation and subrogation (third-party claims).

In order to reduce costs and at the same time maintain customer satisfaction, management set a number of objectives, as follows:

- prompt settlement time;
- higher client satisfaction;
- reduced settlement cost;
- increased productivity.

Management had also developed a number of performance indicators to keep track of the company's progress. However, despite their best intentions and efforts, the problems persisted. In fact, the harder they tried, the worse the problems became.

Frustrated by its lack of success, the management team sought the help of the MIT System Dynamics Group. The team met regularly with the System Dynamics Group for several months and looked at problems more fundamentally. Management soon realised that they had treated many of their problems as *disjoint* and had created *separate solutions* for them.

Using systems thinking tools, facilitated by the System Dynamics Group, the Hanover management team was able to transform the disjoint problems into systems models. Later, a 'microworld' and an associated 'learning laboratory' were developed to transmit the learning to the entire company.

In using the systems methodology, it became clear that management had implicitly adopted two responses (unstated strategies) to relieve the chronic time pressures of the claims department. While these responses were not in the form of written policies, they were nevertheless understood by the staff as the operating norm of the company. The two responses were:

1 work faster: spend less time per claim;

2 work harder: work longer hours, take fewer and shorter breaks, etc.

Over time, these responses had produced the desired effects but had also caused serious unintended consequences. The unintended consequences were, however, masked by long time delays and hidden cause-and-effect relationships. In this section we examine these responses and their effects on the organisation. First, we describe each effect individually and then we combine them into an overall CLD. The first effect, or the 'productivity' loop, is shown in Figure 3.20(a).

Figure 3.20(a)   The productivity loop

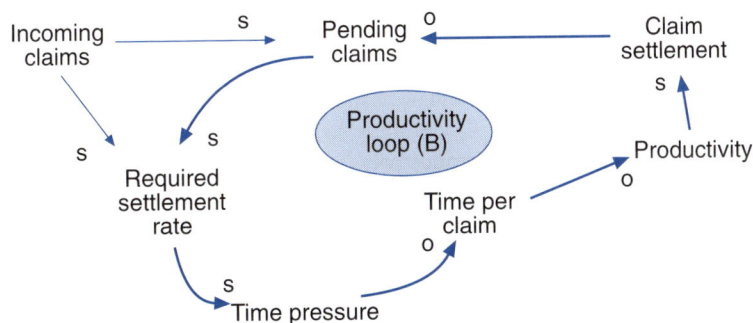

The productivity loop goes like this: as the influx of incoming claims increases, the employees feel greater time pressure. This causes the assessors (also called adjusters – people who investigate and settle claims) to spend *less* time on each claim. This results in *higher* productivity that, in turn, will increase the number of claims settled and hence *reduce* pending claims. This will ease pressure on the required settlement rate. As we started with a *higher* required settlement rate and ended with a *reduced* settlement rate, this is a balancing (counteracting) loop. This can be verified by the three (odd number) 'o' signs in this loop.

The increased time pressure also increases the required work intensity, and hence leads to greater productivity. This is another balancing (relieving) effect shown as the work week loop in Figure 3.20(b).

Figure 3.20(b)   The work week loop

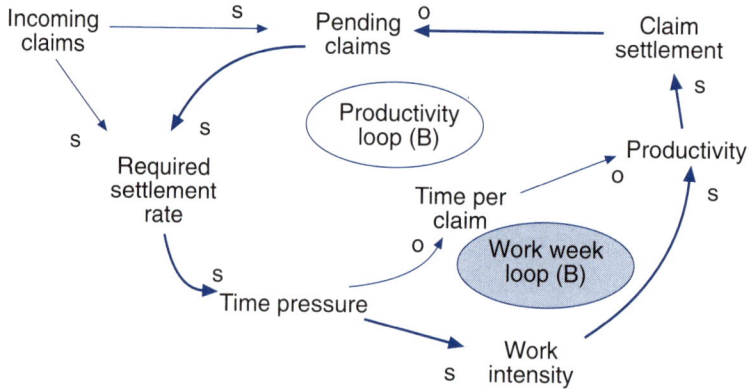

Increasing work intensity means working longer hours, taking shorter and fewer breaks, etc. If this persists, it will soon lead to staff fatigue, burnout and poor health, which has an adverse effect on productivity. This reinforcing vicious cycle is shown in Figure 3.20(c). Note that this loop is the outer 'circle', starting with pending claims to burnout and back to pending claims.

Figure 3.20(c)   The burnout loop

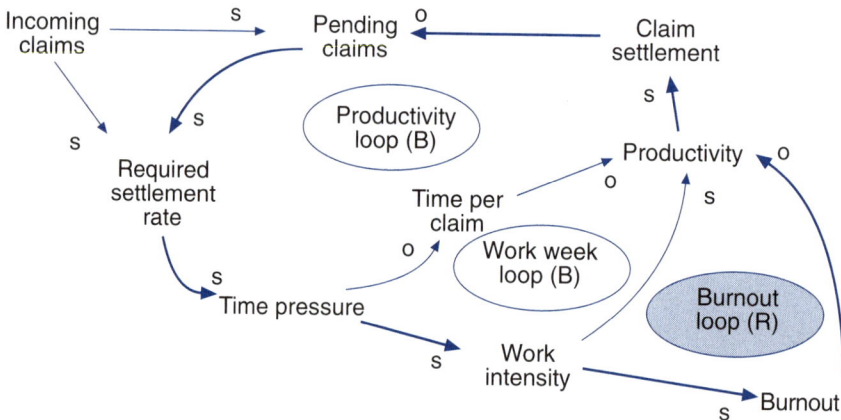

Persistent burnout increases staff turnover, which has a negative impact on assessing resources (capacity). This, in turn, reduces time available and causes even greater time pressure. This effect is shown as the turnover loop in Figure 3.20(d).

Figure 3.20(d) The turnover loop

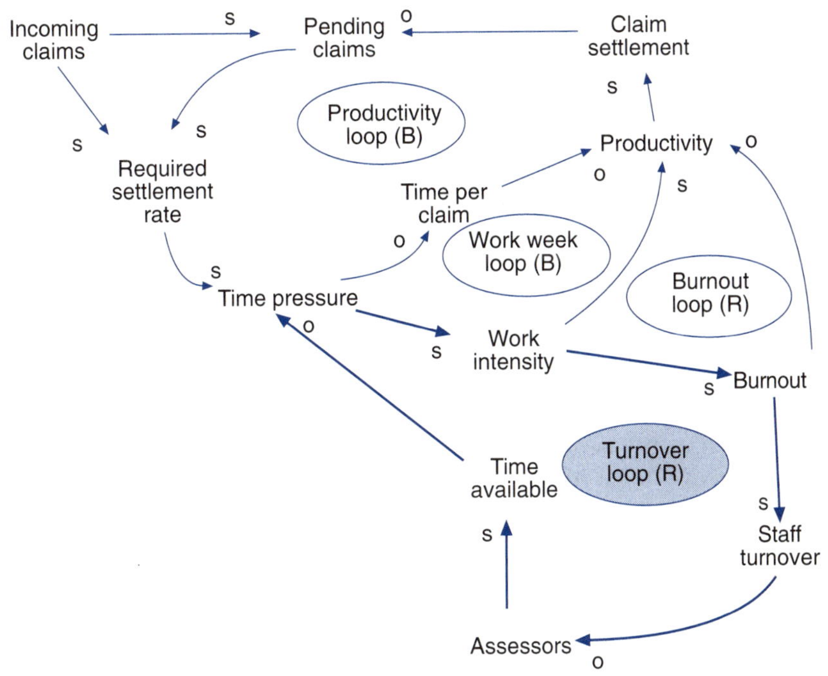

Figure 3.20(e) The settlement cost loop

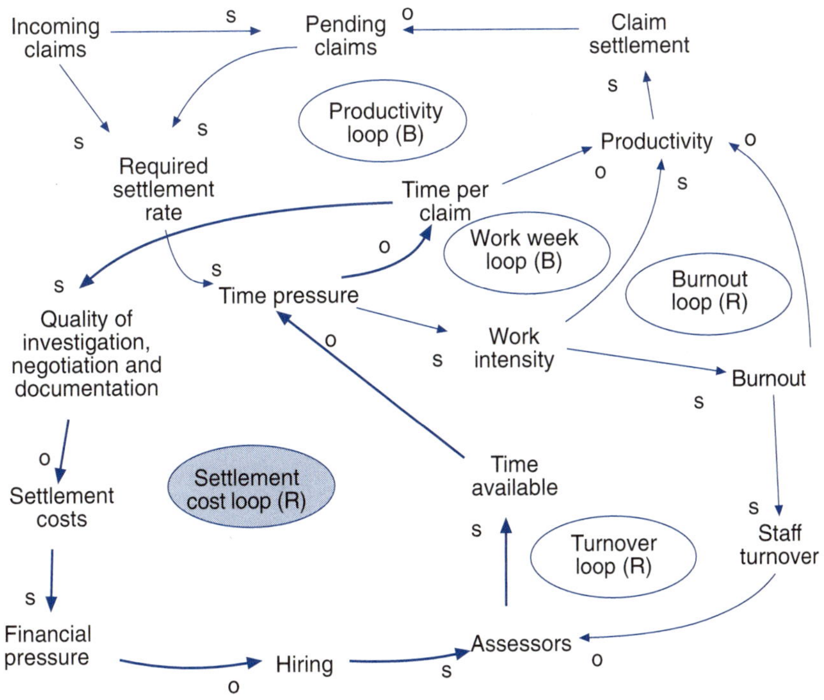

In addition to the productivity-related effects, increased time pressure has a significant but *invisible* effect on quality. This is because, as time pressure increases, assessors tend to spend less time per claim. This means inadequate investigation, poor documentation, and spending less time with customers – therefore not developing a rapport with them. This generally results in higher settlement costs because assessors tend to overcompensate the customers to make up for their own inadequate investigation and delayed actions. In other words, they give the claimants the benefit of the doubt – a 'safe' strategy to keep the customers happy and avoid the possibility of complaints and perhaps even litigation.

Surprisingly, this strategy has often yielded the reverse outcome. Often, the customers who have been overcompensated feel that they could have asked for more! This leaves them with a sense of suspicion about the insurance company and an overall feeling of dissatisfaction: a case of a 'fixes that fail' archetype.

Higher settlement costs increase the financial pressure on the company and make the recruiting of new staff less likely, thus exacerbating the time pressure even further. This effect is shown as the settlement cost reinforcing loop in Figure 3.20(e) on the previous page (starting with time pressure, moving to time per claim, to quality of investigation, and back to time pressure).

Figure 3.20(f)   The capacity loop

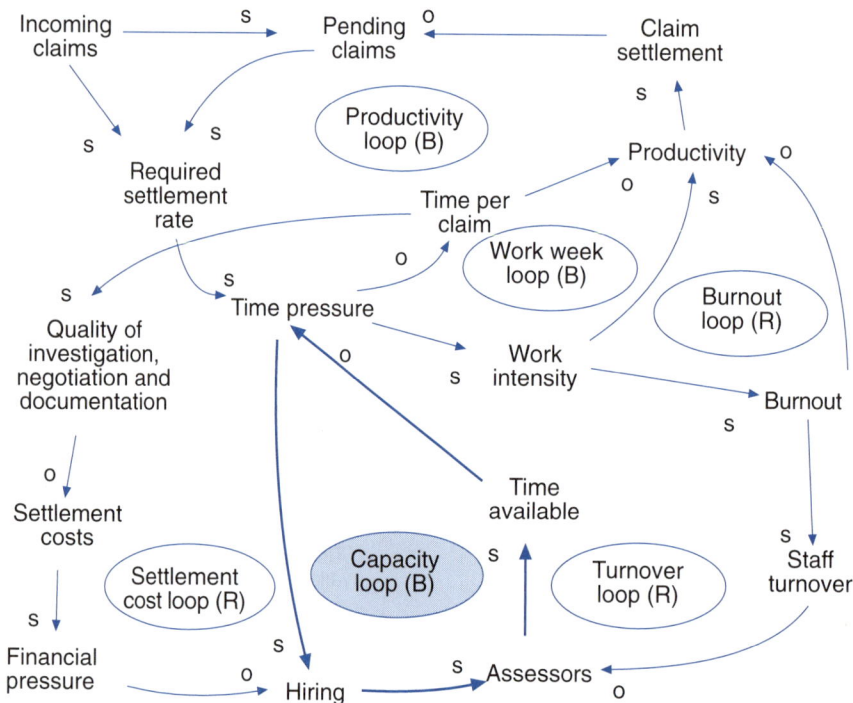

The actions and their associated effects discussed so far represent short-term fixes and their unintended consequences: that is, 'fixes that fail' archetypes. In contrast, the fundamental strategies for dealing with increasing workload are:

1 to improve/re-engineer processes;

2 to add capacity;

3 to do both.

In this case, Hanover Insurance, having carried out process improvements, had only one option left: to increase assessing capacity by hiring new assessors. In the insurance industry, this is the most expensive and hard-to-train staff resource and yet hiring new assessors was the only viable long-term solution to increase capacity. Ironically, Hanover had the highest ratio of assessors per claim at the time – it was the industry benchmark for this activity. However, this exercise suggested a need for even greater assessing capacity at a time when the firm and the entire industry were under intense pressure to cut costs.

Ultimately, Hanover management took the brave action of adding more assessing resources despite their industry lead and the financial pressure they were under; a powerful example of commitment to 'best practice' philosophy. This 'fundamental solution' is shown as the capacity loop in the overall causal loop diagram in Figure 3.20(f).

Learning summary

The Hanover case highlights the strategic 'blind spots' from which organisations often suffer and the pitfalls that organisations frequently fall into. Prior to undertaking this exercise, Hanover management believed that external causes were responsible for the multitude of problems that beset their firm. The systems thinking and modelling showed that the established management practices contributed to and even worsened the very problems that they set out to solve. To transmit the learning of this exercise to the whole organisation, a computer simulation model (microworld) was created. This microworld and the associated learning laboratory was extensively used by Hanover staff to learn the dynamics of claims operations and to experiment with various assumptions and hypotheses (scenario planning). Additionally, the simulation model allowed the staff to quantify the effect of changes. For example, it showed that increasing investigation and negotiation quality could lead to a reduction of between 5% and 20% in settlement costs.

The question arises why such seemingly obvious consequences of actions are not evident to management. The answer is that, for one thing, people responsible for organisations (i.e. managers) do not often see the entire (big) picture at once, either spatially or temporally. In other words, today's organisations are divided into divisions or functions, isolated by physical barriers and often conflicting objectives. This fragmentation masks the *dynamics* of interrelationships and leads to a lack of cohesion among the parts. The result is an underdeveloped and underperforming organisation. Jay Forrester, the creator of the System Dynamics discipline, states that organisations are at only about 5% of their learning potential (Forrester, 1994).

A second reason is that the human mind can only deal with a limited degree of complexity.[6] As the number of 'variables' in a system increase and their relationships become 'messier', the human mind fails to 'see' the web of relationships and the interplay amongst these variables.

We use binoculars and telescopes to extend our vision and computers to speed our calculations; similarly, we need special tools to extend our thinking ability. Systems thinking and modelling tools are the binoculars and telescopes of the mind that help us 'see' the otherwise invisible details and complexity in organisations. They clarify foggy views and bring to focus distant pictures – they bring the future into the present. Never before have these tools been so crucial to organisational development and advancement.

Notes

1 KJ stands for Jiro Kawakita, the Japanese anthropologist who originally devolved this techniques in the 1960s. Affinity Diagrams are a derivation of KJ developed by the GOAL/QPC Group.

2 Most of the examples in this section are adapted from MIT's Core Competency Course on Learning Organisations (Kim, 1995).

3 *Time*, 15 June 1998: 41.

4 This case is based on 'Clifford's Security Trucks' by B. Smith and D. Wolfden (1994: 151–153).

5 This case is based on the article 'Systems Thinking and Organisational Learning: Acting Locally and Thinking Globally in the Organisation of the Future,' by P.M Senge and J. D. Sterman, in *Transforming Organisations*, T. Kochan and M. Useem (eds.), Oxford University Press, 1991.

6 This is referred to as 'Bounded Rationality' by H.A. Simon (1982).

REFERENCES

Brassard, M. (1984) *The Memory Jogger Plus – Featuring the Seven Management and Planning Tools.* GOAL/QPC, Methuen, MA.

Eaves, D. (1992) The Tragedy of Commons. *Systems Development,* Part 2: 2. Department of Information Systems, Monash University.

Forrester, J. (1994) *Building a Foundation for Tomorrow's Organizations.* Systems Thinking in Action Video Collection, Vol. 1. Pegasus Communications Inc., Cambridge, MA.

Hardin, G. (1968) The Tragedy of the Commons. *Science,* 162: 1243–1248.

Hodgson, A.M. (1994) Hexagons for Systems Thinking. In Sterman, J.D. and Morecroft, J.D.W. (eds). *Modelling for Learning Organisations.* Productivity Press, Portland, Oregon.

Kauffman, D.L. Jr. (1980) *Systems 1: An Introduction to Systems Thinking.* (Innovative Learning Series). Future Systems Inc., Minneapolis.

Kim, D. (1995) Core Competency Course on Learning Organisations. MIT, Cambridge, MA.

Kreutzer, D.P. (1995) FASTBreak: A Facilitation Approach to Systems Thinking Breakthroughs. In Chawla, S. and Renesch, J. (eds). *Learning Organizations: Developing Cultures for Tomorrow's Workplace,* pp. 229–241. Productivity Press, Portland.

Richardson, G. (1997) Problems in CLDs Revisited. *System Dynamics Review:* 247–252.

Senge, P.M. (1990) *The Fifth Discipline: The Art and Practice of the Learning Organization.* Doubleday/Currency, New York, NY.

Simon, H.A. (1982) *Models of Bounded Rationality.* MIT Press, Cambridge, MA.

Smith, B. and Wolfden, D. (1994) in *The Fifth Discipline Fieldbook*, Nicholas Brealey Publishers.

Vennix, J. (1996) *Group Model Building: Facilitating Team Learning using System Dynamics.* John Wiley, Chichester.

Chapter **4**

Dynamic modelling

OVERVIEW

In the previous chapter, we discussed the development and use of causal loop models. In this chapter we show how these causal loop models can be converted into dynamic simulation models, using the *ithink* modelling software.[1] However, firstly we present some of the reasons why someone might want to develop a simulation model, followed by an overview of the dynamic modelling process, and a more detailed presentation of some of the key aspects of dynamic modelling. Such key aspects include the construction of stock flow diagrams, developing a simulation model, and simulating model behaviour. Some of these steps are illustrated by means of the development of a simple population model. Model validation, sensitivity analysis, and policy and strategy analysis are also covered in more detail. Finally, a technical appendix is provided, which includes an overview of the simulation process and the simulation parameters, plus some special functions used in constructing system dynamics models.

Why construct a simulation model?

Although causal loop modelling is very powerful, as discussed in the previous chapter, there are a number of advantages to be gained from developing a computer simulation model to investigate more deeply the dynamic issues that are of concern to management. These advantages include the following.

1 More information can be contained in a computer simulation model than in a conceptual model.

2 Causal relationships and assumptions can be formulated clearly and unambiguously.

3 Once the model has been validated, it can be used reliably to simulate alternative model experiments without manual errors.

4 Assumptions can be altered easily for different experiments.

5 Experiments can be performed readily with different structures and policies.

6 Sensitive parameters or assumptions can be located quickly through repeated simulations.

7 Uncertainties and errors can be incorporated into the model explicitly.

8 Graphical and tabular output can be communicated easily to management or model users.

9 The model provides a laboratory tool for learning about the behaviour of the real world.

In addition, the system dynamics[2] approach to modelling, which is the general approach to dynamic modelling used in this book, has the following advantages.

1 Causal loop diagrams (and/or stock flow diagrams) are formulated to show the nature and direction of the relationships within the system being modelled. These diagrams also assist the modeller in gaining a better understanding of the system and they act as a powerful form of communication within the organisation.

2 Decision rules or policies can be varied during the simulation as they are formulated to depend on the state of the system at the time, rather than being specified as constant relationships as happens in the case of static simulation models. In other words, system dynamics models incorporate the feedback effects of past actions on the state of the system and this information can be used in current decision making.

3 Both non-linear and linear relationships can be included.

4 Physical and information delays are easily incorporated.

5 Information can be included for which adequate statistical data may not be available; for example, 'soft' behavioural relationships can be modelled readily.

In summary then, the system dynamics approach to modelling, with its emphasis on describing (by means of causal loop diagrams) and formulating equations (in a quantitative model) for each cause-and-effect relationship, is good example of the 'open box' approach to policy modelling. Greenberger has emphasised the advantage of the 'open box' approach when communicating the results of policy models to decision makers:

> 'The typical policy model is not designed for ease of communication with the decision maker. Even the model builder may have difficulty comprehending fully the essential working of the model. Ideally, the model should be presented to the policy maker, not as a "black box" with assumptions and data feeding into the left and results coming from the right, but as an "open box" whose inner workings are sufficiently simplified, exposed, and elucidated to enable the policy maker to trace the chain of causality from input to output on at least an elementary fundamental level.'
>
> (Greenberger, cited by Richels (1981: 52))

The dynamic modelling process

The general approach in a systems thinking and modelling intervention involves five major phases: problem structuring; causal loop modelling; dynamic modelling; scenario planning and modelling; and implementation and organisational learning. This chapter deals with the 'dynamic modelling' phase. The steps involved in this phase are summarised in bold in Table 4.1 and they will be expanded on in subsequent sections of this chapter. Although these steps are presented in a linear fashion, they can be undertaken iteratively. In some cases, it may not be necessary to follow all the steps in a particular dynamic modelling intervention. The other phases and steps in the systems thinking and modelling process are provided in Table 4.1 to emphasise the wider context within which dynamic models are developed.

The steps of the dynamic modelling process summarised in Table 4.1 will now be briefly outlined, using a simple population model to illustrate some of the main points. However, it is important to emphasise that dynamic modelling can only take place effectively after the problem structuring phase has been completed. Also, certain aspects (depending on the particular intervention) of Phase 2, causal loop modelling, are normally completed prior to the computer modelling stage.

Table 4.1   Systems thinking and modelling process

Phases	Steps
1 Problem structuring	1 Identify problems or issues of concern to management 2 Collect preliminary information and data
2 Causal loop modelling	1 Identify main variables 2 Prepare behaviour over time graphs (reference mode) 3 Develop causal loop diagram (influence diagram) 4 Analyse loop behaviour over time 5 Identify system archetypes 6 Identify key leverage points 7 Develop intervention strategies
3 **Dynamic modelling**	1 **Develop a systems map or rich picture** 2 **Define variable types and construct stock-flow diagrams** 3 **Collect detailed information and data** 4 **Develop a simulation model** 5 **Simulate steady-state/stability conditions** 6 **Reproduce reference mode behaviour (base case)** 7 **Validate the model** 8 **Perform sensitivity analysis** 9 **Design and analyse policies** 10 **Develop and test strategies**
4 Scenario planning and modelling	1 Plan general scope of scenarios 2 Identify key drivers of change and keynote uncertainties 3 Construct forced and learning scenarios 4 Simulate scenarios with the model 5 Evaluate robustness of the policies and strategies
5 Implementation and organisational learning	1 Prepare a report and presentation to management team 2 Communicate results and insights of proposed intervention to stakeholders 3 Develop a microworld and learning lab based on the simulation model 4 Use learning lab to examine mental models and facilitate learning in the organisation

Develop a systems map or rich picture

This step involves developing a high-level systems diagram of the problem situation which shows the main sectors and the initial boundaries for the potential simulation model. There are a number of forms that this high-level map can take, including a high-level *ithink* systems map, a general sector diagram, and a rich picture.

● High-level *ithink* systems map

This involves developing an upper layer diagram in the *ithink* computer software (or other system dynamics software, e.g. Powersim) which shows the main sectors in the potential simulation model and the physical flows and information linkages between these sectors. However, this diagram can be produced by hand or with general purpose software. Examples of *ithink* systems maps are provided in Case figure 4.1 for the Mainland Beer distribution model, and Case figure 5.2 for the Telecommunications business unit strategy model. Initially this high-level map is produced showing just the main sectors, and the physical and information linkages are added as the detailed modelling proceeds.

● General sector diagrams

These are more general diagrams which show the relationships between the main sectors, variables and stakeholders in the system of interest. An example of a sector diagram is provided in Figure 4.1 which shows the relationships between the inputs, outputs and outcomes expected by government for a proposed model of the search activity of the New Zealand Customs Service (Cavana and Clifford, 1999). In this case a simulation model was not developed because of the lack of suitable data and appropriate outcome measurements. However, the study did assist with the introduction of systems thinking concepts into the strategic planning process at New Zealand Customs.

Figure 4.1   Sector diagram for the proposed customs search

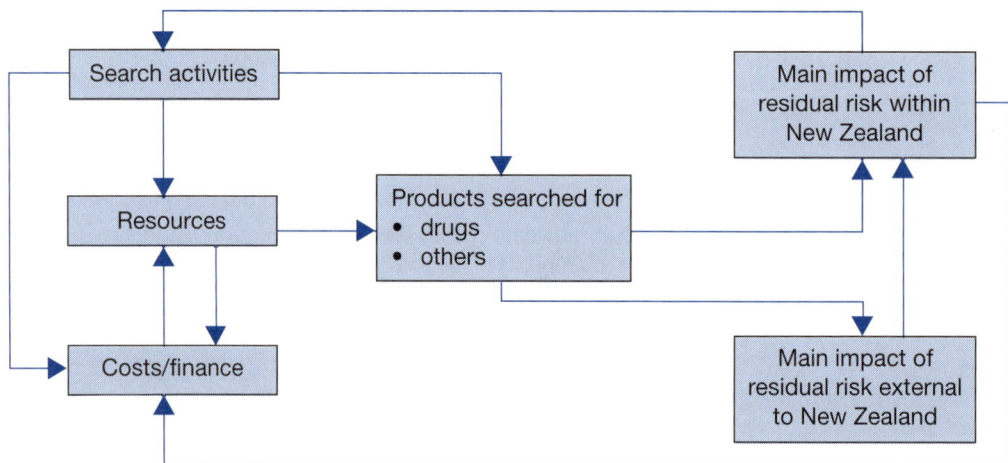

(Source: Cavana and Clifford, 1999: 9)

● Rich pictures

Rich pictures were developed by Peter Checkland (1981) as part of his Soft Systems Methodology. A rich picture, or situation summary, generally involves a diagrammatic representation of the main variables and issues involved in the system of interest. An example of a rich picture is provided in Figure 4.2, for a New Zealand farm woodlot model. This system dynamics study (Cavana et al., 1996) involved evaluating a range of measures for controlling possums and gorse and examining their impact on the potential volume and value of wood expected to be produced from a farm woodlot in the Wellington region. The rich picture was found to be a very useful aid to help establish the boundaries for the problem area.

Figure 4.2   Rich picture for the Makara Farm woodlot

(Source: Cavana et al., 1996: 183)

Define variable types and construct stock flow diagrams

The essential feature of a system dynamics model is the way in which the system being analysed is described in terms of stocks (also called levels), flows (rates), converters (auxiliaries), and the feedback loops formed by these variables. The way in which these variables represent a system is critical to the dynamics of the system.

- **Stocks** are accumulated quantities within the system, such as cash, inventory, population, level of knowledge, or averaged (smoothed) statistical data, such as average sales rate, average cash inflow and average birth rate. Stocks describe the condition of the system and they would continue to exist even if all the flows in the system were brought to a halt. In the *ithink* computer simulation package, the symbol for a stock (or level) is:

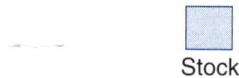

Stock

- **Flows** are the changes to the stocks that occur during a period of time (e.g. revenue earned during the month, wood grown on trees over the year, interest earned on a bank account during the quarter). The flows in the system (alternatively called rates) are usually the outcomes of decisions by management or external (exogenous) forces outside management's control. They cannot be observed at a single point in time, except by accumulation or averaging – both of which create stocks. In the *ithink* computer simulation package, the symbol for a flow (or rate) is:

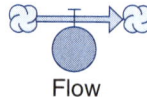

Flow

- **Converters** or auxiliary variables are the other variable types including constants, graphical relationships, and behavioural relationships. Converters are intermediate variables and can be substituted into flow equations if desired. The advantage of converters is that they break complex flow equations into simpler components and make the model easier to understand. In terms of understanding the way in which the system works and can be modelled, converters are very important and are significant components of the system structure. Examples of converters are provided in the simple population model presented on pp. 63–66 and pp. 70–73. The converters are the constants 'birth fraction' and 'life expectancy'. In sensitivity analysis (pp. 70–73), the life expectancy parameter is converted into a graphical relationship depending on the level of the population. In the *ithink* computer simulation package, the symbol for a converter is:

Converter

● Stock flow diagrams

A stock flow diagram is generally constructed from a causal loop diagram, although in some cases it may be easier to conceptualise the system being considered by going direct to the stock flow diagram. This is particularly the case where the system consists of some clearly defined stocks and flows in and out of these stocks.

If a simplified causal loop diagram has been developed in Phase 2 of the systems thinking and modelling process, it can be converted to a stock flow diagram, although generally more detailed variables are included in the stock flow diagram.

Figure 4.3(a) shows a causal loop diagram of a simple population system, where population is increased by births and depleted by deaths. Births depend on the current population and the current average percentage of new births each year and deaths depend on the current level of the population and the average life expectancy.

The *ithink* stock flow diagram for this system is provided in Figure 4.3(b). In the *ithink* stock flow diagram the boxes (rectangles) represent stocks or levels; the circles attached to double lines in or out of stocks represent flows or rates; the remaining circles represent

Figure 4.3   Causal loop and stock flow diagrams for a simple population model

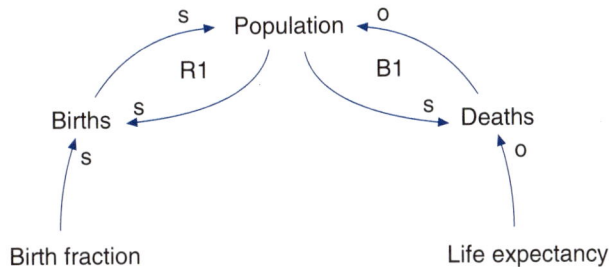

(a)   Causal loop diagram

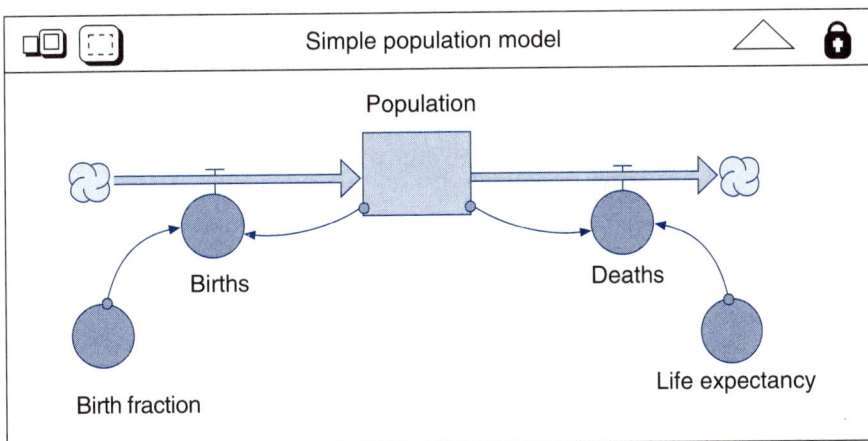

(b)   Stock flow diagram

converters containing other relationships, constants, parameters or graphs; the single-line arrows are called 'connectors' and they show the links between the variables; and the clouds represent variables outside the system being modelled.

Note that the double lines represent the 'physical' flows in the system, and not the influence or effects of the physical flows, which are shown by single lines (i.e. connectors). For example, the arrow from 'deaths' to 'population' in Figure 4.3(a) with the 'o' (opposite symbol) by the head is represented by a physical flow out of the 'population' stock in Figure 4.3(b). In general feedback loops can only be fully identified and analysed from causal loop diagrams (e.g. B1 and R1), and not from stock flow diagrams.

Collect detailed information and data

In this step, more detailed information is collected, e.g. initial values for stocks, parameter values for auxiliary variables, graphs and constants. This information can come from observations, interviews, meetings with managers, company records, historical records and archives, statistical publications, survey responses, media reports, and so on.

Sometimes a stock flow diagram is developed and more detailed information and data are collected before the computer modelling and equation writing begin. However, these steps are more often executed in tandem, and modelling and data collection proceed simultaneously.

Develop a simulation model

A computer simulation model of the problems/issues being investigated is constructed, based on the causal loop diagrams or stock flow diagrams (both of which depend on the early stages of the problem structuring phase, i.e. problem/issue identification and reference mode behaviour of the main variables). Initial values are identified for the stocks (levels), parameter values are identified for the relationships, and the structural relationships between the variables are determined using constants, graphical relationships and mathematical functions where appropriate.

The behavioural relationships are estimated on the basis of historical data where appropriate, and 'soft' relationships are formulated from discussions with managers and stakeholders. This frequently involves formulating graphical relationships between variables or the use of statistical methods to determine relationships between variables.

This stage involves using specialised computer packages like STELLA, *ithink*, POWERSIM, DYNAMO, DYSMAP, COSMIC or VENSIM.[3]

Model building should proceed using a systematic approach, and the simulation output should be checked at each stage to validate/confirm the model behaviour in order to capture 'understanding' of the model behaviour and consolidate the learning from the model development.

The *ithink* equations for the simulation model, developed from the stock flow diagram in Figure 4.3, are presented in Figure 4.4. This model has been documented to give the source and background information for each parameter or equation. Model documentation provides a good 'trail' so that company teams or other model users are able to follow the logic and assumptions of the model.

Figure 4.4   *Ithink* equations for the simple population model

Simple population model

Stocks:

Population(t) = Population(t – dt) + (Births – Deaths) * dt

INIT Population = 100 {people}

DOCUMENT: The initial population of a small island in the South Pacific.

Flows:

Births = Population*Birth_fraction {people/year}

DOCUMENT: The annual birth rate (ie the number of people born each year).

Deaths = Population/Life_expectancy {people/year}

DOCUMENT: The annual death rate (ie the number of people dying each year).

Converters:

Birth_fraction = 0.03 {fraction/year}

DOCUMENT: The average percentage of people born each year on the island, expressed as a fraction of the total population.

Life_expectancy = 70 {years}

DOCUMENT: The average life expectancy of people living on the island.

● **Stock equation**

In Figure 4.3(b) on p. 63, population is modelled as a stock. This stock is represented by the following equations:

$$\text{POPULATION(t)} = \text{POPULATION(t – dt)} + (\text{BIRTHS – DEATHS}) * \text{dt}$$

$$\text{INIT POPULATION} = 100 \text{ \{people\}}$$

The first equation states that population at the present time (i.e. 't') is equal to the population at the previous time (i.e. t – dt), plus the births less the deaths that have occurred during the period (i.e. dt) since the population level was previously calculated. (The simulation interval, dt or DT, is discussed in the technical appendix to this chapter.)

The second equation indicates that the initial value of population was 100 people at the beginning of the simulation. Dimensions (or units of measurement) are provided here for each variable in brackets at the end of each equation. Dimensions should be provided as a means of clarifying how the variable is measured. For example, population is measured in terms of 'people', whereas births are measured in terms of 'people per year' in this model.

● Flow equations

Flow equations are generally the policy statements in the system. They reflect the rate at which the system will change during the forthcoming simulation interval of time (i.e. the next DT).

An example of a flow equation from the simple population model is:

$$\text{DEATHS = POPULATION/LIFE\_EXPECTANCY \{people/year\}}$$

This states that the number of deaths in the following time interval is equal to the population divided by the average life expectancy. This variable is measured in terms of the number of people who die per year. For example, if there were 100 people and if their average life expectancy were 70 years, then we would expect that the number of deaths in the next period (i.e. the next year if DT = 1) would be 100/70 = 1.43. In other words, on average, 1.43 people would die during the next year. Now if the simulation interval (DT) were set to half a year (DT = 0.5), then although the annual rate of deaths would still be 1.43 people per year, the actual number of deaths during the period would be:

$$\text{DT*DEATHS = 0.5 * 1.43 = 0.71.}$$

● Converter equations

Converters (or auxiliary variables) are intermediate variables, graphical relationships and constants. In the simple population model shown in Figure 4.4, two converters are provided: BIRTH FRACTION and LIFE EXPECTANCY. They are both modelled here as constants, although we will alter the assumptions about LIFE EXPECTANCY being a constant in the sensitivity analysis section.

Simulate steady-state/stability conditions

The initial value for the beginning of the simulation run is selected (e.g. a year, '1990', or a time zero, '0'), and the unit of time for the simulation (e.g. hour, day, week, month, year, etc.) is specified. Select the simulation interval (DT) (e.g. 0.25, 0.5, 1.0) and the time horizon for the simulation run (i.e. the length of the simulation). The model is then simulated over time and graphical and tabular output is produced.

In the simple simulation model set out in Figure 4.4 we have specified the simulation to commence in the year 2000, with a simulation interval of 0.25 years (DT = 0.25), and a simulation length of 100 years.

Generally the first step towards validating the behaviour of the model is to get the model into a steady-state equilibrium by setting all the inflows equal to the outflows from the stocks.

In the case of the simple population model there is only one stock, namely population. So to get the model into equilibrium we set the inflows to the stock equal to the outflows at the beginning of the simulation run. That is:

BIRTHS = DEATHS

However,

BIRTHS = POPULATION * BIRTH FRACTION and

DEATHS = POPULATION/LIFE EXPECTANCY

Setting these two flows equal to each other gives:

POPULATION * BIRTH FRACTION = POPULATION/LIFE EXPECTANCY

Dividing both sides by POPULATION we get:

~~POPULATION~~ * BIRTH FRACTION = ~~POPULATION~~/LIFE EXPECTANCY

or

BIRTH FRACTION = 1/LIFE EXPECTANCY

Since LIFE EXPECTANCY = 70 years,
we set the BIRTH FRACTION = 1/70 and run the model to get the following equilibrium results for the main variables.

Figure 4.5   Preliminary validation run with the simple population model

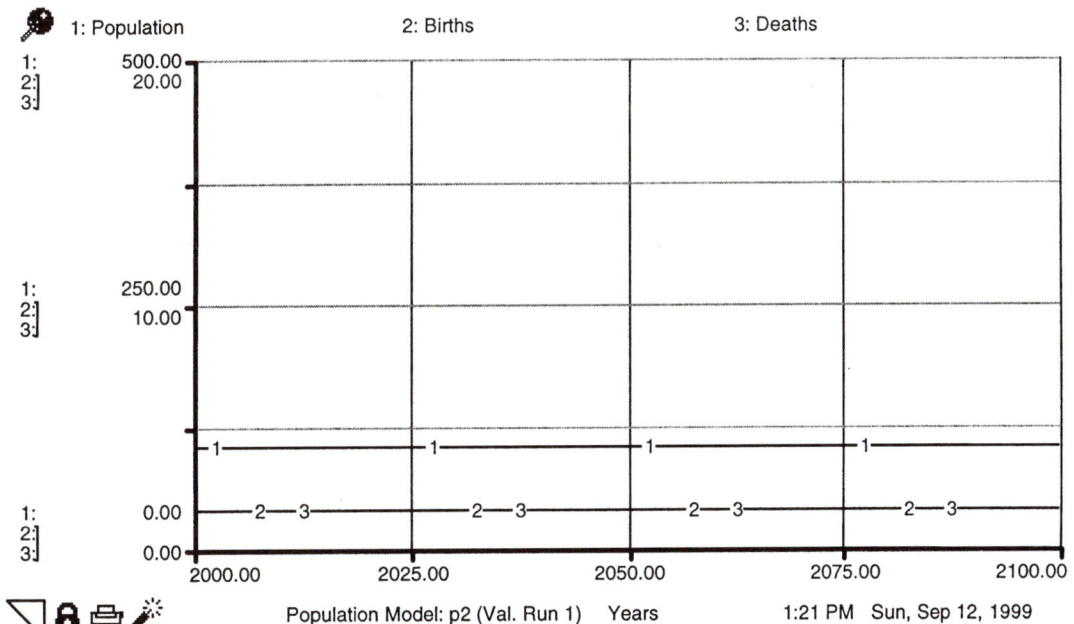

1: Population   2: Births   3: Deaths

Population Model: p2 (Val. Run 1)   Years   1:21 PM Sun, Sep 12, 1999

The model output graphs are annotated as follows. The graphed variables are listed across the top of the diagram. Each variable is assigned a number that relates to a similarly numbered line in the diagram space. On the vertical axis, each numbered variable is associated with a scale, which shows the minimum, middle and maximum values.

For example, in Figure 4.5, variable 1 refers to POPULATION, which has a minimum value of 0 (zero), a middle value of 250, and a maximum value of 500.

Reproduce reference mode behaviour (base case)

This involves putting in provisional values for the parameters at first, to try and reproduce the general pattern of the reference mode. More accurate and detailed parameter values are obtained later and these are inserted into the model. The reference mode is reproduced – this is generally called the base case.

The graphical and tabular output for the base case of the simple population model are provided in Figure 4.6 and Table 4.2 respectively. These figures show that population is increasing exponentially over the simulation run, due to the fact that births exceed deaths for each time period in the simulation run. The tabular output is printed here at 10-yearly intervals, to provide a summary of the numerical data. However, when validating the model, the output should be printed for every point of time that the model is simulated, until such times that the mechanics of the model have been thoroughly checked.

Figure 4.6 Base case graphical output for the simple population model

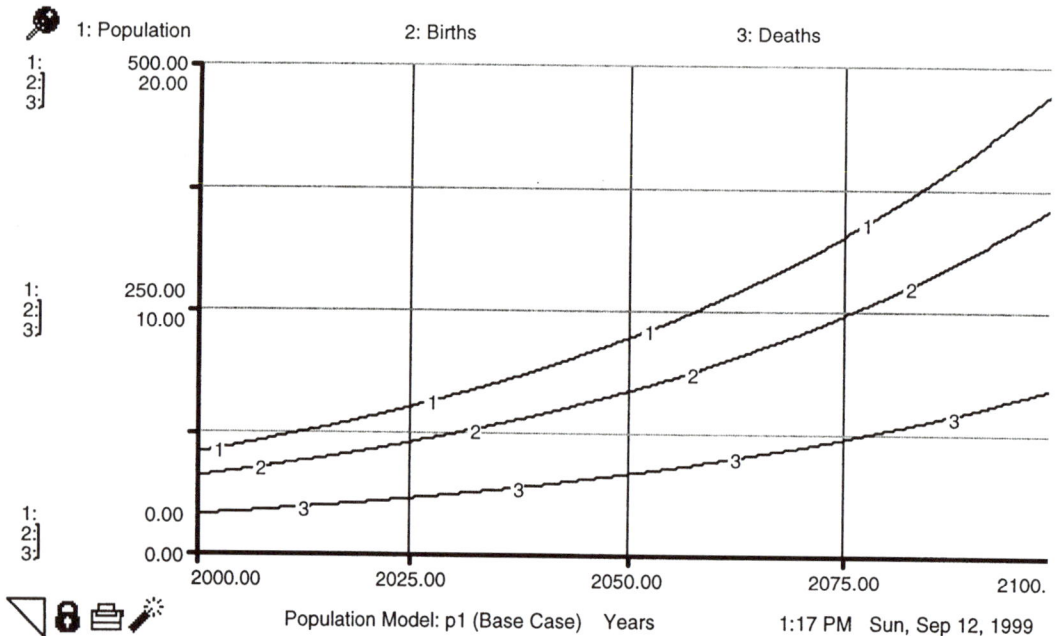

Table 4.2   Base case numerical output for the simple population model

Base Case				
1:30 PM Sun, Sep 12, 1999 Population Model (Base Case)				
Years	Population	Births	Deaths	
2000.00	100.00	3.00	1.43	
2010.00	116.98	3.51	1.67	
2020.00	136.84	4.11	1.95	
2030.00	160.08	4.80	2.29	
2040.00	187.26	5.62	2.68	
2050.00	219.06	6.57	3.13	
2060.00	256.26	7.69	3.66	
2070.00	299.77	8.99	4.28	
2080.00	350.67	10.52	5.01	
2090.00	410.22	12.31	5.86	
2100.00	479.87	14.40	6.86	

Validate the model

Before a model can be used for policy analysis or any other use, the model team (i.e. the users or management) must have sufficient confidence in the 'soundness and usefulness' of the model (Forrester and Senge, 1980: 210). There is no single test which serves to 'validate' a system dynamics model. Rather, confidence in a dynamic simulation model accumulates gradually as the model passes more tests and as new points of correspondence between the model and empirical reality are identified (Forrester and Senge, 1980: 209).

The usual process by which this confidence is generated is called 'validation'. Coyle (1983: 362) has outlined the main tests which should be used to validate a system dynamics model. These include:

1   verification tests, which are concerned with verifying that the structure and parameters of the real system have been correctly transcribed into the model;
2   validation tests, which are concerned with demonstrating that the model actually generates the same type of behaviour that would be expected from the real system;
3   legitimation tests, which are applied to determine that the model follows the laws of system structure or any generally accepted rules.

The purpose of applying these rigorous tests is to show that there is nothing in the model that is not in the real system and nothing significant in the real system that is not in the model. More recently, Coyle (1996: 96–97) has suggested a number of steps or guidelines which could apply to all models to help build confidence in them. These guidelines include the following.

- The causal loop diagram must correspond to the statement of the problem. (Coyle refers to 'influence diagrams' rather than 'causal loop diagrams'.)
- The equations must correspond to the causal loop diagram; in particular the 's' or 'o' signs in the equations must match the signs in the causal loop diagram. (Coyle uses the symbols '+' and '-' instead of 's' and 'o' respectively to indicate the direction of the linkages in an 'influence' or causal loop diagram – see p. 27.)
- The model must be dimensionally valid, i.e. the dimensions (or units of measurement) of the variables on the right-hand side of the equation should be able to be converted to the dimension of the variable on the left-hand side of the equation. Some simulation packages do this automatically. Generally, the dimension of the variable on the left-hand side of the equation is shown in brackets after each equation.
- The model must not produce any unrealistic values, such as negative births.
- The behaviour of the model must be plausible – what it does should be what we expect it to do – and it must be possible to confirm the values at which it stabilises by simple arithmetic. These particular tests are harder to apply to a complex model than to a simple one, but they are necessary in all cases.
- The model should maintain 'conservation of flow'. This means that the total quantity of a variable which has entered and left the system together with what is still there should be accounted for.

Additional tests that we have found very useful are the following.

- Determining whether each equation in the model has been fully documented. Typically this would involve providing a managerial (or 'real world') interpretation of each equation plus referencing the source of the relationship or the parameter values used where appropriate.
- Determining whether the model behaves 'properly' when subjected to extreme conditions. This is done by subjecting the flow equations to STEP or PULSE functions (see Richmond and Petersen, 1997).

Perform sensitivity analysis

Normally some of the initial conditions, parameter values and structural relationships (equations) are estimated using uncertain or imperfect information when constructing simulation models. However, if the model is to be used with confidence, then it is important to know, as part of the validation process, how the model will behave if the uncertain parameter values are varied over a reasonable range. The procedure by which these tests are performed is called sensitivity analysis and the purpose of sensitivity analysis is to see how much the system's quantitative (numerical) and qualitative (graphical) behaviour changes if the uncertain parameter values are altered. Coyle (1977: 193) suggests that 'the aim of a sensitivity analysis is to conduct a programme of simulation experiments to identify the sensitive parameters'.

If some parameter changes appreciably alter model behaviour then more effort is needed to improve the estimates of the sensitive parameters. Alternatively, the model may need formulation so that it relies on more precisely known parameters (Tank-Nielsen, 1980: 188).

Several methods of performing sensitivity analysis are available, but we have found the method set out below very useful.

1 Select those parameters or groups of parameters which are considered most likely to affect the behaviour of the model, or whose estimation was based on more imprecise or uncertain information than that of other parameters.

2 Modify the values of each separate group of parameters by a certain percentage (for example, plus or minus 10% or 25%) at a time, and conducting the corresponding simulation runs.

3 Identify those parameters which, when changed, significantly affect model behaviour.

4 Analyse whether the behaviour changes are justified using existing knowledge or common sense.

Suitable variables to monitor (graphical behaviour and performance measures) over the simulation run should be determined, and all parameter values and graphical relationships identified.

Now classify parameters either as internal ones (that is, subject to management's control – e.g. how quickly people are hired, what discounts are offered, how much inventory is held), external ones (outside management control – e.g. market growth rate, exchange rates, tax rates) or combined ones (e.g. staff's response to policy changes).

Overall the main purpose of sensitivity analysis is to find the key leverage points in the system – i.e. the points where small changes to the parameter values cause considerable changes to the behaviour of the model or to the values of the outcomes (performance measures).

● Population example continued

One example of an external sensitivity experiment[4] would be the introduction of a relationship between population and life expectancy in the simple population model. This involves adding a link between these variables shown in the causal loop diagram in Figure 4.7(a). By making 'life expectancy' an endogenous variable (rather than a constant 70 years) a further balancing loop (B2) is created, linking population – life expectancy – deaths and population. Hence this loop also acts to control the growth-producing reinforcing birth loop (R1).

The variable 'life expectancy' has now been converted into a graphical relationship (shown in Figure 4.8 on p. 73) that declines as the population grows for this small island. This is based on the assumption that the 'population carrying capacity' for this small Pacific island is limited. Once the population reaches a certain level, it is assumed that famine and disease will lower the average life expectancy (hence the declining curve as the population increases).

Figure 4.7 Diagrams showing the structural change to the simple population model
(a) causal loop diagram
(b) stock flow diagram

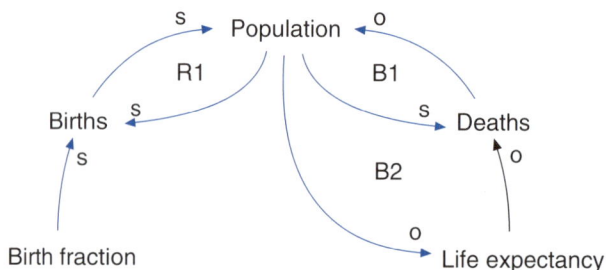

(a)   Causal loop diagram

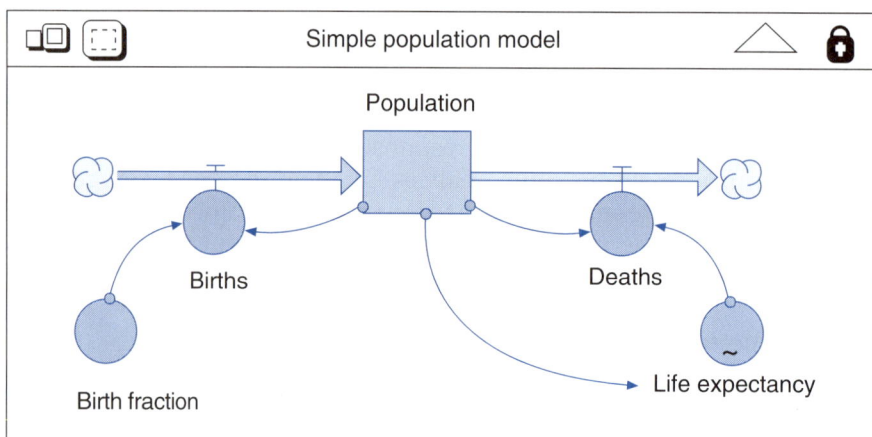

(b)   Stock flow diagram

The graphical output for this sensitivity test is provided in Figure 4.9 on p. 73. We have extended the length of the simulation run for this experiment to see when the population settles at its steady state or equilibrium value. This occurs after about 150 years, when the population reaches a level of about 300 people, with about 9 people being born and dying each year (compared with an exponentially growing population of 480 people after 100 years in the base case (from Table 4.2)). However, the average life expectancy has dropped from 70 years in the base case to about 34 years in this experiment. This could result from a much higher infant and child mortality rate, because of the deprived conditions brought about by the population being at a much higher level than the island's ideal carrying capacity (of about 100–125 people). Of course this model experiment suggests the need for policy analysis to help the Pacific island overcome its problems!

Figure 4.8   Graphical representation between population and life expectancy

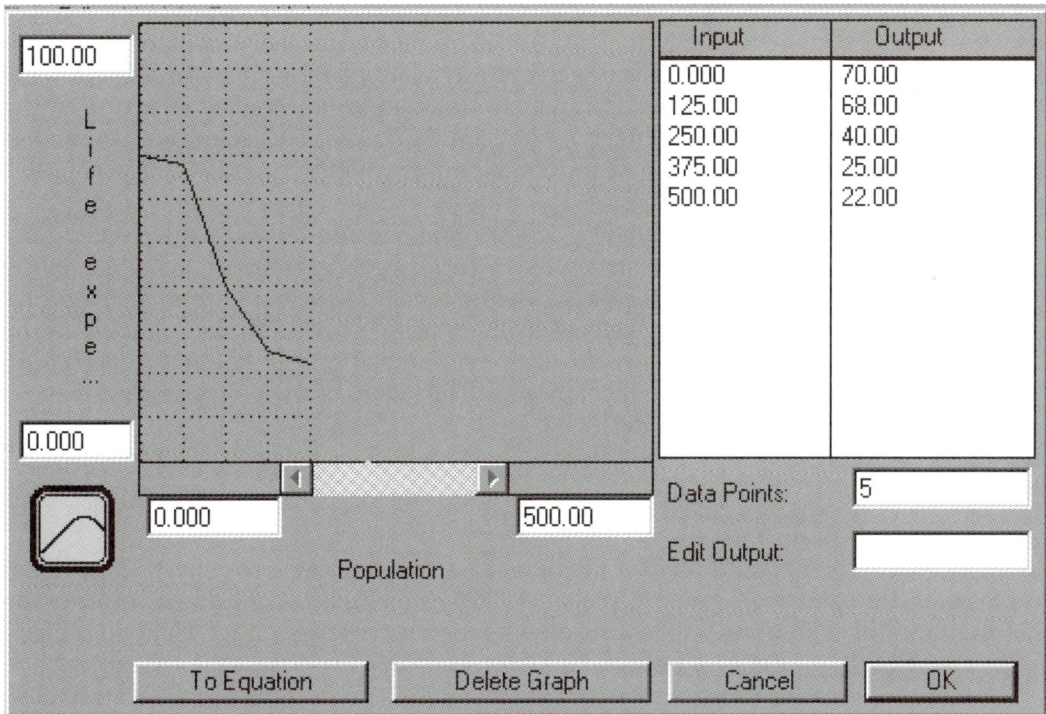

Figure 4.9   Behaviour of the simple population model with structural change to life expectancy

Design and analyse policies

In system dynamics models, policy analysis is an extremely important part of the modelling process. Usually this involves performing a carefully planned range of policy experiments with the model; varying the policy parameters or changing the policy structure of the model (i.e. by adding or deleting linkages between variables). The example discussed in Part II, Case 4 (the 'Mainland Beer distribution model') provides a good example of policy analysis in a dynamic simulation model.

The first stage of policy analysis is to simulate the model with different policy parameters, by keeping the model structure fixed. Then make structural changes to the model to examine the effects of different policies on the decision-making stream emerging from the model. It is important to systematically develop policies by testing them in the model and closely examining the graphical and numerical output before proceeding to the next stage of policy or strategy development. The extent of the policy analysis clearly depends on the purpose of the model.

Develop and test strategies

Strategies are combinations of policies intended to achieve strategic objectives. If the initial problem is a strategic issue, then it is likely to involve more than one functional area in the organisation, and its solution will require co-operation across these areas. Hence it is likely that strategies (or groupings of policies) may be necessary to address the issues.

A strategy development matrix can be developed to help design consistent strategies. These can then be tested with the aid of the model. Strategy development and analysis are illustrated in Case 5 – the telecommunications business unit case.

Subsequent modelling stages

In the next chapter we discuss planning and modelling scenarios, and testing the robustness of the designed policies and strategies to variations in scenarios.

In subsequent chapters we discuss the role of implementation in the organisation and the use of learning laboratories (or microworlds) based on system dynamics models to extend the learning further into the organisation.

However, implementation of dynamic models is an ongoing process, as the modelling work is generally undertaken with different stakeholders in the organisation, and the learning and insights are transferred 'seamlessly' or continuously throughout the modelling process, rather than 'delivered' in a final report at the end.

Nevertheless, it is still very important to produce a final report with a fully documented model to leave with management and the organisation for reference and ongoing learning. Also, many of the 'systems thinking and modelling' skills required for the dynamic modelling intervention are passed on to the organisation during the process.

Technical appendix[5]

Model simulation

The essential idea in simulating a dynamic system is that of calculating the values for its stocks at each of a sequence of points covering the required length of time. This requires knowledge of:

1 the values of the stocks at their starting points – the 'initial conditions';
2 the flows for the intervals separating the points on the time scale at which the values of the stocks are to be calculated;
3 a means of calculating the converters and then the flows to give the next values of the stocks.

The sequence of calculation is, therefore:

1 stocks;
2 converters;
3 flows calculated from stocks and converters or as delayed earlier flows.

Note that circular loops of converters and flows should not be formed, because that will create a set of 'simultaneous equations' that cannot be simulated sequentially. Hence the circular loop will have to be broken with a stock or an averaged (smoothed) flow.

Simulation parameters

■ Simulation interval (DT)

The gap between successive values of stocks is called the simulation interval, and is DT time units long. In calculating stocks, DT is expected to give a reasonable approximation to a very small interval between calculations. Obviously, this is a question of relative size and DT will, therefore, depend on the magnitude of time delays modelled in a particular simulation.

If DT is too large, the delays become unstable because the internal stocks acquire or lose too much of the quantity being delayed and this leads to large fluctuations in the output rate. To prevent instability from delays so as to ensure that the output from the model delays approximates reasonably closely that of the system delays, the value chosen for DT should either be one quarter of the smallest first-order delay (one half prevents instability and one tenth gives good accuracy, so one quarter is a good compromise), or one twelfth of the smallest third-order delay period specified in the model.

In general, DT should be selected as follows:

$DT \leq min \ (DEL/4n)$

where DEL = length of the delay
n = order of the delay
min = select the minimum of (DEL/4n) if two or more delays are present in the model

Rounding error can occur when DT is successively incremented to produce the passage of TIME. This may lead to uncertainty about the exact times of occurrence of time-related functions and events. However, such uncertainty can be avoided by making DT the decimal equivalent of an exact binary fraction, for example 0.5, 0.25, 0.125 or 0.0625.

■ TIME

The variable TIME, which gives the values of time during a simulation, is a stock built into most simulation packages and does not need to be defined. TIME starts at a value equal to zero and is incremented by each DT during the simulation. However, TIME can be specified to start at any point other than zero, by initialising TIME.

■ LENGTH

LENGTH represents the total duration of the simulation, in whatever time units are selected. Most simulation packages will continue to run, calculating a new value every DT, until the end of the simulation run is specified. The LENGTH of the simulation run or planning horizon will depend on the model purpose. For example, the model purpose might be detailed short-term analysis, medium-term policy analysis, or longer-term strategic analysis. The concepts of short, medium, and long term vary according to the industry or the particular situation. However, a rule of thumb is that the simulation LENGTH should be long enough for the system being modelled to achieve stability.

Special functions in dynamic modelling

■ Delay functions

One of the most important classes of functions in system dynamics modelling are delays, because of the influence they have on the dynamics of a system. Delays fall into two categories: material (or physical) and information. Material delays occur, for example, between the time construction of a house is started and completed, or between the time goods are ordered and delivered. Examples of information delays are the lag effects of sales, prices and interest rates that arise from averaging these data. (The underlying pattern of sales is not altered, as 'averaging' smooths out information about the sales values.) However, the difference between these two categories of delay does not normally affect the numerical results. These examples show that a delay involves the presence of at least one other level within the system. For example, between the time house construction is started and completed, houses would be in a state of 'being constructed'.

A simple first-order or exponential delay consists of an inflow rate, a level at which the material is held during the delay duration, DEL, and an outflow rate. More complicated delays can be constructed by considering the outflow rate of the first delay to be an input rate to another first-order delay. The outflow rate of the second delay is final outflow. The two delays are said to be cascaded and, jointly, comprise a second-order delay. If DEL is the average total time that an entity spends in a second-order delay, each of the two first-order delays is given a delay duration of DEL/2.

Figure 4.10 demonstrates the effect of the output responses of first-order, third-order and twelfth-order delays to a step increase of an input of 100 units after two months, with a total delay time of two months (e.g. for a production process where there is an average delivery/production time). The higher the order of delay, the closer it resembles a pipeline delay.

Figure 4.10 Behaviour of information and material delays to a step increase

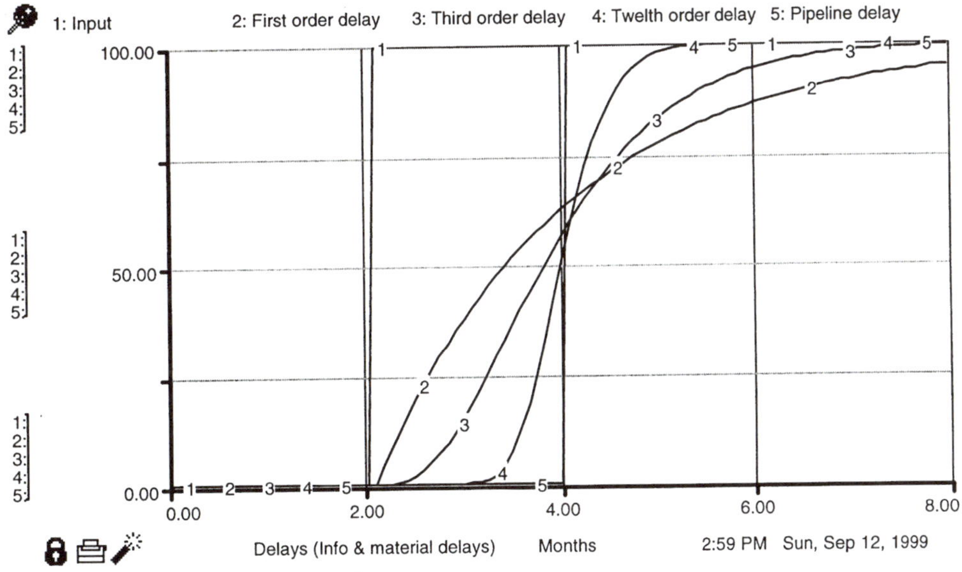

(Source: based on Richardson and Pugh, 1981: 109)

◼ Graphical functions

One of the most useful groups of functions provided by simulation software are the graphical functions. They allow any non-linear functional (or graphical) relationship between two variables to be expressed in terms of a graph. This can be done by drawing the curve to be input, choosing a series of equally spaced points on the horizontal axis, reading off the values from the curve and then entering them, in order, in the table (for example, see Figure 4.8 earlier in the chapter – repeated as Figure 4.11 on p. 78). The equally spaced points have to be chosen so that the straight lines drawn between the points defined on the curve would provide a reasonable approximation to the actual curve.

The *ithink* equations for this graphical relationship are:

Life_expectancy = GRAPH(Population)

(0.00, 70.0), (125, 68.0), (250, 40.0), (375, 25.0), (500, 22.0)

These equations are generated automatically by the *ithink* package, once values have been inserted on a graph pad as in Figure 4.11. On the first line of the equation, 'life expectancy' is referred to as the dependent variable, and 'population' is referred to as the 'independent' variable, i.e. the value of 'life expectancy' depends on the value of 'population'. The brackets on the second line of the equation indicate the coordinates on the graph (for example, see Figure 4.11). The first value in the brackets (called an 'argument') indicates

Figure 4.11 Graphical representation between a population and life expectancy

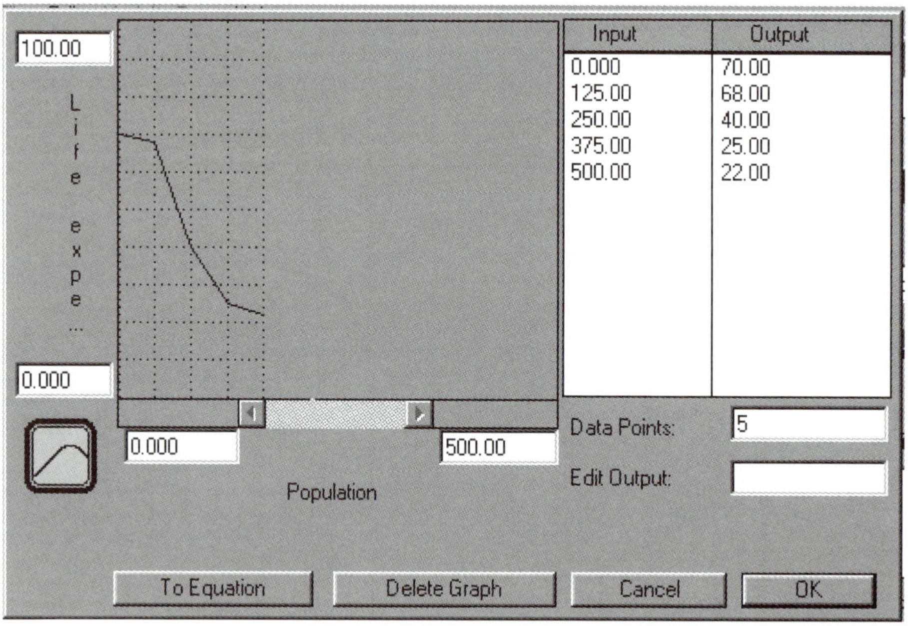

the value on the 'x' or horizontal axis (i.e. the value of the 'independent' variable), and the second value or argument in the brackets indicates the value of the point on the 'y' or vertical axis (i.e. the 'dependent' variable). For example, the coordinates of the first point (0.00, 70.0), indicates that when population is 0 (zero), then life expectancy is 70 years. Similarly, the next point (125, 68.0) indicates that at the point where population is 125 people, then life expectancy will be 68 years, and so on. This graphical relationship can be changed by sensitivity analysis. In the base case, life expectancy was assumed to be a constant 70 years, irrespective of the population level. The same result can be achieved by setting a straight line in the graph with life expectancy equal to 70 years, at all population levels.

Notes

1 The *ithink* Analyst software (outlined in Richmond and Petersen, 1997) was used in this book.

2 For more information on system dynamics refer to Forrester (1961), Coyle (1996), Mohapatra *et al.* (1994), Morecroft and Sterman (1994), Roberts *et al.* (1983), Senge (1990), and other titles listed in reference section below.

3 See Coyle, 1996, Appendix A, for a full discussion of these packages.

4 Strictly speaking, this change to external structure of the model is an example of a scenario experiment, which will be discussed fully in Chapter 5.

5 Much of the material on pp. 75–76 is obtained from Cavana, R.Y. and Coyle, R.G. (1982) *DYSMAP User Manual.* University of Bradford Printer, UK.

REFERENCES

Cavana, R.Y. and Clifford, L.V. (1999) The matrix, the spiderweb and the influence diagram: developments in systems thinking at the New Zealand Customs Service. *Graduate School of Business and Public Management Working Paper Series 3/99.* Victoria University of Wellington, Wellington

Cavana, R.Y., Lee, M.W., Bennett, J. and Taylor, R.J. (1996) Possum and gorse control on a farm woodlot in New Zealand: a system dynamics analysis. *Asia-Pacific Journal of Operational Research* (13): 181-207.

Checkland, P. (1981) *Systems Thinking, Systems Practice.* Wiley, Chichester.

Coyle, R.G. (1977) *Management System Dynamics.* Wiley, Chichester.

Coyle, R.G. (1983) The technical elements of the system dynamics approach. *European Journal of Operational Research,* 14: 359–370.

Coyle, R.G. (1996) *System Dynamics Modelling: A Practical Approach.* Chapman and Hall, London.

Coyle, R.G. and Morecroft, J.D.W. (1999) Special Issue: System Dynamics for Policy, Strategy and Management Education. *Journal of the Operational Research Society,* 50(4).

Forrester, J.W. (1961) *Industrial Dynamics.* MIT Press, Cambridge, Mass.

Forrester, J.W. and Senge, P.W. (1980) Tests for building confidence in system dynamics models. *TIMS Studies in the Management Sciences,* 14: 209–228.

Mohapatra, P.K.J., Mandal, P. and Bora, M.C. (1994) *Introduction to System Dynamics Modelling.* Universities Press (India), Hyderabad.

Morecroft, J.D.W and Sterman, J.D. (eds). (1994) *Modelling for Learning Organizations.* Productivity Press, Oregon.

Powersim. (1994) *User's Guide and Reference.* ModellData AS, Norway.

Richardson, G.P. (1991) *Feedback Thought in Social Science and Systems Theory.* University of Pennsylvania Press, Philadelphia.

Richardson, G.P. and Pugh III, A.L. (1981) *Introduction to System Dynamics Modelling with DYNAMO.* Productivity Press, Mass.

Richels, R. (1981) Building good models is not enough. *Interfaces,* 11(4): 48–54.

Richmond, B. and Petersen, S. (1997) *An Introduction to Systems Thinking.* High Performance Systems, Hanover.

Roberts, N., Andersen, D.F., Deal, R.M., Grant, M.S. and Schaffer, W.A. (1983) *Introduction to Computer Simulation: a System Dynamics Modelling Approach.* Addison Wesley, Reading, Mass.

Senge, P. (1990) *The Fifth Discipline: The Art and Practice of the Learning Organization.* Doubleday Currency, New York.

Tank-Nielsen, C. (1981) Sensitivity analysis in system dynamics. In Randers, J. (ed.). *Elements of the System Dynamics Method.* MIT Press, Cambridge, Mass.

Vennix, J.A.M. (1996) *Group Model Building: Facilitating Team Learning Using System Dynamics.* Wiley, Chichester.

Wolstenholme, E.F. (1990) *System Enquiry: A System Dynamics Approach.* Wiley, Chichester.

Chapter 5

Scenario planning and modelling

OVERVIEW

This chapter begins with an overview of scenario planning and some guidelines on developing and using scenarios. This is followed by a brief summary of the Foresight Project and an outline of the national scenarios that have been prepared as background to developing research, science and technology strategies for the New Zealand government. An introduction to scenario modelling is then provided, followed by a brief overview of a dynamic simulation model that has been developed to model scenarios for the New Zealand wine industry.

Introduction to scenario planning

The term 'scenario' has entered the everyday language of managers in all sectors of the economy and it has been heavily popularised by the media. In earlier times, a scenario was a term more related to the theatrical scene than the business world. The Oxford Dictionary[1] defines scenario as '**1** an outline of the plot of a play, film, opera, etc., with details of the scenes, situations, etc. **2** a postulated sequence of imagined events.' The author Jules Verne wrote futuristic stories (i.e. scenarios) of human beings travelling to the moon and into the depths of the ocean, well before such travel became possible. Similarly, social commentators such as Aldous Huxley and George Orwell wrote stories (scenarios) about the future state of society, with the intention of warning people how things could turn out if society developed along 'undesirable' paths.

During World War II, scenario planning became popular with military strategists analysing potential deployment of military resources, personnel and weapons. Scenario planning was further popularised in the 1950s by Herman Kahn, a well known futurist from the Rand Corporation and Hudson Institute. 'Kahn was best known for his scenarios about nuclear war, in which he advocated that people should "think about the unthinkable" so that, if nuclear war did become imminent, society would be less vulnerable and less likely to slide into a holocaust' (De Geus, 1998: 57).

More recently, scenario planning was introduced to the business world by business planners at the Royal Dutch Shell Group. In the late 1960s and early 1970s, planners at Shell developed a process of preparing a range of stories about future potential states of the business environment, and communicating these stories and their implications to management within the Shell Group. This enabled Shell's management to be better prepared for the 1973 oil crisis than the other international oil companies. Also, scenario planning provided Shell management with substantial competitive insights again in 1981, 'when other oil companies stockpiled reserves in the aftermath of the outbreak of the Iran-Iraq war, Shell sold off its excess before the glut became a reality and prices collapsed.'[2]

Scenario planning should not be confused with forecasting, or single path projections. Although forecasting does have its place in managerial decision analysis, history is littered with 'forecasts' from famous people and experts that have proved to be totally wrong. Figure 5.1 summarises some of these.

Figure 5.1   Some expert 'forecasts'

'The phonograph … is not of any commercial value.'
Thomas Alva Edison, inventor of the phonograph, c. 1880

'Heavier-than-air flying machines are impossible.'
Lord Kelvin, British mathematician, physicist, and president of the British Royal Society, c. 1895

'There is no likelihood man can ever tap the power of the atom.'
Robert Millikan, Physics Nobel Prize, 1923

'Who the hell wants to hear actors talk?'
Harry M. Warner, Warner Bros., 1927

'A severe depression like that of 1920–1921 is outside the range of probability.'
The Harvard Economic Society, 16 November 1929

'I think there is a world market for about five computers.'
Thomas J. Watson, chairman of IBM, 1943

'There is no reason for any individual to have a computer in their home.'
Ken Olson, president, Digital Equipment Corporation, 1977

'We don't like their sound. Groups of guitars are on the way out.'

Decca Recording Co. Executive, turning down the Beatles in 1962

'No matter what happens, the US Navy is not going to be caught napping.'

Frank Knox, Secretary of the Navy, 4 December 1941, just before the Japanese attack on Pearl Harbour

'With over fifty foreign cars already on sale here, the Japanese auto industry isn't likely to carve out a big slice of the US market for itself.'

Business Week, 2 August 1968

(Source: Cerf and Navasky, 1984)

These 'forecasts' almost provide sufficient reason to consider multiple futures! Scenario planning provides a framework to help managers understand the forces driving their businesses, rather than relying on forecasts presented to them with a hidden set of assumptions and judgements incorporated into a set of figures that become a substitute for thinking about the future. In short, scenario planning attempts to capture the richness and range of future possibilities, stimulating decision makers and managers to consider changes they would otherwise ignore. At the same time, it organises those possibilities into stories that are easier to grasp and use than huge volumes of data. Above all, however, scenarios are aimed at challenging managers' mental models and their prevailing mindsets.

In particular, organisations that face the following conditions will benefit from scenario planning:

- 'uncertainty is high relative to managers' ability to predict or adjust;
- too many costly surprises have occurred in the past;
- the company does not perceive or generate new opportunities;
- the quality of strategic thinking is low (i.e. too routinised or bureaucratic);
- the industry has experienced significant changes or is about to experience such change;
- the company wants a common language and framework, without stifling diversity;
- there are strong differences of opinion, with multiple opinions having merit;
- competitors are using scenario planning.'

(Schoemaker, 1995: 27)

A scenario is not a forecast or an intention to describe a certain future state, but it is intended to provide a possible set of future conditions.

> 'A scenario can present future conditions in two different ways. It can describe a snapshot in time, that is, conditions at some particular instant in the future. Alternatively, a scenario can describe the evolution of events from now to some point of time in the future. In other words, it can present a "future history". This latter approach is generally preferred by those engaged in policy analysis and choosing strategy, because it provides cause-and-effect information. Indeed, preparing scenarios as a future history requires that a possible evolution of events and trends be described as an integral part of the scenario.'
>
> (Becker, 1983: 96)

Becker also identifies three distinct purposes for using scenarios:

1 to estimate if various policies and actions can assist or prevent the conditions of a scenario from coming about;
2 to assess how well alternate policies and strategies would perform under the conditions depicted, i.e. to estimate risks in choosing certain courses of action; and
3 to provide a common background for various groups or individuals involved in planning within an organisation.

Developing and using scenarios

Pierre Wack (1985: 140) stresses that 'scenarios must help decision makers develop their own feel for the future of the system, the forces at work within it, the uncertainties that underlie the alternative scenarios and the concepts useful for interpreting key data.'

The main building blocks for constructing scenarios are illustrated in Figure 5.2 and more detailed steps in scenario construction are provided in Table 5.1. It should be noted that there are many alternative ways of constructing scenarios,[3] but the method outlined here appears the most consistent with the subsequent use of simulation modelling for testing the assumptions, internal consistency and future implications of the scenarios.

Figure 5.2   Building blocks for scenarios (Schoemaker, 1995)

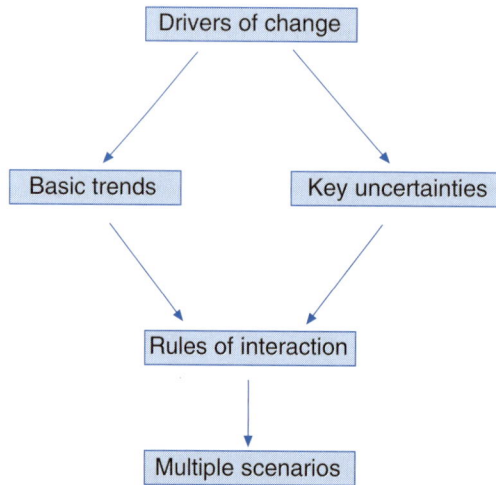

Some guidelines for using scenarios are provided by Steven Schnaars (1987: 104–114). These guidelines include the following.

- The most important part of scenario analysis is to think about the problem. It is important to think about the assumptions that underlie the scenarios. Obtaining accurate assumptions is far more important than selecting the 'best' method of constructing scenarios.

- The most difficult issue in scenario analysis is how to reduce a large number of potential future outcomes to a few plausible scenarios. Two methods have been proposed.

  a If the number of key factors is small and only a small number of future values are provided for each factor, it is possible to examine all the combinations and select a few plausible scenarios from this set. The scenarios can be selected to represent either optimistic or pessimistic outcomes, or some dominant 'theme' of the future environment.

  b If the number of factors is large then a preferred approach is to decide whether the scenarios will represent an optimistic or pessimistic view of the future, or some dominant 'theme' of the future environment. Once the tone of the scenarios is set, future values of the factors are formed that conform to this tone.

- In either case, avoid assigning probabilities, as they give a misleading sense of precision. Scenarios represent possibilities, not probabilities. Instead, formulate the scenarios using either the 'optimistic/pessimistic' format (see step 5 in Table 5.1) with or without a 'surprise-free' scenario, or 'theme' them according to some dominant aspects of the future environment. A 'surprise-free' scenario consists of a set of assumptions about the future that all stakeholders can accept as being realistic.

Table 5.1   Steps in scenario construction

1   Define the issues you wish to understand better in terms of **time frame, scope** and **decision variables**... Review the past to get a feel for degrees of uncertainty and volatility.

2   Identify the major **stakeholders** or **actors** who would have an interest in these issues, both those who may be affected by it and those who could influence matters appreciably. Identify their current roles, interests and **power** positions.

3   Make a list of current **trends** or **predetermined elements** that will affect the variable(s) of interest. Briefly explain each, including how and why it exerts an influence. Constructing a diagram may be helpful to show interlinkages and causal relationships (*e.g. a causal loop diagram*).

4   Identify key **uncertainties** whose resolution will significantly affect the variables of interest to you. Briefly explain why these uncertain events matter, as well as how they interrelate.

5   Construct two **forced scenarios** by placing all positive outcomes of key uncertainties in one scenario and all negative outcomes in the other. Add selected trends and predetermined elements to these extreme scenarios.

6   Next assess the **internal consistency** and **plausibility** of these artificial scenarios. Identify where and why these forced scenarios may be internally inconsistent (in terms of trends and outcome combinations).

7   Eliminate combinations that are not credible or are impossible, and **create** new scenarios (two or more) until you have achieved internal inconsistency. Make sure these new scenarios bracket a wide **range of outcomes**.

8   Assess the revised scenarios in terms of how the key **stakeholders** would behave in them. Where appropriate, identify topics for further study that would provide stronger support for your scenarios, or might lead to revisions of these **learning scenarios**.

9   After completing additional research, re-examine the internal consistencies of the learning scenarios and **assess** whether certain interactions should be formalised via a **quantitative** model... (*such as a system dynamics simulation model*).

10 Finally, reassess the ranges of uncertainty of the dependent (i.e. target) variables of interest, and retrace Steps 1 through 9 to arrive at **decision scenarios** that might be given to others to enhance their decision making under uncertainty (*or used to test strategies and generate new ideas*).

(Source: Shoemaker, 1993: 197. We have added the words in italics.)

- In most situations, two to four scenarios are sufficient, although there is a lack of consensus in the literature about how many scenarios are desirable. Most authors agree that three scenarios are usually the best, as long as one is not regarded as being 'most likely'.

- Scenarios should be limited to assessing future environmental states. They should not include plans, or the market response to plans, because of the additional uncertainties that this would introduce.

- Generally, scenarios should be targeted to applications of a narrower scope, that include a smaller number of factors which are fairly easy to identify but very difficult to predict.

- Scenario analysis is best suited for longer time horizons, where the accuracy of forecasting deteriorates more rapidly.

- Scenario analysis offers the greatest advantages over other methods when uncertainty is high, and historical relationships are unreliable, or when the future is likely to be affected by events that have no historical precedents.

How can you determine whether your final scenarios are any good?

Schoemaker (1995: 30) suggests that the first criterion is relevance.

'To have impact, your scenarios should connect directly with the mental maps and concerns of the user (e.g. senior executives, middle managers, etc.). Second, the scenarios should be internally consistent (and be perceived as such) to be effective. Third, they should be archetypal. That is, they should describe an equilibrium or a state in which the system might exist for some length of time, as opposed to being highly transient. It does an organisation little good to prepare for a possible future that will be quite short-lived. In short, the scenarios should cover a wide range of possibilities and highlight competing perspectives (within and outside the firm), while focusing on interlinkages and internal logic within each future.'

Based on the experiences at British Airways, the most important guidelines for success in introducing scenario planning are the following.

- 'Gain support from the top level in the company and build it into the existing planning processes from the start.

- It is a major exercise – plan it well, take the time to do the design and research properly and show progress along the way.

- Treat the exercise as a learning process. Consult as many people as possible in the development process so they feel ownership with the final product.'

(Moyer, 1996: 180–181)

Case

Scenarios from the New Zealand Foresight Project

The following project and associated scenarios are presented here as they are widely regarded as exemplary applications of scenario generation in New Zealand.

The Foresight Project[4]

The Foresight Project is an initiative led by the Ministry of Research, Science and Technology (MORST) about New Zealand's future and the role of research, science and technology in that future. The project has:

- encouraged an ongoing process of strategic thinking across diverse sectors, groups and communities within New Zealand, with particular attention to science and technology needs and opportunities for the future;
- guided the development of a new set of priorities for the Government's investment in research, science and technology to take effect in the year 2000.

A wide range of individuals, groups and organisations has become involved in the Foresight Project. Throughout 1998, MORST encouraged sector groups, sharing common interests and a concern for the future, to develop strategies toward the future through the use of foresight principles and tools. Later, participating sector groups submitted their strategy work to MORST so that it could use that information in developing criteria for public investment in research, science and technology.

The Foresight Project has four overlapping phases:

Phase 1: Establishing a context for thinking about future knowledge needs

Phase 2: Sector strategy development

Phase 3: Government decision making about new priorities and investment strategies

Phase 4: Begin to implement new priorities and investment strategies

Foresight scenarios

MORST has developed three national scenarios which are consistent with the various ways in which underlying social, environmental and economic trends could unfold in New Zealand and globally.[5]

They were designed to stimulate Foresight participants to think about the choices facing New Zealand as a nation. Scenarios are thinking devices, and sectors were encouraged to use them as part of a process for arriving at a vision of a desirable future and the outcomes and competencies required to reach it. The three scenarios are the following.

- 'Possum in the glare'
- 'Shark roaming alone'
- 'Nga Kahikatea reaching new heights'.

These scenarios depict different views of New Zealand in 2010. It is important to recognise that they represent three of many possible scenarios that may be constructed. The three scenarios respond differently to the following 'key drivers':

- fundamental technological change – waves of new technologies will enable huge productivity gains and open up new opportunities to address economic, social and environmental challenges;

- globalisation – the integration of the world's economies will mean a new ethos of openness, enabling free movement of people, ideas, goods and services;

- environmental quality – there is growing concern about a range of environmental tensions, for example the reduction in biodiversity, climate change, our ability to manage waste, and sustainable resource use;

- social and demographic trends – these include an ageing population, increasing urbanisation, changing family structures and work patterns, and an increasing recognition of the importance of social capital in creating wealth.

The introductory paragraphs for each of these scenarios, as set out in the MORST document, *Building Tomorrow's Success,* are provided below.

Scenario 1: Possum in the glare

New Zealand is caught like a possum in the glare of the oncoming future. But possums are hardy creatures, and New Zealand muddles along by finding new markets for traditional agricultural products, and combating falling prices with new production technologies. New Zealand has postponed thinking beyond the inevitable unsustainability of this situation. Skills and attitudes remain suited to the economy and society of the past 50 years. An entrenched underclass develops, and society is deeply divided. Auckland, to other New Zealanders, is like another planet. We become very vulnerable to risks of many kinds – economic, social and environmental …

Scenario 2: Shark roaming alone

After a period of economic difficulty, New Zealand has adapted quickly to keep up with the changes of the early 21st century. Rapid uptake of new technology and the Internet, and the success of the entrepreneurial approach have made us a highly individualised society of sharks. New Zealand is diverse and entrepreneurial, but sharply divided and lacking in social cohesion, and although economically the nation's health is sound, socially it is in great danger …

Scenario 3: Nga Kahikatea reaching new heights

Around the world, there is much interest in the social change that has occurred in New Zealand over the first decade of the 21st century. What distinguishes New Zealand from other countries is a strong and widely shared sense of purpose and a national intent. A nation of Kahikitea, standing together …

What can we learn from these scenarios?

The three scenarios highlight some choices ahead, and challenge participants to think about how they might deal with these choices. Some examples of questions about such choices and decisions are given below.

- Possum in the glare. How will we fare if we simply wait for the future? Are the consequences suggested realistic? What could be done to avoid the undesirable consequences?

- Shark roaming alone. How important are agility and entrepreneurialism in achieving success? Will agility and entrepreneurialism enable us to achieve prosperity and well-being as a knowledge society? How will such attributes influence social cohesion?

- Nga Kahikatea: reaching new heights. How important is social cohesion? Is working co-operatively vital for social cohesion? How does a commitment to a cohesive society influence economic and environmental outcomes?

    Using scenarios to think about these and other questions, it is possible to develop a vision of a 'desirable future', and an understanding of key decisions and strategies that will be necessary to move towards that future. Just as the MORST project team has developed national scenarios, this process can be applied at other levels: for individuals, groups and sectors. In Part 3 of *Building Tomorrow's Success* (MORST, 1998), the project team outlines the use of scenarios within the context of a process for developing a view of a desirable future for individual sectors of the New Zealand economy.

Scenario modelling

The process outlined by Schoemaker (1993: 197) for developing scenarios is summarised in Table 5.1 (see p. 85). A dynamic simulation model is most useful during stages 6, 9 and 10 of the process, i.e. to test the internal consistency and consequences of a range of scenarios. In addition, a dynamic simulation model can be used to design and analyse the implications of policies and strategies against the backdrop of the scenarios developed. The process involved in developing a simulation model has been outlined in Chapter 4 and will not be repeated here. In the next section, we briefly outline a dynamic simulation model that has been developed to evaluate scenarios for the New Zealand wine industry. A more detailed case study involving scenario modelling and strategy development for a business unit in the telecommunications industry in New Zealand is provided in Part II of this book, as Case 5.

⟫ **Case**

Scenario modelling for the New Zealand wine industry[6]

Case overview

This case provides an overview of scenario modelling for the wine industry in New Zealand. The background to the wine industry is briefly outlined, and an overview of the causal loop structure of the model is provided. Several scenario and policy experiments involving the model are discussed, as are some conclusions regarding the value of the model for wine industry stakeholders.

Background

The national vineyard, the size of which is one of the most important determinants of the size of the wine industry, has grown from 387 hectares (ha) in 1960 to 6000 hectares in 1991. In 1960, the industry comprised fewer than fifty family-owned vineyards, each with its own production facility for wine. Production totalled 4.1 million litres, 84% of which was 'fortified' wine (sherry and port).

Heavy investment in the industry by New Zealand and overseas brewers and liquor distributing companies during the 1960s and 1970s assisted the development of a few larger wine companies. With the development of these large wineries came the concept of contract grape growing – something which persuaded farmers to plant vines. In 1960, 96% of grapes were grown by wine producers themselves, a figure which had declined to 44% by 1980, to 30% by 1984, and to 25% by 1989.

The need for co-ordination within the industry gave rise to the formation of the Wine Institute of New Zealand (WINZ) in 1976. WINZ receives its authority from the Winemakers' Act 1976, which provides for compulsory membership of WINZ for those holding a licence to make grape wine. However, WINZ has no power to control the actions of its members.

Production of wine is heavily influenced by climatic conditions since these affect the size of the harvest. For example, the yield of 13.4 tonnes per hectare in 1983 was followed by a yield of 8.9 tonnes per hectare in 1984 due mainly to substantial changes in weather conditions. This was equivalent to a potential reduction of 24 750 tonnes (or over 30%) in the 1984 harvest of grapes. Notwithstanding climatic variations in the harvest size, there was a significant divergence between production, based on the harvest from producing vineyards, and the quantity of wine which the market could absorb. This led to increased stock-holdings which in 1985 reached a maximum for the industry of 84 million litres, or the equivalent of nearly two years' sales.

Figure 5.3 summarises some of the main statistics associated with the wine industry in New Zealand in the period from 1981 to 1992. As can be seen, the industry has been characterised by considerable fluctuations during this period.

Figure 5.3 Wine statistics (million litres)

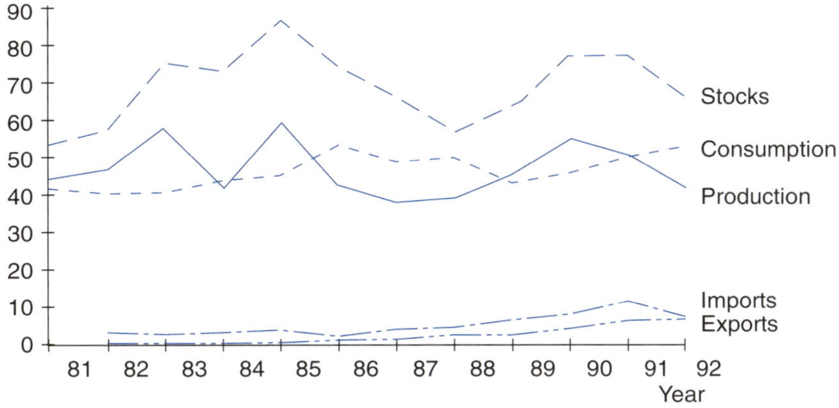

Model overview

This case provides an overview of a system dynamics model which has been developed to analyse the dynamic behaviour related to the New Zealand wine industry. This model was intended to be used to gain greater understanding of the forces shaping the industry and to help support the role of the Wine Institute within the industry. Also, the model can be used to determine the effects of environmental and policy changes on the industry, including the impact of variations in annual grape yields, excise duties and price movements.

For the sake of simplicity, the preliminary model has been constructed on an aggregate basis – using New Zealand as a single vineyard and market, and assuming grapes to be homogeneous. Figure 5.4 on the following page shows the simplified causal loop diagram for the New Zealand wine industry.

As stated in Chapter 3, the symbol | | indicates the presence of a significant material or information delay in the relationship. Five major (simplified) causal loops are apparent. Loops B1 to B4 are balancing (i.e. they generate goal-seeking behaviour) and loop R1 is a reinforcing loop (i.e. it generates growth or collapse behaviour).

For example, Loop B1 (a balancing loop) indicates that if wine stocks are increased by, say, an increase in production, then this will lead to a decrease in wine prices, which in turn will lead to an increase in consumption and hence decreased stock levels in the future. Therefore, actual stock levels are being controlled to match target levels by adjustments to wine prices and consumption levels.

Based on this causal loop diagram, a computer model[7] was constructed using the STELLA II dynamic simulation modelling package (Richmond, Petersen and Boyle, 1990) on a personal computer. This model has been reproduced as an *ithink* simulation model and appears in the technical appendix to this chapter.

Figure 5.4 Simplified causal loop diagram of the New Zealand wine industry preliminary model

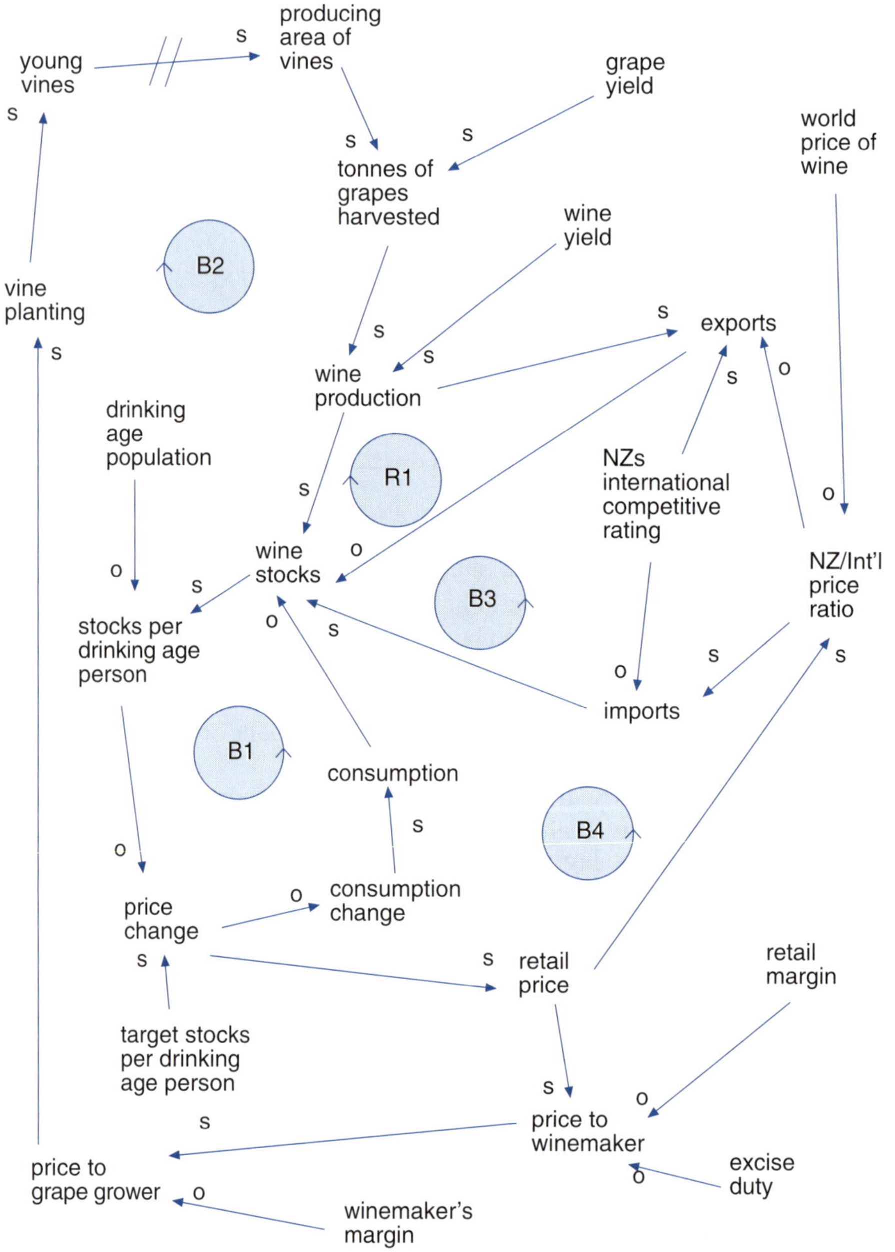

Scenario modelling

There are several variables in the model which can be changed to reflect possible environmental changes in the 'real world'. These changes give rise to several model scenarios, four of which will be illustrated here. They are changes to the wine excise duty; to New Zealand's international competitiveness; to the target stocks per drinking age person; and to the wine industry structure.

However, in this case each of the scenarios will be presented separately, rather than combined as in the telecommunications business unit case in Part II (Case 5). These scenarios can be followed in conjunction with Figure 5.4 on p. 92.

Scenario 1 Wine excise duty

Historically, high taxes and duties have been inflicted on consumers of alcohol and tobacco. The Wine Institute of New Zealand lobbies, on the one hand, for a reduction in indirect taxation, and on the other for moderation in the consumption of wine, so as to minimise the social damage which alcohol can cause, and maintain an image for wine that is better than the image of either beer or spirits. At the same time, the anti-alcohol lobby is seeking higher taxes on alcohol. Indirect taxes could either rise or fall in the future, with consequent effects on wine consumption.

In 1988, the excise duty on wine was increased from $1.32 to $1.50 per litre, and this was to be inflation-adjusted every six months. In 1992, the rate was $1.70 per litre.

Figures 5.5(a) and 5.5(b) show the sensitivity to the 1999 excise duty changes of between $1.20 (line 1 on the graphs) and $2.20 (line 5), in steps of 25c. When the duty is increased to or reduced from $1.70, the rate of planting changes in the opposite direction. However, the long-term New Zealand retail real prices of wine also change in the same direction as the initial change in excise duties. Note that the model does not assume an immediate short-term adjustment to changes in excise duties, although there are long-term effects due to changes in supply and demand.

Figure 5.5(a)   Excise duty changes – effect on vine plantings

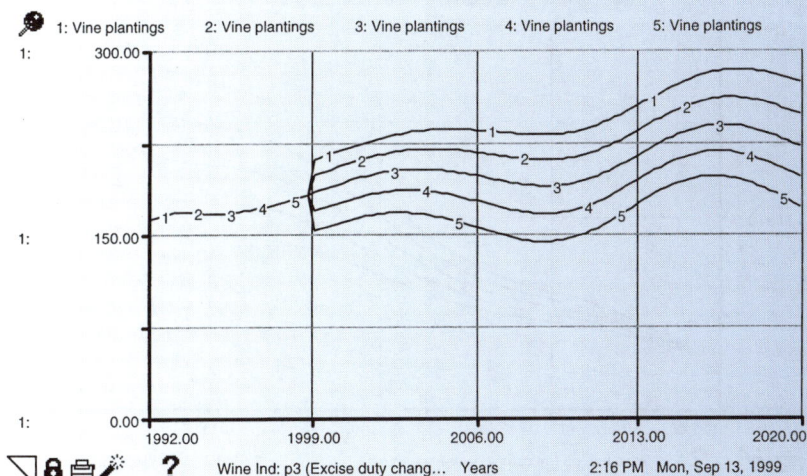

Figure 5.5(b) Excise duty changes – effect on New Zealand wine prices

Scenario 2   New Zealand international competitiveness

This variable sets the rate at which New Zealand's trading competitiveness changes. Initially set at 0, indicating that New Zealand's competitiveness remains at 1991 levels, an increase to, say, 0.01, indicates an improvement of 1% per annum.

New Zealand's international competitiveness could change due to exchange rate fluctuations, an increase or decrease in tariffs in countries importing New Zealand wine, an increase or decrease in tariffs in New Zealand on imported wine, or a world-wide shortage of wine.

Figure 5.6(a) Changes in international competitiveness – effect on wine exports

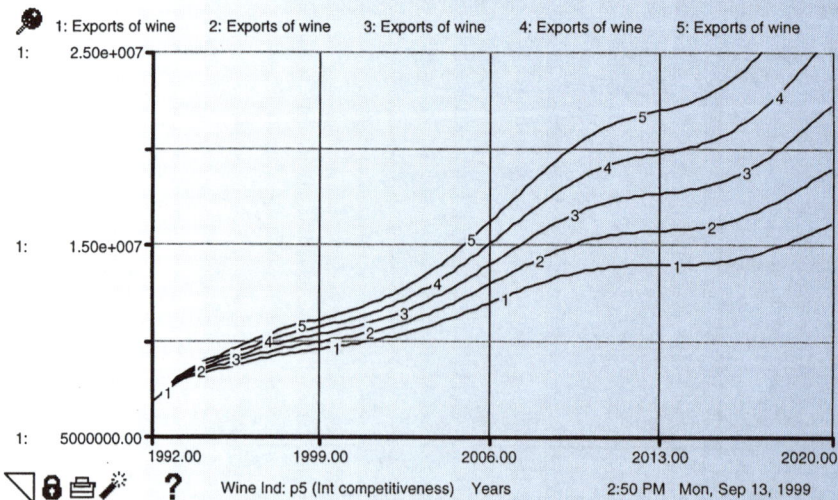

Figures 5.6(a) and (b) show the effects on wine exports and New Zealand retail prices of the following constant annual changes in New Zealand competitiveness: (1) –1%; (2) –0.5%; (3) 0; (4) +0.5%; (5) +1%. As New Zealand becomes more competitive, exports increase and imports decrease, resulting in reduced stocks and rising prices.

Figure 5.6(b)   Changes in international competitiveness – effect on New Zealand wine prices

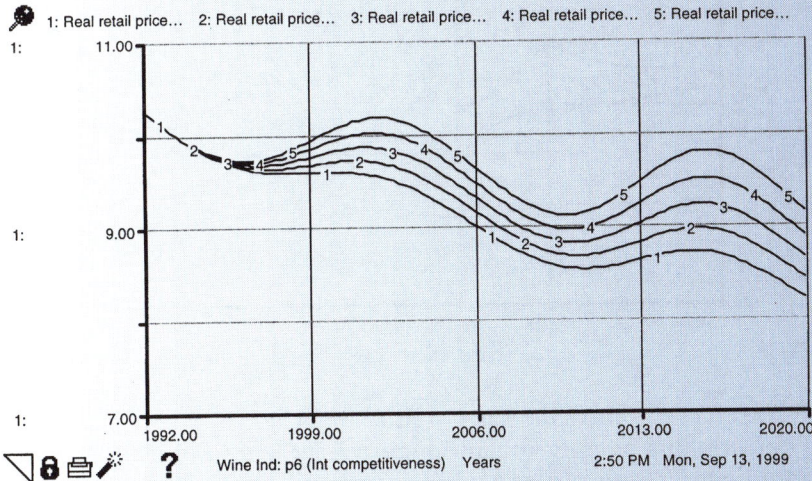

Scenario 3   Target stocks per drinking age person

Historically, this stock level has oscillated around 40 litres per drinking age person (DAP), but this could change. A rationalisation of wine distribution which has the effect of increasing the efficiency of this part of the industry will allow the target to fall. Alternatively, a reduction in distribution efficiency could cause the target level to be increased.

Figure 5.7(a)   Target stocks per drinking age person (DAP) constant

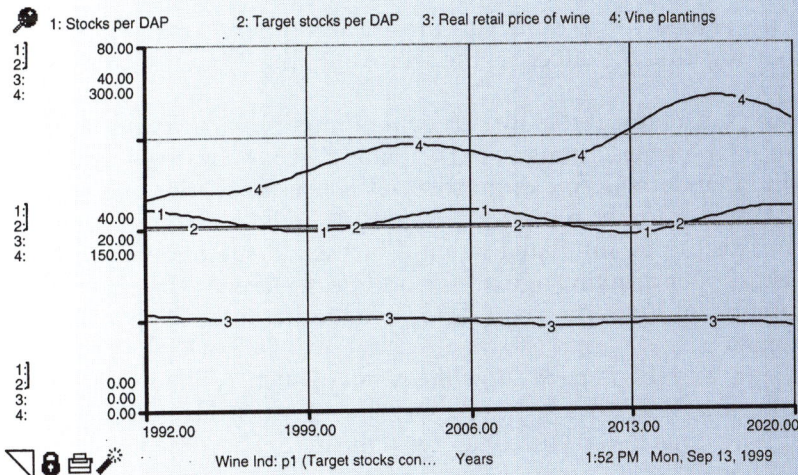

Figure 5.7(b)   Target stocks per drinking age person (DAP) falling

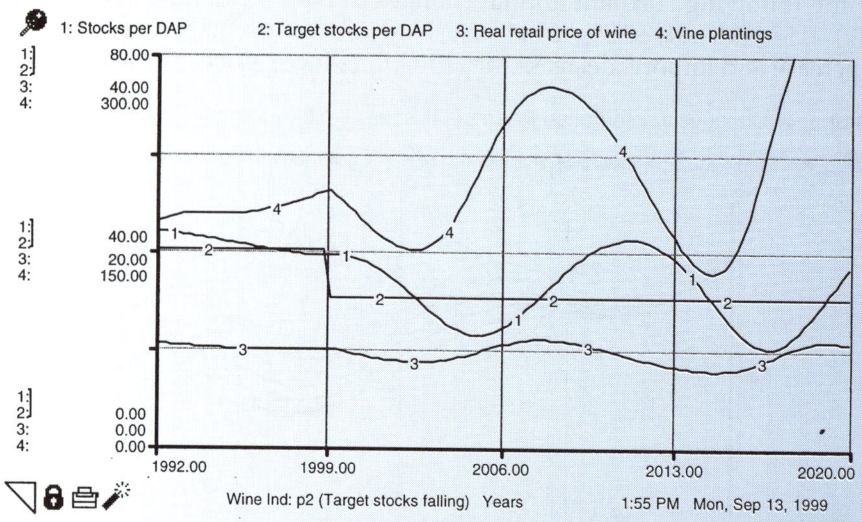

1: Stocks per DAP   2: Target stocks per DAP   3: Real retail price of wine   4: Vine plantings

Wine Ind: p2 (Target stocks falling) Years   1:55 PM Mon, Sep 13, 1999

Figure 5.7(a) on p. 95 shows the current situation if stocks of wine remain constant at 40 litres per drinking age person, and Figure 5.7(b) shows the effect of the target dropping rapidly to 30 litres per drinking age person in 1999. This drop immediately precipitates a price decrease (stimulating consumption) and a decrease in the planting rate. The net effect of such a rapid change in policy is to increase the magnitude of the swings in all the industry variables.

It should be noted that the Wine Institute does monitor stock levels, commenting to industry members on whether the levels are considered high or low, and thus becomes an important agent of change.

Scenario 4   Effects of changes to industry structure

The model developed so far replicates historical industry trends. It is worthwhile, however, investigating the effects of the removal of the Wine Institute (WINZ) from the industry.

WINZ can play a critical role by surveying industry participants and publishing the results of such surveys. Industry participants are thus able to use this information in their individual decision-making processes concerning price and planting rates. Removal of WINZ from the industry could result in delays in the provision of such information. This can be simulated by introducing a delay of one year between the variables – stocks per drinking age person and price change. The effect of this is that aggregate pricing information would be delayed rather than being available quickly to decision makers.

Figures 5.9(a) and (b) on p. 98 show the result of such a change. These graphs are directly comparable with the base case shown in Figures 5.8(a) and (b) on p. 97, and it is obvious that the oscillations in the model become more dramatic as a result of the change.

Figure 5.8(a)   Base case

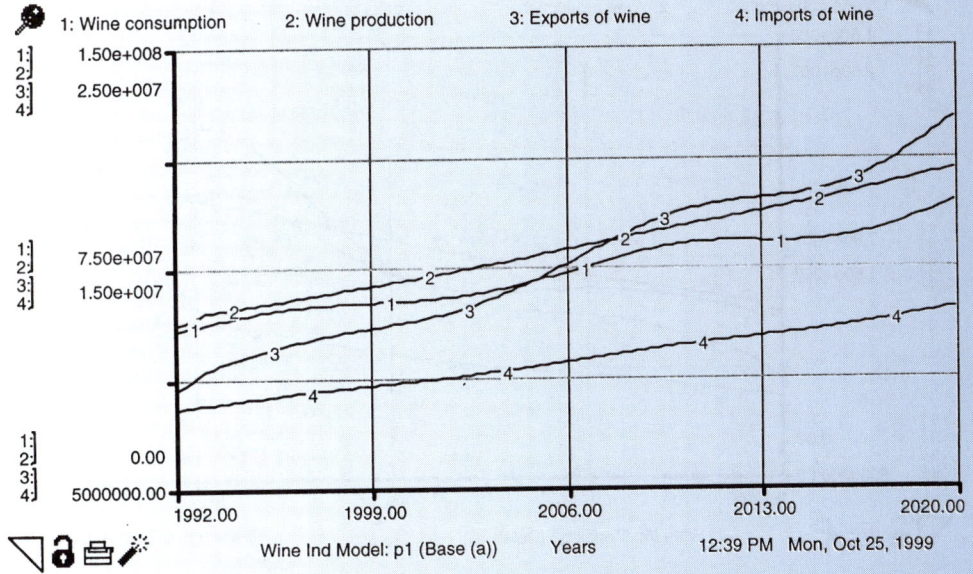

1: Wine consumption   2: Wine production   3: Exports of wine   4: Imports of wine

Wine Ind Model: p1 (Base (a))   Years   12:39 PM   Mon, Oct 25, 1999

Figure 5.8(b)   Base case

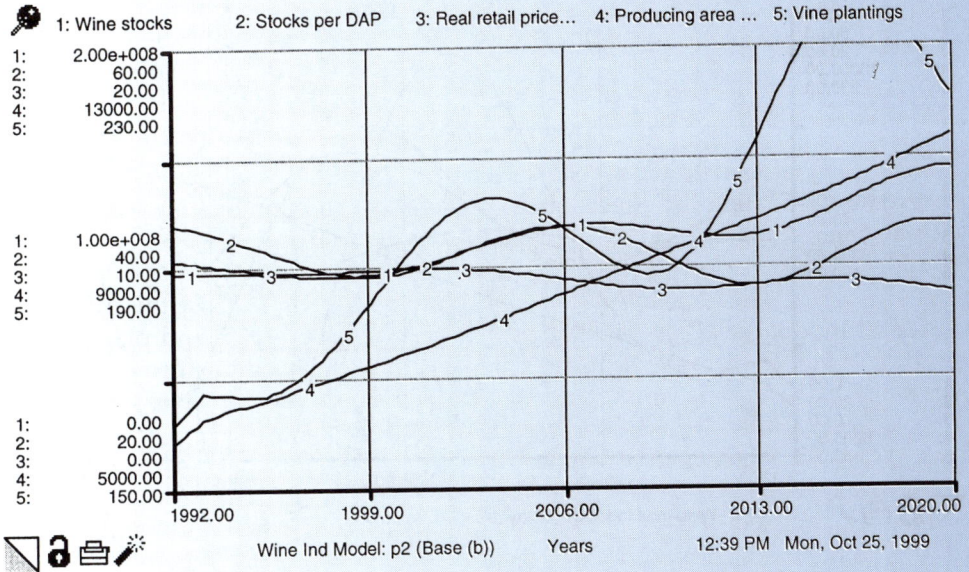

1: Wine stocks   2: Stocks per DAP   3: Real retail price...   4: Producing area ...   5: Vine plantings

Wine Ind Model: p2 (Base (b))   Years   12:39 PM   Mon, Oct 25, 1999

Figure 5.9(a)   Effect of a delay in information

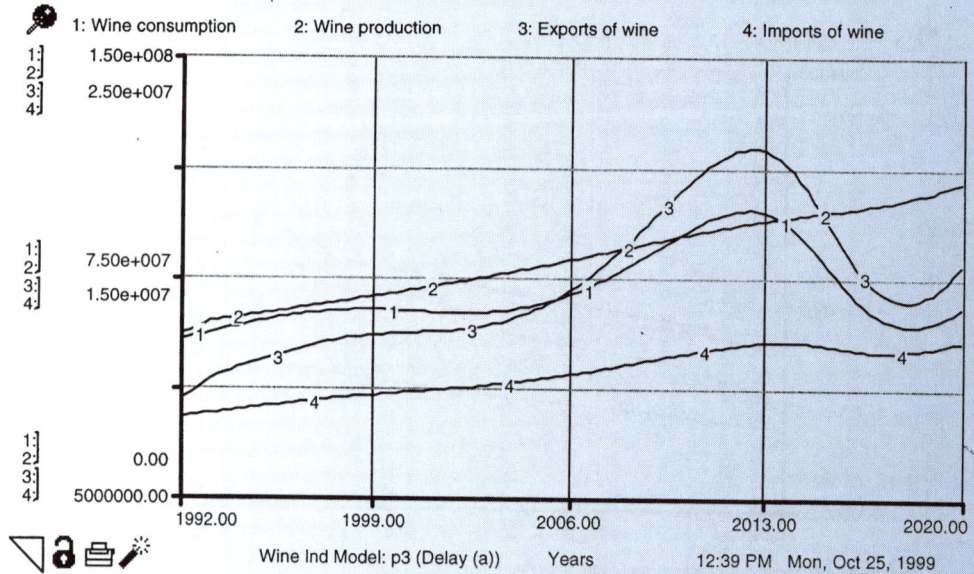

1: Wine consumption   2: Wine production   3: Exports of wine   4: Imports of wine

Wine Ind Model: p3 (Delay (a))   Years   12:39 PM   Mon, Oct 25, 1999

Figure 5.9(b)   Effect of a delay in information

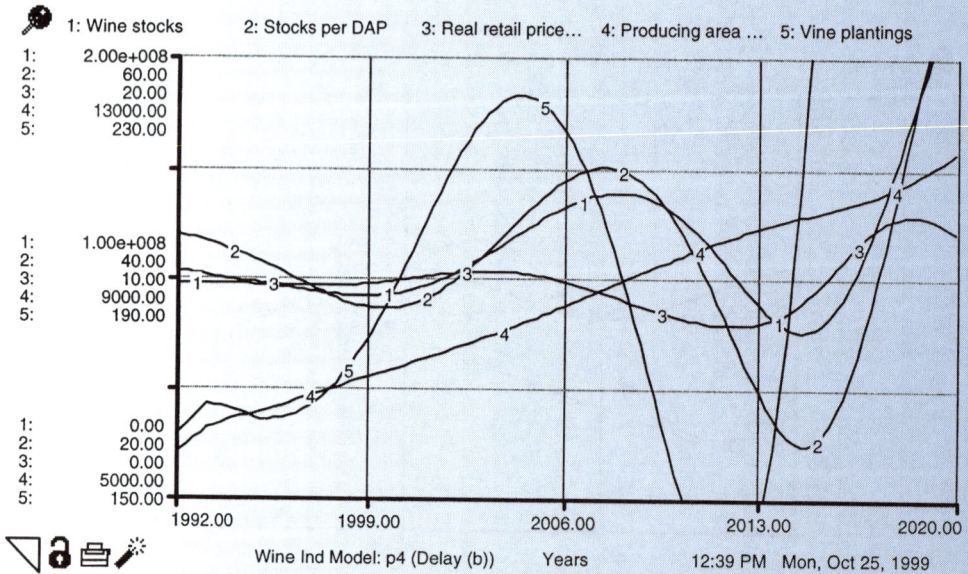

1: Wine stocks   2: Stocks per DAP   3: Real retail price...   4: Producing area ...   5: Vine plantings

Wine Ind Model: p4 (Delay (b))   Years   12:39 PM   Mon, Oct 25, 1999

Conclusions

The wine industry is characterised by high sunk costs, both in the winery and the vineyard. Growers are reluctant to abandon the harvest or to remove vines, even when prices are low. As long as the cost of harvesting grapes is lower than the revenue which they generate (machine harvesting results in relatively low costs), growers will harvest and sell the crop. This factor, together with the delay of three years before vines mature, results in a 'ratchet' effect on grape supply. This leads to periods of an oscillation between oversupply and undersupply of wine, causing wide fluctuations in prices in the longer term.

The type of dynamic simulation model discussed here would allow stakeholders in the wine industry to undertake scenario analysis to gain three important insights:

a anticipation of the long-term impact of environmental changes (e.g. excise tax changes, international price and currency movements, government policy changes, etc.);

b assessment of the impact of structural and policy changes within the wine industry (e.g. changes in target stocks, information effects of industry structure, planting decisions, etc.); and

c the understanding that cyclical changes are normal and may be short-term ones. These 'normal' cyclic changes can be seen clearly in the model output provided above, and thus may allow growers and wine makers to make more informed long-term strategic decisions concerning grape and wine supply.

Technical appendix: Equations for the wine industry model

Consumers_price_index(t) = Consumers_price_index(t - dt) + (Change_in_CPI) * dt

INIT Consumers_price_index = 1 {fraction}

DOCUMENT: This is a 1992-based CPI figure.

INFLOWS:

Change_in_CPI = Expected_inflation*Consumers_price_index {fraction/year}

Consumption_per_drinking_age_person(t) = Consumption_per_drinking_age_person(t - dt) + (Change_in_consumption) * dt

INIT Consumption_per_drinking_age_person = 24 {litres/person/year}

DOCUMENT: In 1992 the consumption of wine per drinking age person was 24.0 litres.

INFLOWS:

Change_in_consumption = Consumption_per_drinking_age_person*Percentage_change_in_consumption {litres/person/year/year}

Drinking_age_people(t) = Drinking_age_people(t - dt) + (Change_in_drinking_age_people) * dt

INIT Drinking_age_people = 2208000 {persons}

DOCUMENT: In 1992 the number of drinking age people (population between 16 and 64) was 2.208 million. This represented 63.9% of the total population.

INFLOWS:

Change_in_drinking_age_people = Drinking_age_people*(0.016-step(0.002, 1996)) {persons/year}

DOCUMENT: Between 1988 and 1992 the average increase in the drinking age population was 1.6% p.a. After 1996 the increase in drinking age population is expected to slow to around 1.4% p.a. (According to data from the New Zealand Department of Statistics). (The number of drinking age people is assumed to be the New Zealand population between the ages of 16 and 64.)

Maturing_area_of_vines(t) = Maturing_area_of_vines(t - dt) + (Vine_plantings - Vines_reaching _maturity) * dt

INIT Maturing_area_of_vines = 400, 180, 119 {hectares}

TRANSIT TIME = 3

INFLOW LIMIT = INF

CAPACITY = INF

DOCUMENT: This conveyor (special stock type) represents the stock of planted grape vines before they mature to producing grape vines. Historical data and interviews with grape growers has indicated that the average time to maturity is three years. As initial values must be set in the conveyor, the areas planted in grapes three years before the simulation starts (simulation starts in 1992) must be entered.

Year	Area planted in wine grapes (hectares)
1989	400
1990	180
1991	119

INFLOWS:

Vine_plantings = Area_planted_per_year {hectares/year}

DOCUMENT: This is the total area of grape vines planted in each year (in hectares).

OUTFLOWS:

Vines_reaching_maturity = CONVEYOR OUTFLOW

DOCUMENT: The area of vines reaching maturity each year, and capable of bearing grapes for harvesting. {hectares/year}

New Zealand_International_competitiveness(t) = New Zealand_International_competitiveness(t - dt) + (Change_in_competitiveness) * dt

INIT New Zealand_International_competitiveness = 1 {fraction}

DOCUMENT: This represents New Zealand's competitive trading status. If the $NZ falls then this competitive rating will increase. Other factors that may influence this are a shortage of wine in world markets or an increase in the world price of wine. If this figure = 1 then the *status quo* (i.e. 1992 competitive ratings) will apply. If this figure increases then New Zealand will become more competitive in world markets, exports will increase and imports will decrease.

INFLOWS:

Change_in_competitiveness = New Zealand_International_competitiveness*0 {fraction/year}

DOCUMENT: This figure is initially set to 0 to represent no change in New Zealand's relative trading position. If, for example, it is changed to 0.01 then New Zealand's competitive position will improve by 1% per year.

Producing_area_of_vines(t) = Producing_area_of_vines(t - dt) + (Vines_reaching_maturity) * dt

INIT Producing_area_of_vines = 5800 {hectares}

DOCUMENT: In 1992 the producing area of wine grape vines in New Zealand was 5800 hectares.

INFLOWS:

Vines_reaching_maturity = CONVEYOR OUTFLOW

DOCUMENT: The area of vines reaching maturity each year, and capable of bearing grapes for harvesting {hectares/year}

Real_retail_price_of_wine(t) = Real_retail_price_of_wine(t - dt) + (Change_in_real_price) * dt

INIT Real_retail_price_of_wine = 10.23 {$/litre}

DOCUMENT: The 1992 retail price of wine was $10.23 per litre. The real price is based on 1992 dollars.

INFLOWS:

Change_in_real_price = Real_retail_price_of_wine*Percentage_change_in_real_price {$/litre/year}

Wine_for_distribution_and_storage(t) = Wine_for_distribution_and_storage(t - dt) + (Wine_production - Exports_of_wine - Transfers_to_stock) * dt

INIT Wine_for_distribution_and_storage = 55200000 {litres}

DOCUMENT: Exports come out of this stock, and the remainder is transferred to storage in wineries and to distribution channels. In 1992, 55.2 million litres of wine was produced in New Zealand (5800 hectares of producing vines * 12.4 tonnes/hectare * 767 litres of wine/tonne).

INFLOWS:

Wine_production = Tonnes_of_grapes_harvested*Average_wine_yield {litres/year}

DOCUMENT: The volume of wine produced each year (in litres) is equal to the volume of wine grapes harvested (in tonnes) * the average yield of wine produced per tonne of wine grapes.

OUTFLOWS:

Exports_of_wine = Exports_per_year {litres/year}

DOCUMENT: The total exports {litres} of New Zealand wine per year.

Transfers_to_stock = Wine_for_distribution_and_storage-Exports_of_wine {litres/year}

DOCUMENT: This is the volume of wine {litres} produced each year that is not exported.

Wine_stocks(t) = Wine_stocks(t - dt) + (Transfers_to_stock + Imports_of_wine - Wine_consumption) * dt

INIT Wine_stocks = 96400000 {litres}

DOCUMENT: In 1992, 96.4 million litres of wine were stored in wineries and distribution channels.

INFLOWS:

Transfers_to_stock = Wine_for_distribution_and_storage-Exports_of_wine {litres/year}

DOCUMENT: This is the volume {litres} of wine produced each year that is not exported.

Imports_of_wine = Imports_per_year {litres/year}

DOCUMENT: The volume of wine {litres} imported into New Zealand each year.

OUTFLOWS:

Wine_consumption = Consumption_per_drinking_age_person*Drinking_age_people {litres/year}

DOCUMENT: This is the total consumption of wine (in litres) by New Zealanders per year.

Actual_retail_price = Real_retail_price_of_wine*Consumers_price_index {$/litre}

DOCUMENT: This is the retail price of wine adjusted by CPI to represent the actual dollar price of wine in any one year.

Area_planted_per_year = Producing_area_of_vines*Planting_as_percentage_of_producing_area {hectares/year}

DOCUMENT: This is the area planted in new vines per year.

Average_grape_yield = 12.4 {tonnes/hectare/year}

DOCUMENT: Between 1988 and 1992 the average yield (tonnes of grapes per hectare of producing area) was 12.4. The standard deviation over this period was 1.0 tonnes per hectare.

Average_wine_yield = 767 {litres/tonne}

DOCUMENT: Between 1988 and 1992 the average yield (from a tonne of wine grapes was 767 litres. The standard deviation was 7.0 litres per tonne.

Expected_inflation = 0.02 {fraction/year}

DOCUMENT: This variable represents the expected annual percentage change in inflation from 1992 onwards.

Exports_as_percentage_of_production = 0.17*(New Zealand_International_competitiveness/Relative_New Zealand_wine_price) {fraction}

DOCUMENT: In 1992 New Zealand exported 17% of its wine production. If New Zealand increases its trading competitiveness then exports will rise. If the real price of wine in New Zealand decreases then exports will rise (because they would be more competitive in international markets).

Exports_per_year = Wine_production*Exports_as_percentage_of_production {litres/year}

DOCUMENT: The volume of exports per year is equal to exports as a percentage of total consumption * total New Zealand consumption.

Imports_as_a_percentage_of_consumption = 0.16*(Relative_New Zealand_wine_price/ New Zealand_International_competitiveness) {fraction}

DOCUMENT: In 1992 New Zealand imported 16% of its total wine consumption. If the price of New Zealand wine increases then imports will increase. If New Zealand's international competitiveness falls (due to a higher $NZ) then imports will rise.

Imports_per_year = Wine_consumption*Imports_as_a_percentage_of_consumption {litres/year}

DOCUMENT: Wine imports per year is equal to 5% of the current producing area each year.

Maximum_planting_as_percentage_of_producing_area = 0.05 {fraction/year}

DOCUMENT: As growers have limited labour and time resources it is assumed that the maximum area of vines that they can plant each year is equal to 5% of their current producing area.

Minimum_grower_revenue = 4000 {$/hectare}

DOCUMENT: The minimum grower revenue is the revenue per hectare (in constant 1992 dollars) that growers must receive in order to make it worth their while to plant additional vines. This figure will depend on the expected returns from other crops as well as the cost of planting vines.

It is assumed that growers base their planting decision on the prevailing returns from selling grapes. Historical data backs up this assumption as growers tend to plant much more when the price per tonne of grapes is high.

PED = -1.18 {fraction}

DOCUMENT: Price elasticity of demand (consumption) has been determined by calculations using historical data relating to consumption per drinking age person and real retail prices of wine per litre.

Percentage_change_in_consumption = PED*Percentage_change_in_real_price {fraction/year}

DOCUMENT: The percentage change in consumption of wine (litres per drinking age person per year) is equal to PED * the percentage change in the real retail price of a litre of wine. As PED is negative, an increase in real price causes a decrease in consumption.

Percentage_change_in_real_price = Stock_ratio*0.25 {fraction/year}

DOCUMENT: The relationship between stock levels and price changes has been determined to approximate the following formula:
% change in price = (target stock levels/actual stock per drinking person - 1) * 0.25
                 = stock ratio * 0.25

Planting_as_percentage_of_producing_area = if(Revenue_to_grower_per_hectare-Minimum_grower_revenue)<0 then 0 else (1-exp(-(Revenue_to_grower_per_hectare/6000-Minimum_grower_revenue/6000)))*Maximum_planting_as_percentage_of_producing_area {fraction/year}

DOCUMENT: The exponential function is used to ensure that plantings start when the minimum grower revenue is exceeded, planting then rises fairly fast, then tails off when the maximum possible planting as a percentage of producing area figure is approached. If the prevailing revenue received is less than the minimum required to prompt planting, a zero planting rate is assigned.

Real_price_to_wineries = Real_retail_price_of_wine_per_litre*(1-Retail_markup)-Wine_excise_duty {$/litre}

DOCUMENT: The real price to wineries is equal to the real retail price less the retail markup less the wine excise duty.

Relationship_between_winemakers_and_growers_price = 2000 {litres/hectare}

DOCUMENT: This represents the revenue/hectare to grower as a multiple of the real price per litre to wineries.

Relative_New Zealand_wine_price = Real_retail_price_of_wine_per_litre/World_price_of_wine {fraction}

DOCUMENT: This represents the relative price of New Zealand wine to the world price of wine. As the relative price of New Zealand wine increases, imports will tend to the world price of wine. As the relative price of New Zealand wine increases imports will tend to decrease (as they will be more competitive) and exports will decrease (as they will be less competitive with wines from other countries).

Retail_markup = 0.40 {fraction}

DOCUMENT: This is the % of the retail price that represents the retailer's markup.

Revenue_to_grower_per_hectare = Relationship_between_winemakers_and_growers_price*Real_price_to_wineries {$/hectare}

DOCUMENT: The relationship between the revenue winemakers receive per litre of wine and the revenue the growers receive per hectare of grapes harvested is:

revenue per hectare = 2000 * revenue received by winemaker per litre of wine.

This revenue per hectare is in constant 1992 dollars.

Stocks_per_DAP = Wine_stocks/Drinking_age_people {litres/person}

DOCUMENT: This is the total New Zealand stock of wine (in litres) per capita of drinking age population. It gives the relative size of the current wine stocks. (DAP = drinking age person)

Stock_ratio = Target_stocks_per_drinking_age_person/Stocks_per_DAP-1 {fraction}

DOCUMENT: The difference between target and actual stocks (per drinking age person) as a ratio of actual stocks per drinking age person.

Target_stocks_per_DAP = 40 {litres/person}

DOCUMENT: Over the last 10 years the total New Zealand wine stocks per drinking age person has oscillated around 40 litres.

Tonnes_of_grapes_harvested = Producing_area_of_vines*Average_Yield_grape_yield {tonnes/year}

DOCUMENT: The volume of grapes harvested in each year equals the producing area of wine grape vines (hectares) * the average yield in tonnes per hectare.
Note that all the producing vines are harvested each year. Historic data shows that even in very bad times (in terms of the revenue the growers receive) growers have harvested all their grapes.

Wine_excise_duty = 1.70 {$/litre}

DOCUMENT: In 1988 the excise duty on wine was increased from $1.32 per litre to $1.50 per litre. This $1.50 per litre excise duty is adjusted by the CPI. The 1992 excise duty equalled $1.70 per litre, therefore the real duty rate is $1.70 in 1992 dollar terms.

World_price_of_wine = 10.23 {$/litre}

DOCUMENT: This is the price of wine in international markets as of 1992. This figure will not change as exchange rate effects are taken into account in the 'New Zealand international competitiveness' variable.
As 1992 is taken as the base for simulation this figure is set at the real price of New Zealand wine in 1992.

Notes

1   *The Concise Oxford Dictionary of Current English*, 9th ed. (1995) Oxford University Press, Oxford.

2   Shell's approach to scenario planning has been fully documented by Pierre Wack in his two articles in the *Harvard Business Review*: 'Scenarios: unchartered waters ahead', *HBR*, Sep–Oct 1985: 73–90; and 'Scenarios: shooting the rapids', *HBR*, Nov–Dec 1985: 131–142.

3   For example, see the books by Peter Schwartz (1996) *The Art of the Long View*, Currency Doubleday, New York, and Kees van den Heijden (1997) *Scenarios: The Art of Strategic Conversation*, Wiley, Chichester.

4   Full details of the Foresight Project are provided in the document *Building Tomorrow's Success: Guidelines for Thinking Beyond Tomorrow*, Ministry of Research, Science and Technology, Wellington, March 1998. Current details are available on the MORST website: http://www.morst.govt.nz/foresight/fron.html. The material in this section is taken from these two sources.

5   These scenarios, or stories, are summarised in the Annex to *Building Tomorrow's Success: Guidelines for Thinking Beyond Tomorrow*, Ministry of Research, Science and Technology, Wellington, March 1998 and are also available on the MORST website: http://www.morst.govt.nz/foresight/fron.html.

6   A fuller account of this case is provided in a paper by R.Y. Cavana, J.W. Chester and J.F.S. Cooper, 'A policy making framework for the New Zealand wine industry', published in *System Dynamics: An International Journal of Policy Modelling*, IX(1) 1997: 1–19.

7   This model was originally developed for an unpublished 1992 MMBA 571 project report by J.W. Chester and J.F.S. Cooper, 'The Wine Industry – A Dynamic Model', Graduate School of Business and Government Management, Victoria University of Wellington, Wellington.

REFERENCES

Becker, H.S. (1983) Scenarios: a tool of growing importance to policy analysts in government and industry. *Technological Forecasting and Social Change*, 23: 96.

Cerf, C. and Navasky, V. (1984) *The experts speak*. Pantheon, New York.

De Geus, A. (1998) *The Living Company*. Nicholas Brearly, London.

Moyer, K. (1996) Scenario Planning at British Airways – A case study. *Long Range Planning*, 29(2): 180–181.

Richmond, B., Petersen, S. and Boyle, D. (1990) *STELLA II User's Guide*. High Performance Systems, Hanover NH 03755.

Schnaars, S.P. (1987) How to develop and use scenarios. *Long Range Planning*, 20(1): 104–114.

Schoemaker, P.J.H. (1993) Multiple scenario development: its conceptual and behavioural foundation. *Strategic Management Journal*, 14: 197.

Schoemaker, P.J.H. (1995) Scenario planning: a tool for strategic thinking. *Sloan Management Review*, Winter.

Wack, P. (1985) Scenarios: shooting the rapids. *Harvard Business Review*, Nov–Dec: 140.

Chapter 6

Microworlds and learning laboratory

OVERVIEW

This chapter introduces two important tools and technologies of systems thinking, namely microworlds and learning labs. These technologies are presented in relation to two key organisational concepts, i.e. managerial practice field and the learning cycle. We show how the learning lab process can assist with the alignment of divergent mental models and facilitate creating a shared understanding within a group or organisation. We demonstrate the learning lab process through two laboratory *experiences* in a step-by-step fashion. These learning labs represent the dynamics of service quality and human resource planning in the context of two service firms, respectively.

Introduction

Microworlds are 'live' models of real-life situations. They are 'virtual worlds' or 'constructed representations of the real world' (Schön, 1983) in which managers can experience a day in the life of the company. Also known as management flight simulators (MFS), microworlds are constructed in various simulation languages. They compress time and space and allow for interactive experimentation and scenario analysis. Flight simulators and sophisticated computer games are other types of microworld.

The purpose of the microworld is to provide a managerial-friendly interface with the computer model. For managers or users who do not wish to engage in model building, microworlds provide a 'black box' model of reality. This interface can take on a variety of forms depending on the simulation language used. Advanced versions of some simulation packages such as STELLA, *ithink* and POWERSIM allow for convenient construction of microworlds. All microworlds have a control panel, which often looks like the instrument or control panel of an aircraft. An example of a control panel is shown in Figure 6.1. One of the features of control panels is 'sliders'. In Figure 6.1, boxes identified as 'hiring' and 'laying off' are sliders. They represent decision variables of the model. There are also two graphical functions (GF) shown in the boxes on the left of the panel. As discussed in Chapter 4 (see p. 77), GFs represents numerical relationships between two variables. The main graph pad in this panel will show the BOT of output variables or key performance indicators. The smaller boxes below this pad show the final values of these variables at the end of each simulation run.

Figure 6.1   Example of a microworld control panel

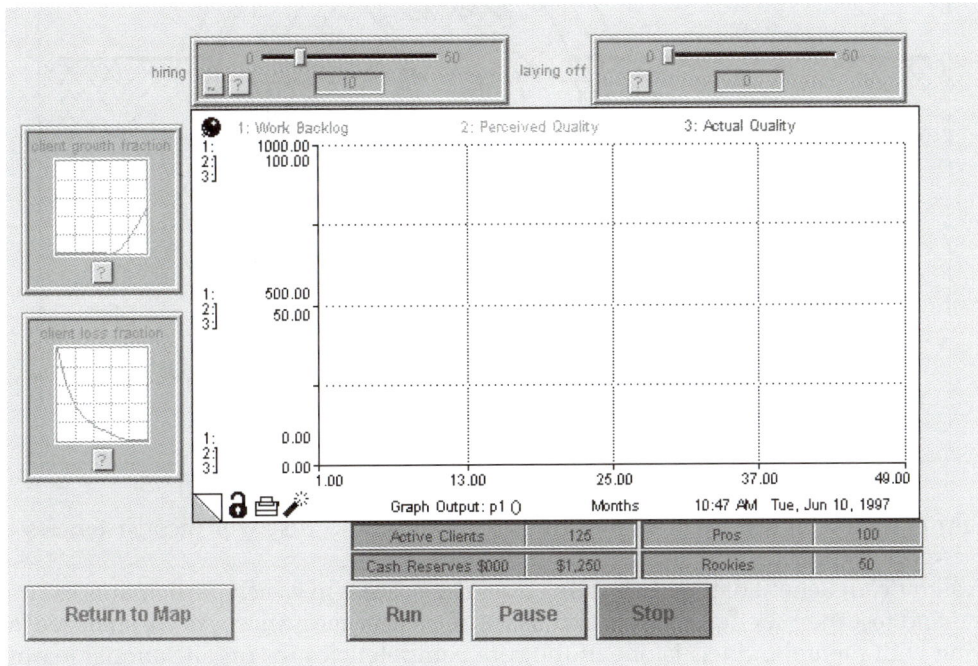

(Source: Service model, *ithink* software)

Learning laboratory (LLab)

Learning laboratory (LLab) is a process as well as a setting in which a group (i.e. a management team) can learn together. The purpose of the learning lab is to enable managers to experiment and 'see' the consequences of their actions, policies and strategies. This often results in finding inconsistencies and the discovery of *unintended* consequences of actions and decisions, *before* they are implemented. Microworlds are the 'engine' behind the LLab.

It must be emphasised that a LLab is distinct from so-called management games. In management games, the players are required to compete – design the 'best' strategy and 'beat' other players or teams. The competitive nature of management games often encourages aggressive and individualistic behaviour with very little regard for team learning and gaining deep insights. The learning lab, in contrast, aims to enhance *learning*, to provide deeper understanding and insights into why systems behave the way they do, to help participants test theories and mental models, and discover inconsistencies and 'blind spots' in policies and strategies.

A significant benefit of the LLab stems from the process in which participants examine, reveal and test their mental models and those of their organisation. As we shall see later, dealing with mental models is one of the core competencies for organisational learning. The LLab can also help participants

- to align strategic thinking with operational decisions;
- to connect short-term and long-term measures;
- to facilitate integration within and outside the organisation;
- to undertake experimentation and learning;
- to balance competition with collaboration.

Managerial practice field

In the last decade, the concepts of 'team' and 'teamwork' have received a great deal of attention. Company after company has reorganised work around a variety of team concepts. From factories to hospitals, *titles* like 'manager' and 'supervisor' have been replaced by *roles* such as 'facilitator' and 'team leader'. Despite this level of attention to team and teamwork the expected benefits have been marginal at best. But why?

Let us consider the working of 'successful' teams. What examples come to mind? Chicago Bulls, France's World Cup soccer team, America's Cup holders Team New Zealand? How about non-sporting 'teams', such as orchestras, ballet companies, astronomers and so on? What do these teams have in common? The answer is that they *practice* a lot more than they 'perform'. Practice means allowing time and space to experiment with new ways, try different approaches and most importantly, make mistakes without the fear of failure. In fact, making mistakes is indispensable to learning. One cannot learn from doing things right all the time! Yet a great deal of organisational energy and attention is devoted to the prevention and masking of mistakes.

What is the *practice field* for management teams? The fact is that the practice field is, by and large, absent from the managerial world. In other words, there is no time and no space for management to 'practice' – to experiment, make mistakes and learn together. In the era of restructuring and downsizing, lack of time is the greatest impediment to managerial and organisational learning. The pace in the modern work environment is so unrelenting that there is virtually no room for managers to slow down, to practice, reflect and learn. The consequence of this lack of practice and learning space is grave, in that most organisations only achieve a small fraction of their potential – about 5%, according to Jay Forrester (1994).

In order to fill this gap, the concept of learning laboratory (LLab) has been developed to provide practice fields for managers. The LLab allows learning to become an integral part of managerial work – it helps learning to become institutionalised. The practice field concept is shown in Figure 6.2 (Kim, 1993).

Figure 6.2   Managerial practice field as a learning system

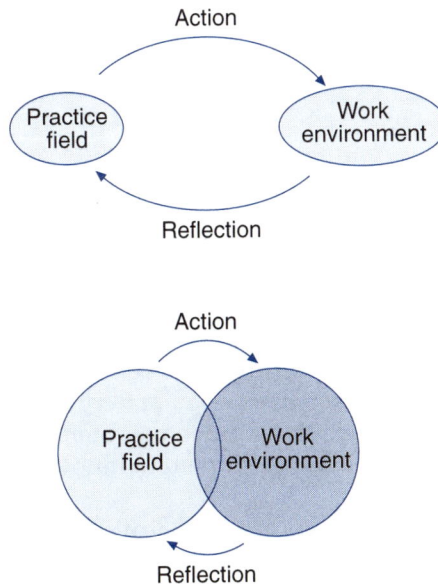

(Kim, 1993)

The learning cycle

The learning cycle is a 'holistic' approach to learning, which goes beyond cognitive learning. The learning lab process follows the three steps that are the elements of a learning cycle. These elements are *conceptualisation* or intellectual learning; *experimentation* or action learning; and *reflection* or emotional learning. This process is analogous to TQM's continuous improvement method known as the Deming cycle or Plan-Do-Check-Act (PDCA). The learning cycle is shown in Figure 6.3.

Figure 6.3   The learning cycle

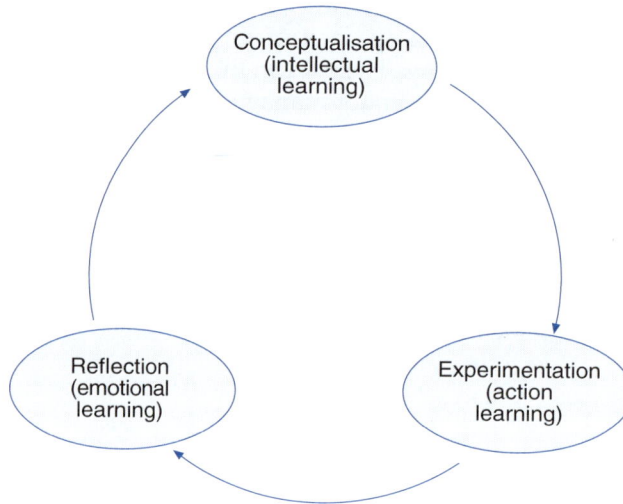

Conceptualisation

This is the learning associated with the mind and the intellect and is also known as cognitive or academic learning. This learning is about developing theories and hypotheses regarding the reasons why things happen as they do. Conceptualisation is also the step in which the learning outcomes from experimentation and reflection get cemented and formalised. It requires fresh and lateral thinking. Many firms are locked into standard industry practices that can be counterproductive to learning. Even popular techniques such as 'benchmarking' and 'best practice' fall short of ideal learning outcomes. Standard industry practices and even the 'best practices' can become an impediment to innovation and thinking 'outside the box'.

Leavitt and Lipman-Blumen (1995) coined the term 'Hot Groups' to refer to groups within organisations that are deeply dedicated to learning. Organisations where Hot Groups flourish, such as Bell Laboratories, place a high value on the 'scientific approach' and search for the 'truth'. These organisations welcome and encourage experimentation with new ideas, and are constantly searching for ways to advance their boundaries.

Experimentation

This refers to 'learning by doing', where new theories and hypotheses are tested in a 'laboratory' environment. Experimentation is the foundation of the 'scientific method'. One of the impediments to this approach is the cost associated with experimentation, and the fact that it is time-consuming. The LLab compresses experimentation time and thereby shortens the learning cycle. Short learning cycles permit a significant increase in the number and speed of experiments and lead to rapid learning. Conventional testing methods are also often too expensive and time-consuming, and prolong experiment time. Management flight simulators and learning laboratories are tools that significantly compress the experimentation time and allow managers to 'see' the implications of policy decisions almost instantaneously.

Long cycle times are a major barrier to experimentation in new product development and in policy analysis. Techniques such as rapid prototyping using stereolithography, a process whereby customers can actually *feel* the product and its characteristics, such as texture, help to shorten the experimentation phase in manufacturing firms (Maani and Benton, 1999).

Reflection

Reflection is the third element of the learning cycle. It allows team members to pause and think through their experiments. It allows one to engage with one's 'feelings' (i.e. assumptions, attitudes, biases, resentments, etc.) in addition to dealing with hard facts and sanitised results. Thus reflection can be thought of as 'emotional learning'. This is perhaps the most neglected area of the learning cycle. Too often management focuses on hard 'data', ignoring the 'emotions' that are attached to this information. As a consequence, loyalties are lost and commitment to management edicts becomes superficial and short-lived.

Story 1: Team New Zealand the America's Cup holders

The desire for experimentation was evident in the Team New Zealand 1995 camp when they decided to launch two similar boats, NZL-38 and NZL-32. The rationale behind this decision was that the two-boat trials would provide the maximum amount of information and improvement over the six months of the 'on the water' campaign (a lot of the ideas for the campaign were tested via on-board computer simulation – their 'learning lab'). Team New Zealand's willingness to experiment stemmed from a constant desire to learn – to test as many questions and scenarios as possible with respect to improving boat speed. As a result, the two-boat campaign led to constant improvements in boat speed.

Team New Zealand used simulation technology to 'experience' design changes. The designers built thousands of different boat shapes and experimented with them under the San Diego wind and wave conditions. The simulation software 'collapsed time' and enabled the design team (including the sailors) to *visualise* the repercussions of new design ideas.

> This process permitted Team New Zealand to 'build' thousands of different boat shapes, and test them to come up with 'the fastest thing on water'.
>
> (Maani and Benton, 1999)

Story 2: Xerox

> Xerox uses video recordings for experimentation. As an integral part of its new product development, management observes videos of the product while in use. Xerox has termed these videos 'unfinished documents'. The viewers are to complete the 'experiment' by suggesting their own ideas for how they might use the new technology and what these uses might entail for the business.
>
> (Maani and Benton, 1999)

Story 3: Royal Dutch Shell

> The importance of emotional commitment is strongly demonstrated by Royal Dutch Shell's Committee of Managing Directors (CMD). The CMD launched a series of workshops designed to shock, energise and mobilise executives into taking new corporate directions. Everyone participating in the workshop was asked to begin the session by spending 20 minutes drafting his or her own resignation. The exercise engaged the executives emotionally. It was the beginning of internalising a *personal* process for change.
>
> (Maani and Benton, 1999)

Aligning mental models through the learning laboratory

Mental models are formed throughout one's life. Family, school, culture, religion, profession and social norms play important roles in this formation. Therefore, modifying one's mental model is not a small matter. The most effective way to check one's mental models is to *experience* alternative realities at first hand and see their implications with a new 'lens'. 'It is never enough just to tell people about some new insight. Rather, you have to get them to *experience* it in a way that evokes its power and possibility' (Brown, 1991: 102–111).

As we observed in the Hanover Insurance case (pp. 48–54), learning lab can play a significant role in clarifying and changing mental models. There are rarely any opportunities in the course of a manager's daily work for him/her to engage in lengthy, drawn-out experimentation. Learning in a 'laboratory' setting is a viable and powerful alternative. Fortunately, advanced computers and sophisticated software have enabled the creation of managerial learning labs where managers can experiment, test their theories and learn rapidly. Learning lab deals with mental models at three levels (Senge and Sterman, 1991), as described below.

1 *Mapping* mental models. This step begins at the conceptualisation phase. Here, the LLab participants articulate and clarify their assumptions, views, opinions, and biases regarding the issue at hand.

2 *Challenging* mental models. The participants identify and discuss inconsistencies and contradictions in their assumptions. This step will begin at the conceptualisations phase and will continue to the experimentation phase.

3 *Improving* mental models. Having conducted experimentation and testing, the participants reflect on the outcomes. This may cause them to alter, adjust, improve and harmonise their mental models.

The laboratory setting provides a neutral and 'safe' space for the participants to create a shared understanding of complex and endemic issues. The following characteristics of the LLab provide a powerful catalyst for alignment of divergent mental models in the organisation.

- The laboratory environment is neutral and non-threatening. The emphasis is on learning and theory building (what we *don't* know), not on winning or display of knowledge.

- Lack of hierarchy. Managers and staff are equal in this environment. The traditional hierarchy is set aside in this laboratory setting.

- The response time is fast. Hence, the feedback cycle is short, which leads to rapid learning.

- There is no cost or 'loss of face' attached to failure. Hence, it is safe to make mistakes. In fact, mistakes provide opportunities for learning.

- People can see the consequences of their actions first hand. No one attempts to convince or teach anyone else or force his or her preconceived views on others. People learn by themselves and through group interactions.

Implications for management

The practice field and the LLab concepts have fresh and challenging implications for managers and their role. They suggest that a leader/manager should think as a *scientist*, be open to and welcome hard questions, experiment with new ideas, and be prepared to be *wrong*. This requires managers to learn systems thinking skills and use them not just for 'solving' problems but as powerful tools for communication, team building and organisational learning. This means that an effective leader is no longer the captain but the 'designer' of the ship (Senge, 1990: 10). Once they have designed a new structure, strategy, policy or procedure then the managers/leaders should allow (i.e. create a practice field for) the staff to experience the new design, and experiment with it and learn for themselves – the outcome is shared understanding and alignment of thought. This is the essence of practice field and learning laboratory theory.

Experience a learning laboratory: Example 1 – Service quality LLab

This example seeks to demonstrate the process of the learning laboratory in the context of a service firm. You, as the manager of the firm, are responsible for strategic decisions on recruitment policy, service quality, and service capacity. This LLab is based on a computer model known as Service Quality Microworld (SQM).[1] The overview map and control panel of the SQM are shown in Figure 6.4 on the following page.

Figure 6.4   Overview map and control panel of SQM

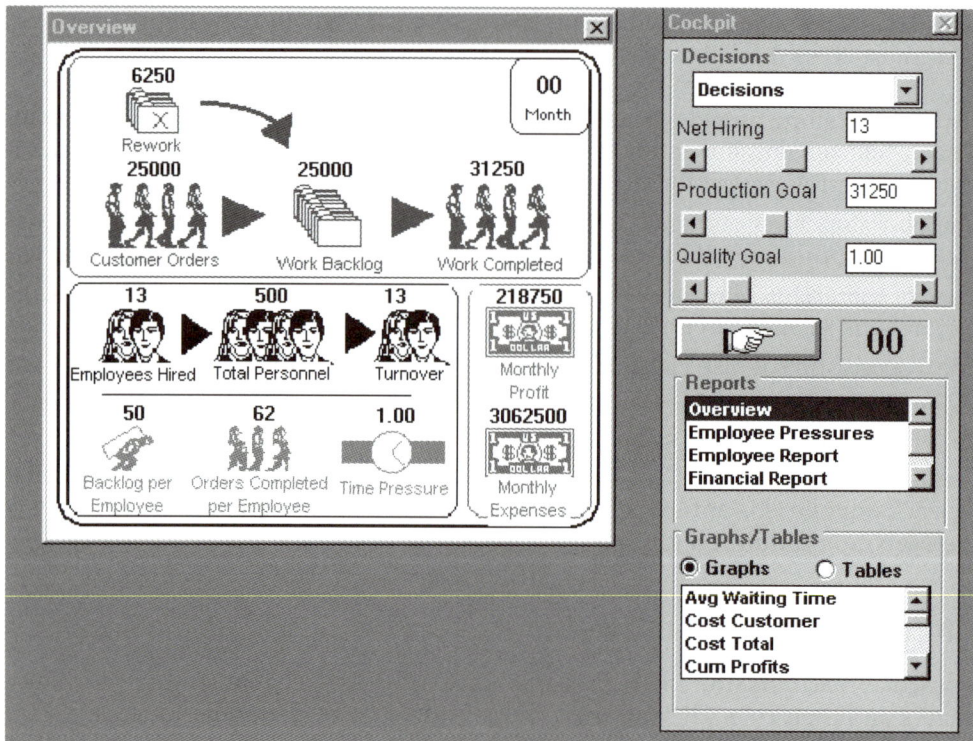

As can be seen on the control panel, there are three decision variables in SQM: Net Hiring, Production Goal, and Quality Goal. A change in any of these variables, such as new hiring or quality improvement, will set off a cycle of events in the system. This change will have a chain effect on internal variables such as workload, productivity, time pressure, burnout and so on. Of course, the greater the scope (number of variables changed at a time) and the magnitude of change, the greater the effects.

In order to illustrate the learning lab process we focus on a single decision variable, namely, *quality goal* as an internal agent for change. There are three quality indicators used in SQM that are defined below.

Quality goal. Quality goal is a decision (or exogenous) variable which reflects management's *desired* level of quality. It is calibrated as an index, where the industry average is set to 1.

Thus, values greater than one indicate above-industry-average quality. The reverse is also true, namely, values of less than one represent below-industry-average quality.

Quality standard. This is an *internal* measure of quality, one that the staff would deliver under normal time pressure and workload intensity. It reflects what management and employees perceive as the acceptable level of quality.

Actual quality. This is the *external* view of quality as seen by the customers. It reflects the actual level of quality that the customers are receiving.

The LLab process

● Step 1: Conceptualise

As an illustration here we explore the relationship between two variables, namely, *quality goal* and *rework*. Now, let us consider the following specific question:

> If quality goal were increased by 10%, how would this affect rework over time?

As a LLab participant, sketch your response to this question on a piece of paper. What does your graph look like? State your assumption about this relationship. In other words, explain why you think the effect will be what you think it will be. Most people would draw a steadily declining pattern like the one in Figure 6.5, since conventional wisdom holds that higher quality should lower rework level.

Figure 6.5 Hypothesised change in rework as a result of a step increase in quality goal

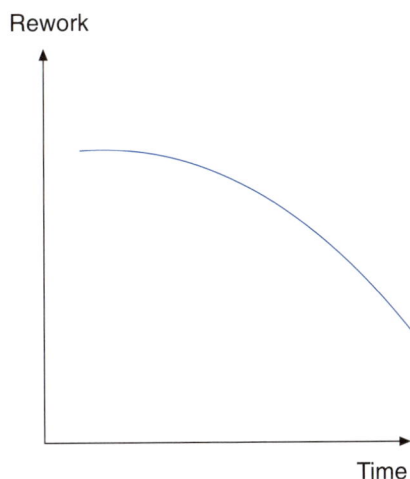

Having completed this step, we can proceed to the next step of the LLab process, i.e. experimentation, to test this hypothesis.

● Step 2: Experiment

This step of the LLab requires experimentation with the microworld. It involves running the SQM model with different values or scenarios for decision variables and reviewing relevant simulated responses (performance indicators). As we can see in the SQM overview, at the beginning of simulation there is a total rework of 6250 units or 12.5 (6250/500) units per employee. The question is how a step increase (i.e. of 10%) in quality goal would change the rework pattern. Figure 6.6 on the following page shows the simulated rework pattern over a five-year simulation run of the SQM model.

Figure 6.6   Simulated pattern of rework after a 10% increase in quality goal

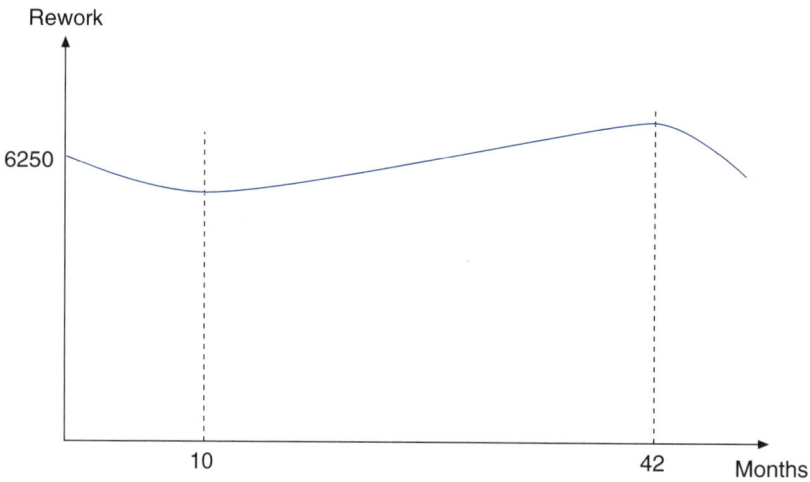

Does this match your graph? Are you surprised to see this pattern? As we can see, the rework level initially drops as expected until period 10 then it begins to rise gradually for a long interval (to period 42) before it starts to fall again. Why doesn't the rework level steadily decline as was expected?

● Step 3: Reflect

In order to answer this question, we need to understand the dynamics between quality goal, quality standard and actual quality. This dynamic is depicted in Figure 6.7.

Figure 6.7   Quality loop

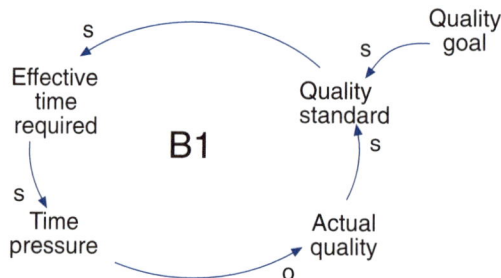

As we can see this is a balancing loop (B1), indicating that a higher quality *goal* will ultimately result in *lower* actual quality and quality standards! This is counterintuitive. Why is it so?

In order to understand this, it is important to keep in mind the distinction between quality *goal* and *actual* quality. While quality goal represents management's desired level of quality, in reality, actual quality begins to improve only after adequate resources (e.g. training, systems and equipment, etc.) have been devoted to product and process improvement. Otherwise, an increase in quality goal will add to staff workload as they will need to work harder to achieve the more demanding quality level. This will increase the time pressure on staff. In a service organisation actual quality means, among other things, fewer errors and mistakes, on-time deliveries, and more fulfilling customer contacts (moments of truth), all of which require more time and greater attention to detail. Expecting higher quality without providing corresponding levels of resources and adequate support systems will increase pressure in the organisation and will, ultimately, lead to increased burnout and staff turnover.

How then does this dynamic affect rework? As we saw above, rework did *not* continually decline as anticipated. How can we explain this? Let us now look at the dynamic between actual quality and rework. This is captured by the following CLD in Figure 6.8.

Figure 6.8   Quality-rework loop

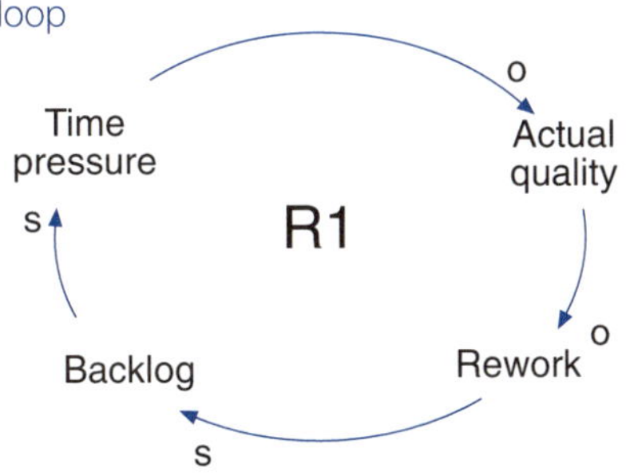

This CLD represents a reinforcing dynamic (R1), showing that once a decline in actual quality begins it will continue and will be exacerbated by growing rework and increasing time pressure. This is because higher rework will increase work backlog and will result in greater time pressure. This creates a vicious cycle as shown in Figure 6.8, which indicates that the harder we push for quality the more rework we get!

Figure 6.9   Quality–staffing loop

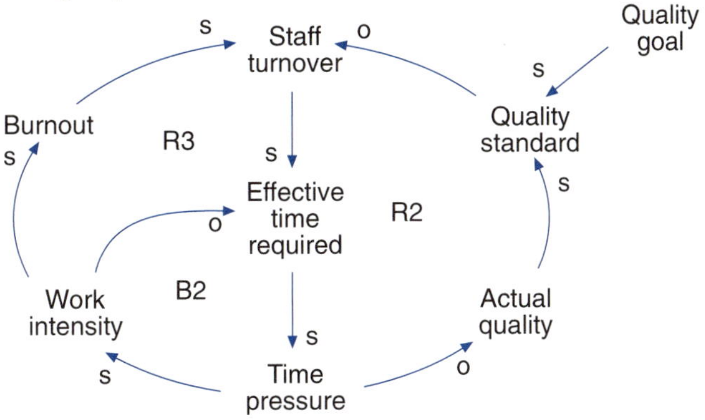

But how come rework did decline *initially* as shown in Figure 6.6? This happened because there is normally some 'slack' capacity (or 'cushion') in the organisation, which absorbs the extra workload and pressure without adversely affecting performance. This occurred here until period 10, before rework started to increase.

But why did rework began to decline again (from period 42)? In order to understand this we need to look at some other variables. A key variable here is staff turnover, which reflects human resource dynamics in the firm. Here, 'staff turnover'[2] is defined as the number of people who leave the company voluntarily. This dynamic is shown in Figure 6.9 on p. 119.

This CLD has three loops. First, there is a reinforcing loop (R2), which indicates that a decline in quality could increase staff turnover. This is because employees' perception of internal quality (quality standard) is an important determinant of their job satisfaction. This CLD also shows the adverse effect of time pressure on staff turnover as a result of higher work intensity and burnout (loop R3). However, there is a balancing force at work here that explains the initial decline in rework discussed above. This loop (B2) shows the effect of increasing work intensity, which initially lowers time pressure, increases actual quality and reduces rework.

Putting these together sheds some light on why the rework level starts to decline toward the end of the simulation run as shown in Figure 6.6. In the SQM model, staff turnover is directly affected by time pressure and quality standard. In this simulation scenario, staff turnover reaches a peak around period 40 then begins to decline from there on. This is a result of the change in personnel mix that would see a declining percentage of experienced staff over time. This reduces the overall turnover (experienced staff tend to leave before new hires do), which will cause rework to decline (from period 42 after a lag effect of 2 months).

Learning summary

What was the lesson here? We started this LLab by asking a 'simple' question regarding the relationship between quality and rework. This may have appeared to have a simple answer too. Not so! As we have seen, this is far from being a simple linear cause-and-effect relationship, as there are complex interdependencies at play here. These interrelationships are shown in the combined CLD in Figure 6.10 below.

Figure 6.10 The combined CLD

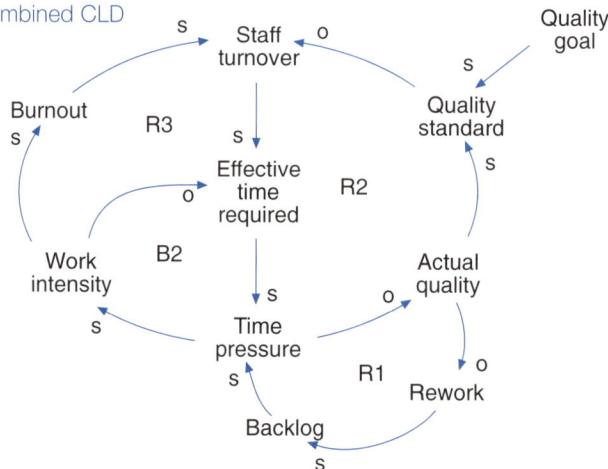

This exercise demonstrated the learning lab process in the context of a simple scenario. The steps of the LLab outlined above can be repeated to address more complex scenarios. This process allows the LLab participants to examine and test their long-held assumptions regarding chronic and complex issues. The outcomes will be shared understanding and group learning.

Experience a learning laboratory: Example 2 – Human resource planning LLab[3]

The objective of this learning lab is to gain a deeper understanding of the dynamics of human resource planning in a professional service firm. The LLab participants are required to manage the HR planning process with a view to creating business growth while maintaining service quality and profitability. The LLab user interface consists of four elements: decision (input) variables, process variables, output variables and parameters. The system map and control panel of this LLab are shown in Figure 6.11 on p. 122.

The explanation of model variables and parameters follows next.

● Decision variables

There are two decision variables in this LLab: Hiring and Layoff. The participants can vary these variables by changing the sliders provided in the control panel within the range provided by the model. The hiring slider represents the number of new hires per month. It should be noted that all new hires start as '*rookies*' and go through a six-month training period. At the same time, there is continuous attrition among '*pros*'. The natural attrition rate is 10%. Therefore, unless we wish to reduce the headcount, we must hire each month to replace those who leave. While hiring is continuous, layoff decisions are effective for a single period only. Since rookies need to be trained by professionals, with every new hiring the total number of professional work hours available for normal client work will decrease initially.

● Process variables

Process variables are those that are directly affected by the hiring and layoff decisions, and in turn, they affect the output variables. In this model, the process variables are Work Backlog, Perceived Quality, and Actual Quality (noted on the graph pad in Figure 6.11b).

● Output variables

Output variables are the selected key performance indicators (KPIs) for the firm. These variables and their initial values are shown below:

- Active clients (125)
- Experienced staff (Pros =100)
- New hires (Rookies =50)
- Cash reserve – this is directly affected by the number of staff since salary is the main component of operating expense. The model assumes that a 'new hire' is only 50% as productive as an experienced staff member in the initial six months of his/her employment.

Figure 6.11 Systems map and control panel of the HR microworld

(a)

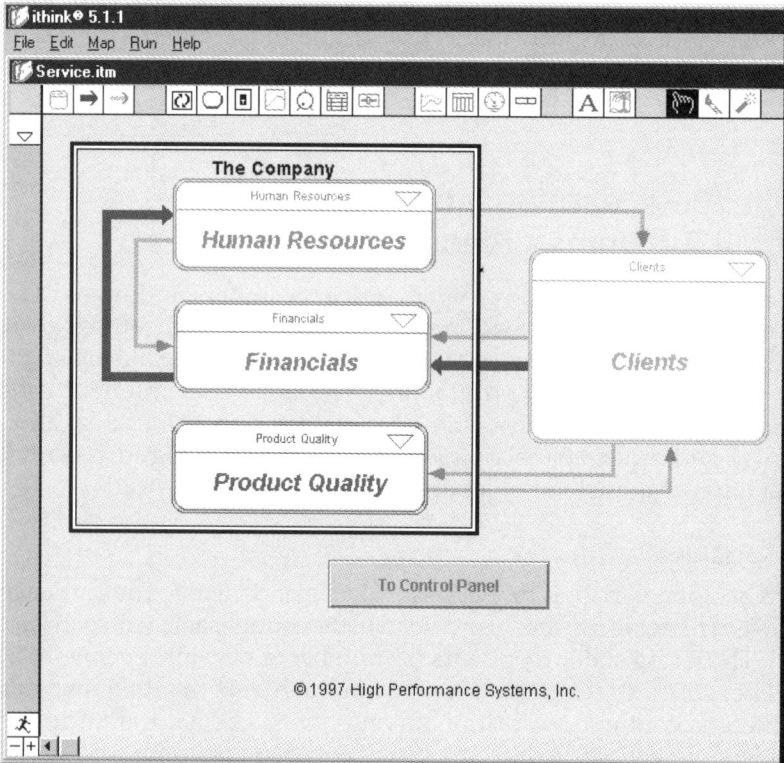

(b)

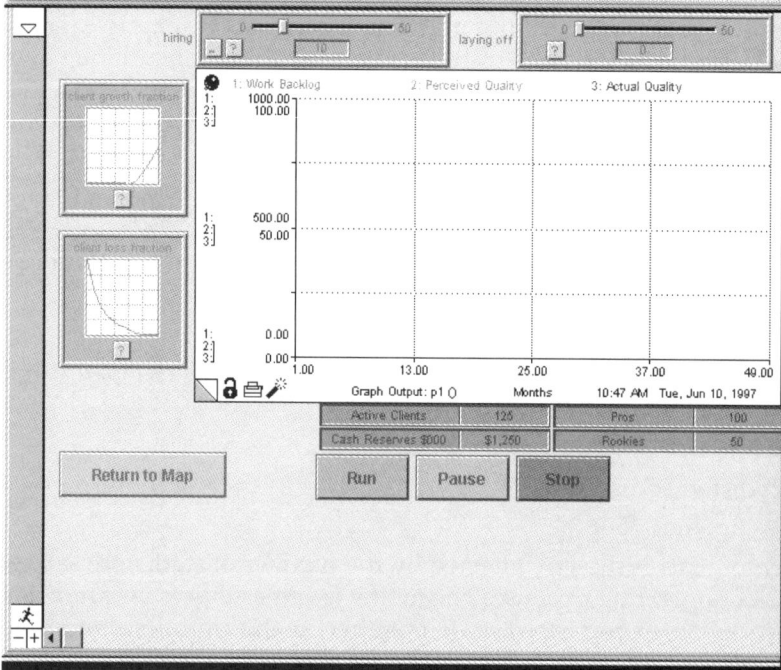

Figure 6.12(a) and (b)   CGF and CLF graphical functions

(a) CGF: The rate at which word-of-mouth brings new clients to the company. As perceived quality increases, so will this fraction. The reverse is also true – as perceived quality decreases, this fraction will also decrease.

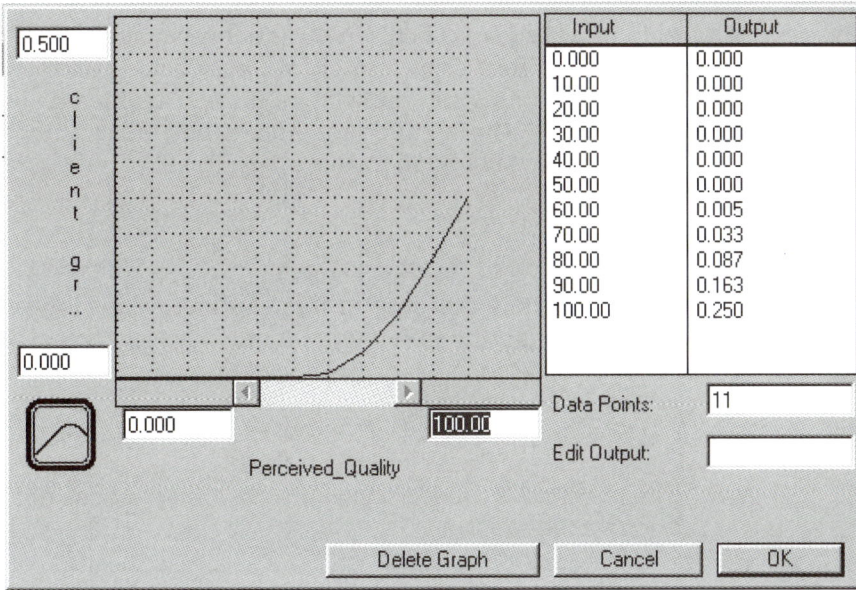

Input	Output
0.000	0.000
10.00	0.000
20.00	0.000
30.00	0.000
40.00	0.000
50.00	0.000
60.00	0.005
70.00	0.033
80.00	0.087
90.00	0.163
100.00	0.250

0.500

client gr ...

0.000

0.000   100.00

Perceived_Quality

Data Points: 11

Edit Output:

Delete Graph   Cancel   OK

(b) CLF: As perceived quality begins to drop, clients will begin to leave at a faster rate. When a client leaves, he/she takes a portion of the backlog with him/her.

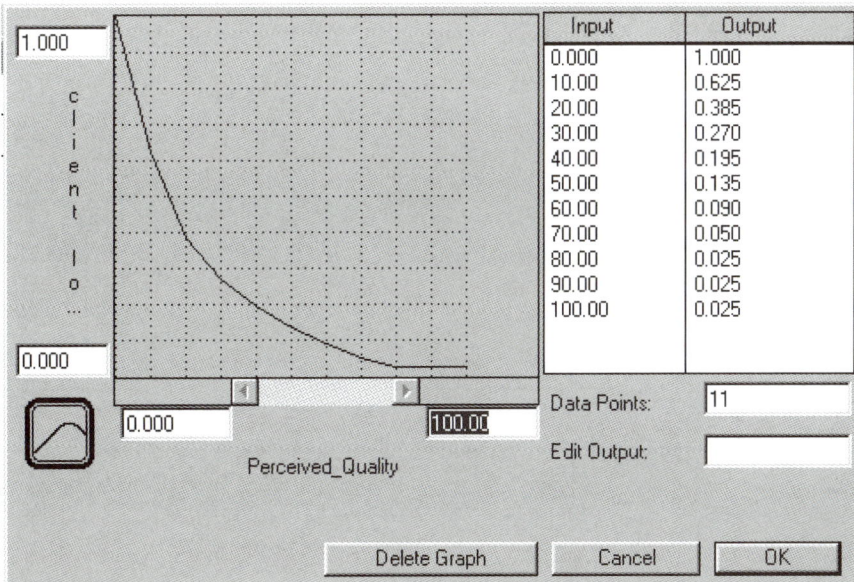

Input	Output
0.000	1.000
10.00	0.625
20.00	0.385
30.00	0.270
40.00	0.195
50.00	0.135
60.00	0.090
70.00	0.050
80.00	0.025
90.00	0.025
100.00	0.025

1.000

client lo ...

0.000

0.000   100.00

Perceived_Quality

Data Points: 11

Edit Output:

Delete Graph   Cancel   OK

● **Model parameters**

The model employs two key parameters described as graphical functions (see Chapter 4):

1 client growth factor (CGF); and
2 client loss factor (CLF).

The CGF relates (the rate of) attracting new clients to the (quality) image of the firm. CLF, on the other hand, determines the rate at which the firm loses clients as service quality deteriorates. The CGF and CLF functions are shown in Figure 6.12 on the previous page. The LLab participants can change these functions and experiment with different assumptions and patterns related to these relationships.

The LLab process

In this LLab we do not explicitly show the steps of the learning cycle. However, these steps are implicit in the process. As in the previous example, we start the LLab with a teasing question (conceptualisation):

What would happen to work backlog if we adopted a constant hiring rate throughout the simulation?

Figure 6.13 Backlog BOT as a result of the constant hiring policy (i.e. 10 per month)

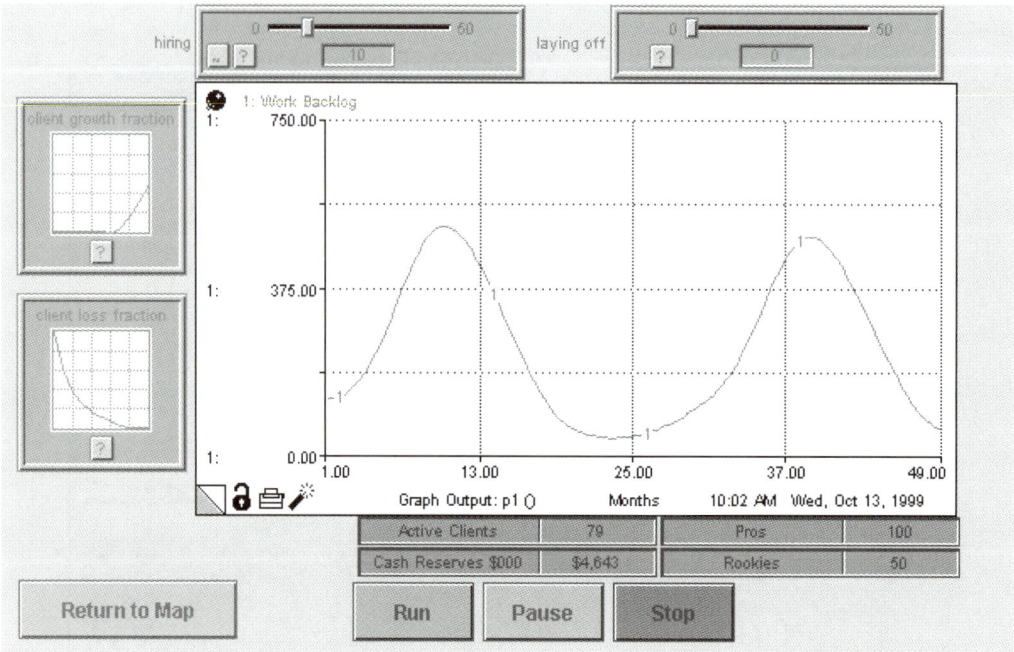

Sketch your response on a piece of paper. Explain and record your assumptions and reasoning. Now, we run the model with a constant hiring rate of 10 new staff per month. As the attrition (leaving) rate is 10% and the initial staff size is 100, this policy should result in a nil net hiring and a constant staff (i.e. pros) size of 100 throughout the simulation duration of four years (48 months). No other variables are changed. The simulation result of this scenario is shown in Figure 6.13.

Is this result different to the one you expected? Why is backlog fluctuating in such cyclical pattern? Why doesn't it decline, grow or stay constant? As we have seen in Chapter 3, cyclical patterns indicate an underlying balancing loop. Before we go any further into this, let us consider another related question:

> What would happen to the backlog pattern if we increased the hiring rate by 50%?

Figure 6.14   Backlog pattern as a result of 50% increase in hiring rate

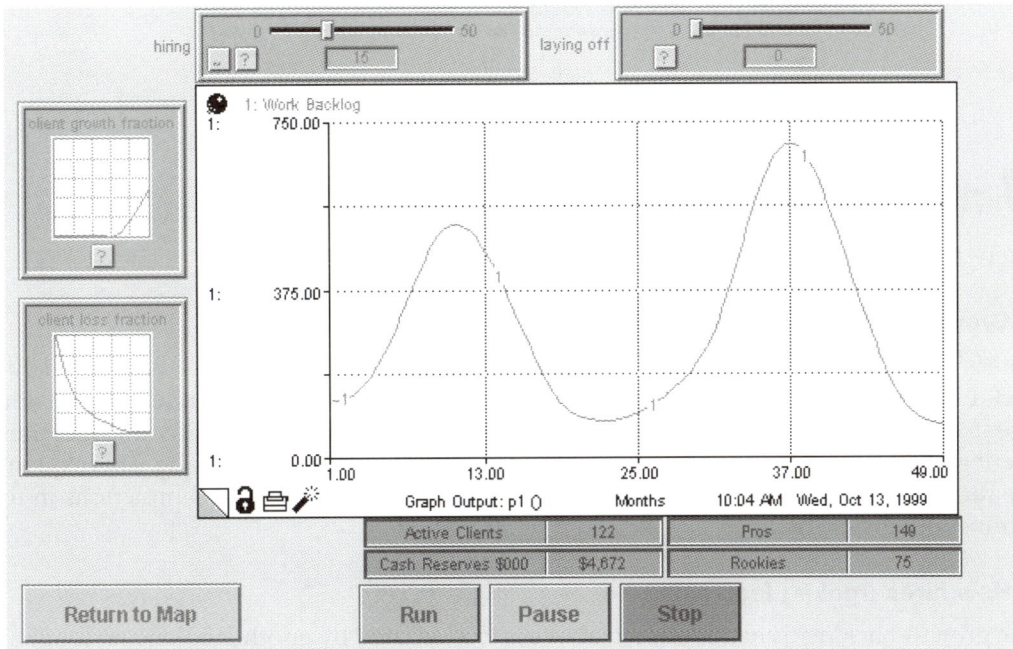

Again, sketch your response on a piece of paper and explain your reasoning. This policy represents a significant increase in the new hiring rate, from 10 per month to 15 per month. Perhaps we expected to see a steady decline in backlog as a result of this increase in hiring rate. Now let us look at the simulation response for this scenario, shown in Figure 6.14.

Surprised again? Not only does the backlog pattern fluctuate, but its oscillations are more pronounced! The range, that is, the difference between the peaks and the lows, increased from 476 jobs to 633 – a 33% increase. Why this exacerbation? To answer this we need to understand the underlying dynamics here. As part of the LLab exercise, can you draw a CLD to explain this phenomenon? A representative CLD is shown in Figure 6.15.

Figure 6.15   The HR dynamics CLD

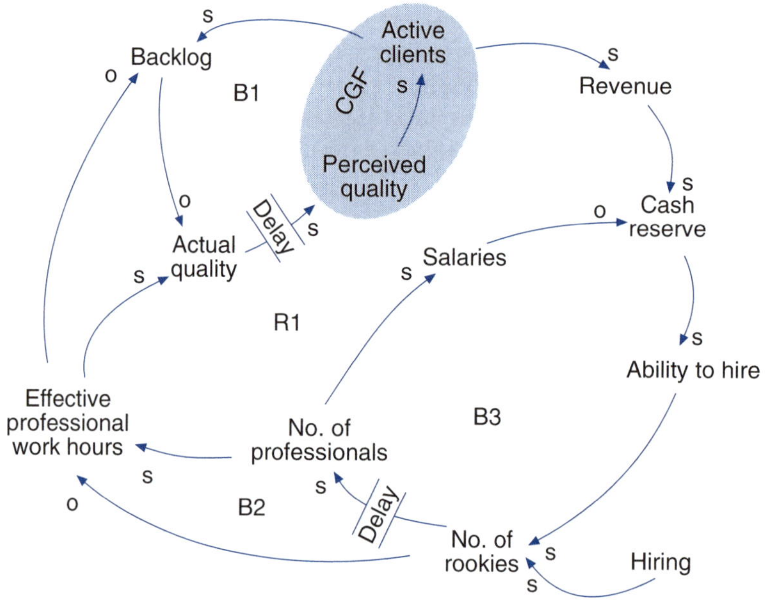

The causal loop

There are four dynamics in this process, and they are described below.

● Growth-backlog loop (B1)

This is a key loop underlying the relationships between backlog, quality and new clients. It is a balancing loop showing that as backlog increases, actual quality decreases and, after some delay, perceived quality also decreases. When perceived quality declines, new client growth begins to contract, which will cause a reduction in the backlog. This explains the fluctuating behaviour of work backlog, due mainly to surges and contractions in the number of new clients.

● New hires (rookie) loop (B2)

The growth-backlog dynamic shown above is exacerbated by another balancing loop, B2. This loop is set off by pulses in new hiring. Each time a new cohort of recruits joins the firm, they bring new dynamics with them. One of these dynamics is the effect on existing staff, specially the experienced staff, as rookies require coaching and on-the-job training by the professionals. This will reduce the effective work hours and the productivity of the professional staff. As the effective number of professional work hours declines, backlog increases, which leads to a reduction in actual quality and ultimately to a smaller client base. As the number of clients decreases, revenue for the firm shrinks, which results in a reduced ability to hire new staff and impedes further growth.

● **Expense loop (B3)**

As the number of professionals grows, salary expenses grow proportionally, which causes a decrease the available cash reserves. Reduction in cash reserves will limit the firm's ability to hire. This creates a negative feedback for the hiring dynamic and hence is a balancing loop.

● **Quality loop (R1)**

There is also a positive feedback or reinforcing loop in this CLD which captures the beneficial effects of new hiring. After the initial training delay, the new staff join the ranks of the professionals. This increases the effective number of staff and available work hours leading to improvements in actual quality and growth of the client base. This increases revenues which enhances firm's financial position and its ability to hire more staff – hence a reinforcing process.

The CLD sheds some light on the fluctuating behaviour of work backlog. This indicates that the existence of three balancing loops keeps the system in a state of 'permanent' pulsation, preventing it from reaching stability. This phenomenon can be confirmed by running the HR model with various hiring rates, all of which will show similar patterns. This raises another question: how can one counter this and reduce variations in the system? In order to answer this, we need to examine the effect of the model parameters or graphical functions. As stated earlier, these parameters determine the effect of quality on client growth or loss. The client growth function is shown in Figure 6.12(a) on p. 123.

This function shows the rate at which perceived quality, through word-of-mouth, brings new clients to the company. That is, as perceived quality increases, so will the client growth factor (CGF). As we can see in Figure 6.12(a), the market (new clients) does not initially respond to an increase in quality. This reflects the fact that clients may expect a certain level of quality as a given. Beyond a certain point (e.g. quality level of competitors), however, increases in quality will attract new clients. This is shown by the steep curve portion of the CGF graph. This has a major influence on the rate of new clients, which, as we have seen above, provides a key impulse to the system, causing the observed fluctuations. To test this effect, in the next run we will reduce this effect by 'flattening' the client growth function and running the model again. This is shown in Figure 6.16 on the following page, together with the simulation output.

As we see, the backlog pattern is 'smoothed' significantly. This highlights the effect of model assumptions on the behaviour of the system.

Discussion

This LLab example demonstrates that the wide fluctuations in work backlog (as well as other performance indicators) were by and large the result of accepting too many new clients at one time. This indicated that the growth loop (B1) had a much stronger impact on the system than had originally been anticipated.

This also indicates that, in reality, leverage lies in *managing* the flow of new clients. This was achieved in the model by 'flattening' the client growth graph. The change made the curve flatter towards the end, which meant new clients flows would be less dependent on quality. In practice, this implies managing the flow of new clients in order to prevent the swings and fluctuations that are caused by a sudden surge of new clients.

Figure 6.16 'Flattened' CGF graph and resulting backlog pattern

(a)

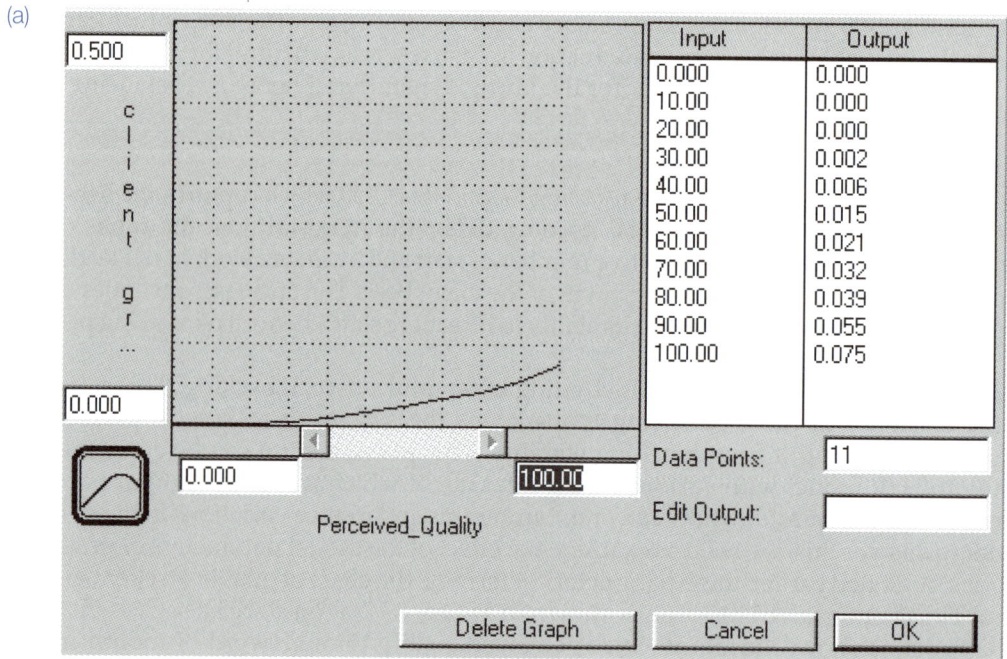

(b)

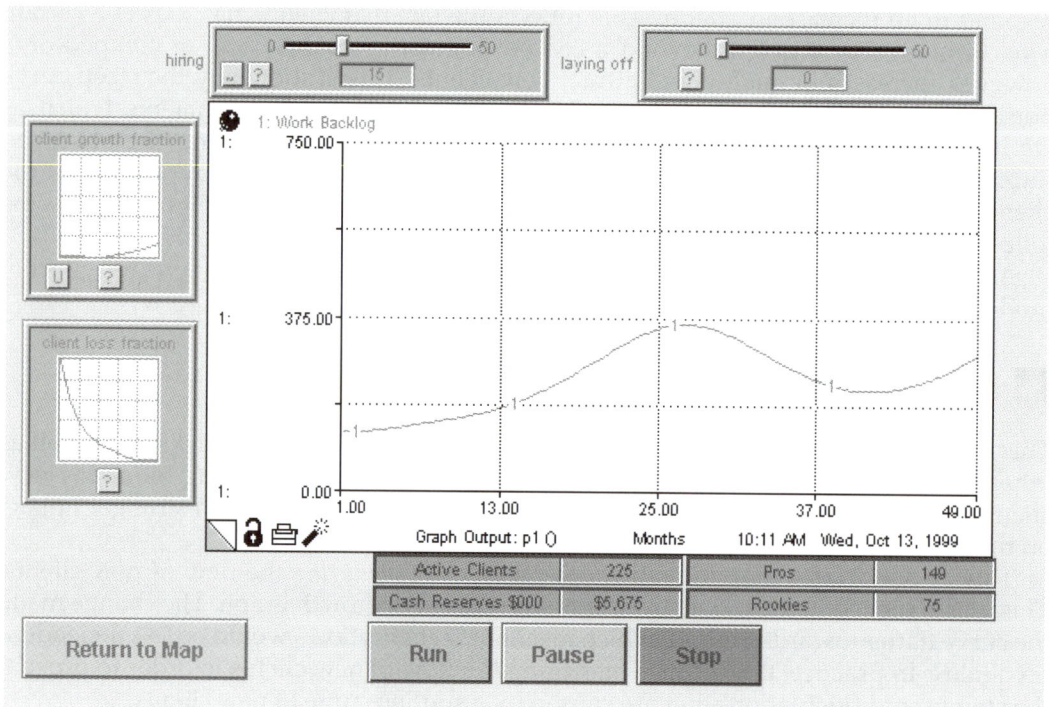

As the results of this LLab confirm, 'managing' the pace of intake of new clients means that excessive work backlogs can be avoided, staff productivity and morale remain more stable, and cash reserves will rise at a relatively steady rate. Other performance indicators also exhibit greater stability over time.

This LLab highlighted the cause of cyclical fluctuations in the model and showed the way to a stable and balanced approach to growth. In summary, this case illustrates that surfacing and testing assumptions and mental models through the learning lab process provide powerful lessons and deeper understanding of the complex dynamics underlying systems. This is the fundamental first step to group and organisational learning.

Notes

1   The SQM model has been developed by the members of the Organisational Learning Center at MIT. It is commercially available through MicroWorlds, Inc. The associated Learning Lab process has been developed by K. Maani.

2   Staff turnover is normally defined as a percentage. The SQM model defines this as an absolute number.

3   This LLab is based on the service model in the *ithink* software and work by D. Dinesh and J. Howcroft, graduate students in systems modelling at the University of Auckland, 1996.

REFERENCES

Brown, J.S. (1991) Research that Reinvents the Corporation. Harvard Business Review, Jan–Feb: 102–111.

Forrester, J. (1994) *Building a Foundation for Tomorrow's Organizations.* Systems Thinking in Action Video Collection, Vol. 1. Pegasus Communications, Cambridge, MA.

Kim, D.H. (1993) The link between individual and organizational learning. *Sloan Management Review,* 35(1): 37–50.

Leavitt, H.J. and Lipman-Blumen, J. (1995) Hot groups. *Harvard Business Review,* 73(4): 109–116.

Maani, K. and Benton, C. (1999) Rapid Team Learning: Lessons from Team New Zealand America's Cup Campaign. *Organisational Dynamics,* 27(4), Spring.

Schön, D. (1983) *The Reflective Practitioner.* Basic Books, New York.

Senge, P. (1990) The Leader's New Work: Building Learning Organisations. *Sloan Management Review,* Fall: 10.

Senge, P. and Sterman, J.D. (1991) Systems Thinking and Organizational Learning: Acting Locally and Thinking Globally in the Organization of the Future. In Kochan, T. and Useem, M (eds). *Transforming Organizations.* Oxford University Press, Oxford.

Service Quality Microworld™. (1994) MicroWorlds, Cambridge, MA: 21–22.

Chapter 7

Systems thinking and the organisation

OVERVIEW

The purpose of this chapter is to present systems thinking in the broader context of organisational learning and to demonstrate its application in real-life organisations. In this chapter we discuss:

- how systems thinking can instil organisational learning;

- how mental models influence learning and organisational alignment;

- how Team New Zealand achieved its phenomenal success in America's Cup Challenge;

- how you can start systems thinking in your organisation;

- how to conduct a systems thinking study.

The chapter will describe the link between systems thinking and organisational learning and the impact of systems thinking on organisational dynamics and performance. We begin by describing the five disciplines of learning organisations. To illustrate these disciplines, we relate them to the story of Black Magic – Team New Zealand's America's Cup campaign. We then outline the steps necessary to introduce systems thinking in organisations and how to gain leverage from mastering it.

Core capabilities of learning organisations

Peter Senge (1992) describes a learning organisation as one 'which is continually expanding its ability to create its future.' He identifies five core capabilities of the learning organisation that are derived from three higher elements. These elements are:

1 creative orientation;
2 generative conversation; and
3 systems perspective.

The capabilities are dynamically interrelated, and collectively they lead to organisational learning. Figure 7.1 shows these core capabilities and their relationships.

Figure 7.1 The core capabilities of a learning organisation

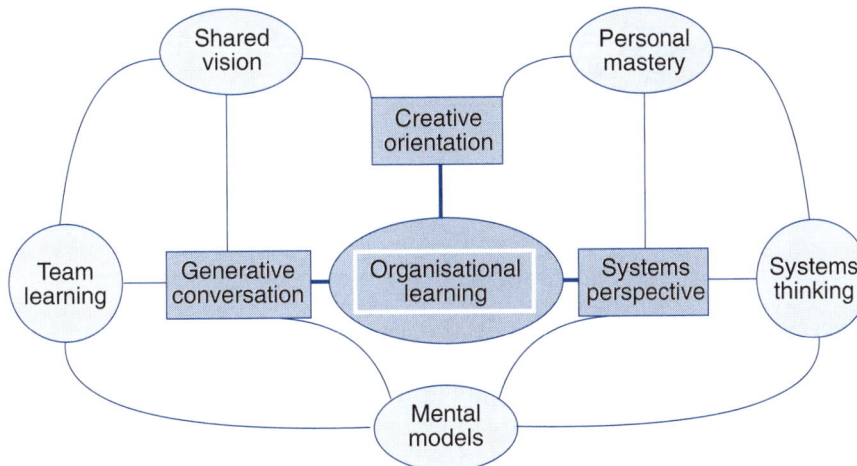

Creative orientation is the source of a genuine desire to excel. It is the source of an intrinsic motivation and drive to achieve. It relinquishes personal gains in favour of the common good. *Generative conversation* refers to a deep and meaningful dialogue to create unity of thought and action. *Systems perspective* is the ability to see things holistically by understanding the interconnectedness of the parts. The foregoing elements give rise to the five core capabilities of learning organisations, namely: personal mastery; shared vision; mental models; team learning and dialogue; and systems thinking. These five disciplines are described below. The importance of learning and its implication for business processes such as new product development are discussed in the final section.

Personal mastery

Personal mastery is the cornerstone and 'spiritual' foundation of learning organisations. It is born out of a creative orientation and systemic perspective. Personal mastery instils a genuine desire to do well and to serve a noble purpose. People exhibiting high levels of personal mastery focus 'on the desired result itself, not the process or the means they

assume necessary to achieve that result' (Senge, 1990). These people can 'successfully focus on their ultimate intrinsic desires, not on secondary goals. This is a cornerstone of Personal Mastery'. Personal mastery also requires a commitment to truth, which means to continually challenge 'theories of why things are the way they are'. Without committing to the truth, people all too quickly revert to old communication routines which can distort reality and prevent them from knowing where they really stand.

Shared vision

It is commonly assumed that in contemporary organisations senior management can develop and impose a vision on employees which they will then follow with *genuine* commitment. This is a fallacy. Imposed vision statements often result in a sense of apathy, complacency and resentment. There needs to be a genuine endeavour to understand what people *will* commit to. For people to commit to something, they must feel a strong interest, even passion, for the outcome. The overriding vision of the group must build on the personal visions of its members. Shared vision aligns diverse views and feelings into a unified focus.

This is emphasised by Arie de Geus when he describes what makes a truly extraordinary organisation. 'The feeling of belonging to an organisation and identifying with its achievements is often dismissed as soft. But case histories repeatedly show that a sense of community is essential for long term survival' (De Geus, 1997). For example, when Apple Corporation challenged IBM, it was in its 'adolescent' years, characterised by creativity, confidence and even defiance. This is similar to the spirit in Team New Zealand when it competed against the bigger-budget syndicates! Within these organisations there is a real passion for the outcome; a common vision for success (Maani and Benton, 1999).

Creating a shared vision is the most fundamental job of a leader (Nadler and Tushman, 1990). By creating a vision, the leader provides a vehicle for people to develop commitment, a common goal around which people can rally, and a way for people to *feel* successful. The leader must appeal to people's emotions if they are to be energised towards achieving the goal. Emotional acceptance of, and belief in, a vision is far more powerful in energising team members than is intellectual recognition that the vision is simply a 'good idea'. One of the most powerful ways of communicating a vision is through a leader's personal example and actions, demonstrating behaviour that symbolises and furthers that vision.

Mental models and leadership

Mental models stem from beliefs, assumptions and feelings that shape one's world views and actions. They are formed through family, education, professional and social contacts and are based for the most part on cultural and social norms. Mental models, however, can be altered and aligned.

Organisations are often constrained by deep-seated belief systems, resulting in preconceived ideas on how things ought to perform. Goodstein and Burke (1991: 10), pioneers in the field of the social psychology of organisations, observed that 'the first step in any change process is to unfreeze the present patterns of behaviour as a way of managing resistance to change'. The leader has a pivotal role in dismantling negative mental models and shaping new ones.

In order to get people to engage in open discussions of issues that affect the organisation, a leader must appeal to their emotions and must get beyond the superficial level of communication. Shell Oil has recently undertaken major changes in the way it encourages leadership. Communications are intended to appeal both personally and emotionally. According to Irv Doty, a manager at Shell, 'When I tried to talk personally about an issue rather than say "here's the answer", it was powerful. It caused me to engage in dialogue with others that resulted in mutual learning on all sides' (Cohen and Tichy, 1997: 71).

The leader must propose and model the manner in which the group has to operate internally. The leader is a ´designer´, and part of that role is designing the governing ideas of purpose and core values by which people will live (Senge, 1990). This provides ample opportunities for leaders to examine their deeply held assumptions about the task, the means to accomplish it, the uniqueness of the people and the kinds of relationship that should be fostered among the people. Only after people have observed and *experienced* the organisational values in practice would these values become the basis for prolonged group behaviour. These values should be manifested first and should be most visible in the leader's own behaviour. Cynicism spreads quickly if people do not perceive the leader to be committed.

In today's knowledge-based organisation, leadership must be distributed and shared to a far greater extent than it was in the past. For example, in the Chicago Bulls basketball team, Michael Jordan changed his role: it became not only that of an individually brilliant player but *also* that of a leader whose job it was to raise the level of play of other team members. After this transition, the Bulls began their record run of championship seasons (Cohen and Tichy, 1997).

Team learning and dialogue

Dialogue results from 'generative conversation', shared vision, and transparent mental models. Dialogue is an essential requirement for organisational learning. It is an exploration of complex issues and creates a deep sense of listening and suspending one's own views. Dialogue centres on the ability of a group to 'see through words'. The word 'dialogue' comes from the Greek words *dia logos,* and it implies that when members of a group talk to one another, the meaning of what they have to say moves through them (Isaacs, 1993).

Constructive feedback is an integral aspect of dialogue. However, personal differences need to be put aside before effective dialogue can ensue. Federal Express adopted 'dialogue improvement' techniques to enhance team learning. Customers commented that Federal Express salespeople became much more attuned to customer needs, did not jump to conclusions so readily, were more willing to hear a customer out, and understood customers' dilemmas better.

Many leaders have strong charisma and are highly eloquent when it comes to presenting their ideas; that's often why they get to the top of the organisation. However, many appear to lack the ability to extract the very best from employees in a non-threatening manner. Without this ability, leaders may miss many good ideas, or might act on many bad ones.

In a group context, encouragement from the leader and mutual encouragement among group members is essential. Comments such as 'Great idea! Let's keep pushing it', or 'OK. So those two alternatives didn't work – let's try the third alternative' (Leavitt and Lipman-Blumen, 1995) keep the group moving forward towards achievement of the task at hand. Such comments, termed 'soft markers', are vital parts of effective group dialogue.

Communication routines in organisations are generally anti-learning and promote mediocrity. For example, a mixed message such as 'Bill, be creative, but for heaven's sake, be careful!' (Argyris, 1992) is a 'defensive routine' (statement) that can stifle innovative thinking. Exposing and unlearning such routines, and understanding the powerful detrimental impact they have on learning, are serious challenges many organisations face if they are to create effective learning environments.

● Separating people from ideas

> 'The essence of all democratic theories of governance is that power flows from ideas, not from people.'
>
> (Senge, 1998: 3)

When people associate themselves with their ideas, egos become involved and defensive routines are enacted. Openness and honesty within a group can create a feeling of security and make it possible for members to challenge one another's ideas. Senge observes 'A team with excellent dialogue consists of members who can separate themselves from their thoughts (i.e. separate ego from thought). They begin to take a creative, less reactive, stance towards their thought. People can help each other become aware of the incoherencies in each other's thought.'

In most organisations, dissent is not only discouraged, it is also punished and generally regarded by employees and managers alike as a 'career ender'. Learning to accept and encourage diversity is one of the key challenges facing managers in learning organisations. If people have been reprimanded in the past for challenging traditional views, it is considerably more difficult to encourage openness and objective criticisms.

Some organisations use a tool called the *container*. The idea is for people in a meeting to imagine a container that holds everyone's hostile thoughts and feelings. Hostility lessens as people discard their personal differences and focus on the task at hand. This enables excellent constructive conversation to emerge, as idea and ego become separated.

For well over a century, Baha'i[1] communities throughout the world have practised the art of 'consultation' as a means of group decision making and community building. Baha'i consultation is based on the following principles that apply universally to all groups and organisations.

- People are detached from their ideas. Once an idea is put forward, it no longer belongs to the proposer, it belongs to the group. This practice helps diffuse egos.

- Truth is the outcome of 'clashes' of *opinions* (not people), just as lightning comes from the impact of charged clouds. But the clash of opinions occurs in a spirit of respect and harmony with a focus on the end result and collective good.

- Unity is more important than absolute 'correctness'. If the group is united, a 'wrong' decision will be corrected in due course.

- Decision making is based on facts, not influence, favouritism or loud assertions.

- All members are equal in worth and dignity – there is no hierarchy within the group.

- Full participation and frank and respectful expression of one's views are encouraged.

- No politicking, lobbying or sub-group colluding is accepted or permitted in meetings or outside.

- The final decision belongs to the whole group. Once a decision has been reached, the process (i.e. the question of who supported or opposed the decision) becomes irrelevant and is at once 'forgotten'. Even the opposers will put their full support behind the decision.

(Kolstor, 1985)

Systems thinking

Systems thinking, the fifth discipline of the learning organisation, is the ability to see things as a whole. It combines the art of seeing interconnections and the science of explaining complexity. A central principle of systems thinking is that a system is the *interaction* of its parts, rather than the sum of the individual parts. Systems thinking can help clarify mental models.

Arie de Geus, referring to a study of the critical success factors of long-surviving and prosperous companies, states: 'Recruits should be judged as much on the basis of their fit with the companies values and principles as they are on their ability to fill the technical requirements of the job' (De Geus, 1997). For example, Team New Zealand, by focusing on compatibility and fit as opposed to pure technical competence, sowed the seeds for a highly effective team environment which led to their phenomenal victory.

Leavitt and Lipman-Blumen (1995) coined the term *hot groups*, in reference to a lively, high-achieving, dedicated group, usually small, whose members are turned on to an exciting and challenging task. They mention that organisations that first devote a lot of time to selecting their people and then allow them plenty of elbow room and opportunities to *interact* are likely to generate groups that will build challenging tasks for themselves. This 'people first' criterion has been used at Bell Laboratories which has been credited with making a host of communication and technological breakthroughs, due in large part to its 'hot groups'.

Rapid team learning

Today, *time* is regarded as a competitive dimension. For example, speed or time-to-market is a critical factor in new product development and customer deliveries. Just-in-time manufacturing, set-up reduction, and quick response time are other examples of time-based management. Faster response time in business processes corresponds to fewer bottlenecks, less rework, fewer queues, and better quality. One of the key objectives of total quality management (TQM) and business process re-engineering (BPR) projects is to reduce time and increase speed. This objective is important today, as organisations must deal with 'critical' decisions rapidly. This both challenges and enhances the ability to learn rapidly.

Product development is one of the key business processes which is often subject to tight timing and can benefit from rapid learning. Product development projects typically operate under extreme time pressures and tight budgetary targets. Successful product development depends upon a close match between market needs and a company's capabilities; mistakes are very costly once mass production and/or service delivery begin.

Rapid product development requires the ability to pull together ideas from both within and outside the organisation in order to produce innovative solutions in a short space of time. This highlights an important point with respect to the speed of team and organisational learning. Bowonder and Miyake (1994) observe that, 'the *nature and dynamics* of people and technology interaction will determine the speed of learning'.

Groups go through the stages of formation, development and cohesion. The learning speed and dynamics change in each stage. Figure 7.2 shows the pattern of learning over the life cycle of the group. As the graph suggests, groups experience an increasing rate of learning in their formative and team-building period (Maani and Benton, 1999).

Figure 7.2   The group learning curve

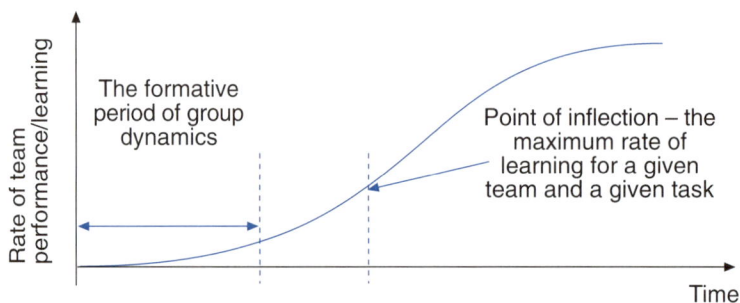

During the formative period, team members develop communication norms and routines (including non-verbal cues, etc.) which can set the pattern for future group dialogue, and hence slow the rate of team learning. In effect, because the team is learning how to learn during the formative period, the rate of learning is not at a maximum. In contrast, the conventional (*individual*) learning curve suggests that the rate of learning continually *decreases* with time.

Beyond the formative period, the rate of group learning can increase sharply until it reaches technological limits. At this point the learning curve will exhibit a diminishing return similar to that proposed by the conventional learning curve of the Boston Consulting Group (BCG).

This phenomenon is amply evident in the case of Team New Zealand, described below, where the elements of learning organisation and rapid learning are discussed in the context of Team New Zealand's America's Cup story. Using Team New Zealand as an example, we show how free-flowing idea generation and communication can lead to rapid improvements in product design and an exceptional end result, once learning processes and effective team dynamics have been established. Team New Zealand's lessons can readily be applied to other organisations.

Case

Black Magic – Team New Zealand's America's Cup story[2]

In the 146-year history of the America's Cup yacht race, teams from outside the United States have won the prestigious prize only twice. Australia was the first to do so in 1983, marking an end to the longest winning streak in sporting history; New Zealand followed suit in 1995. Furthermore, Team New Zealand's unprecedented margin of 41 wins and only one loss in the six-month long race makes this victory unique in the history of the America's Cup Regatta.

The success of Team New Zealand (TNZ) in the 1995 America's Cup campaign has been well publicised. It has been acknowledged that the inspirational leadership of Sir Peter Blake, the strong sense of community apparent within the Team New Zealand camp, the openness of communication between team members, the sustained rate of boat speed improvements, and the uncommon levels of commitment and purpose shown by participants in the campaign were among the key contributing factors to Team New Zealand's success.

The Team New Zealand campaign exhibited many traits that are characteristic of learning organisations. From team selection through to the final race, the Team New Zealand camp was structured from a 'systemic' perspective.

The team

Team selection was based on a fundamentally different premise to that used in previous campaigns. Peter Blake took a 'systemic' perspective towards team selection. As a team member commented, Blake selected a team 'not purely on their skills and abilities, but on how the members were likely to *interact* with each other. The overriding selection criteria was *compatibility*; we had to be able to get along with each other in a variety of situations.'

Too often members of teams such as engineering and product development teams, consisting of technically excellent people, mistrust one another. As a result, communication breaks down and performance falters. This has been the case in previous America's Cup campaigns where the sailors were played off against one another.

In the 1995 America's Cup campaign, Team New Zealand members' emotional intensity was directed towards attainment of a common goal rather than towards achieving conflicting secondary agendas, which cloud the ability of the team members to 'throw themselves´ into successful completion of the task.

The TNZ 1995 campaign was undertaken by a group of individually successful people – a combination which would, in many circumstances, lead to ego battles. What enabled TNZ members to overcome this potential problem and forge a powerful shared vision?

Ownership

From the start, Team New Zealand instilled a sense of ownership within the camp. As the public relations manager commented: 'It was *their* project and everybody in the team had to own it. It wasn't Peter Blake's campaign, it was *theirs*.' Such a sense of ownership provides a powerful force. Personal visions were given a full range of opportunities to develop. Because they felt they 'owned the campaign', the crew members were energised to contribute as much as was humanly possible.

Blake instilled a vision of a sailor-led campaign not by merely talking about it but by actually working as a crew member throughout.

He was instrumental in establishing a highly effective team environment, in which new team members had to discard any baggage from the past and become dedicated to the task at hand. Because Team New Zealand was initiated from scratch, Peter Blake could mould the group norms and communication routines based on a set of common core values. He saw himself as a catalyst for designing the governing ideas and core values by which people would coexist within the confines of the camp. Team New Zealand's core values were:

* meaningful communication ('dialogue');
* integrity;
* everybody having the right to express an opinion;
* playing nicely together and 'sharing your toys';
* no hidden agendas.

These values laid the foundation that facilitated open and complete sharing of information and brought about the high levels of honesty and trust present in the camp. They became an important catalyst for effective team learning.

Stewardship

Blake had a strong sense of *stewardship* towards the Team New Zealand crew. They could see how serious he was about committing to the goal of having *the fastest boat on a given day*. He clearly displayed to all members of the camp that he was willing to go the extra mile. A team member stated, 'We would walk over broken glass to do anything for him'. He had 'a keen appreciation of the impact one's leadership can have on others'. Having him on the boat almost completely removed the gap that normally exists between the management and crew.

This gap between management and crew is analogous to 'the great manufacturing divide' (most commonly between marketing and manufacturing) in many organisations. Often orders are accepted by marketing that cannot be produced within the quoted lead times, or for which the specifications will prove impossible to meet given the current production technology. The result: excessive work in process, large lead times, frequent expediting of orders and a high number of missed due dates.

Blake's relationship on the water with the team skipper, Russell Coutts, established a model for interaction between management and sailors. For example, Blake could see the validity of sailors' suggestions for increased boat speed or claims for dry suits (which may be directly related to increased boat speed). There existed little chance of a disparity between 'production capabilities' and management expectations within the team, given that he worked 'on the shop floor'. If crew members needed dry suits to operate more effectively and hence add to boat/product performance, this could be operationally evaluated from the *perspective of the shop floor*; not by peering through financial or corporate binoculars.

Team New Zealand achieved 'a deliberate process of total communication'. In team meetings there existed no pecking order and no hidden agenda. Reality was perceived from as many different angles as possible; the most insightful view achievable given the combined contributions of *all* team members was therefore obtained. Genuine trust and camaraderie helped facilitate the free flow of information and open dialogue evident in the campaign. A major learning outcome for a crew member was 'how a bunch of guys through *rigorous honesty* can achieve great results'.

Team New Zealand was intrinsically aware of the need to always keep moving forward. This enabled them to transcend any of the secondary agendas that impair group momentum (i.e. having to 'win' a place on the crew). Creating the vision of boat speed; that is, 'to build, modify and sail the fastest boat on a given day'; provided the drive. In contrast to previous campaigns, the 1995 campaign saw the most dramatic increase in boat speed occurring in the last month leading up to the challenger series.

What enabled Team New Zealand continually to generate new and often diverse ideas in an environment of extreme pressure (time, cost and public expectations)? How did Team New Zealand succeed in developing effective team environments whereas a myriad of companies have faltered in this task and have reverted back to 'crowd' or 'herd' behaviour typical of traditional authoritarian hierarchical organisational structures?

Blake actively sought contributions from everyone and discussed *all* the possible ideas before a decision was settled upon. Unconventional solutions were sought, as these could often lead to big gains in a short time, providing they were correct. As a result, all members were encouraged to think on the margin (i.e. 'outside the square') as was evidenced by the receptionist who, at a brainstorming session, selected the best idea for increasing boat speed.

Rapid learning

Team New Zealand was operating under extreme time and budgetary pressures. Moreover, it needed rapid improvement in boat speed during this period. Because of budget limitations, design changes had to be implemented at the launch time. This is comparable to a manufacturing company entering the tooling phase in the product development life cycle. Undoing design modifications once they had been made to the boat could easily 'blow the budget'. A poor design element fitted to the boat could be extremely counterproductive to the campaign goal of increasing boat speed.

Rapid learning was amply manifested throughout the Team New Zealand campaign. A useful analogy to help understand the nature of rapid learning is to view the entire TNZ campaign as a new product development project. In the case of Team New Zealand, sailors (i.e. end users) were an integral part of the design process. 'To achieve a team-oriented culture, traditional management structures were tipped upside down, and the sailing team, who were the customers, were placed at the pyramid's apex.' The design team worked on the above-deck layout and systems with a core group of 'yachties' right up until the race day. The sailors accepted any design change that would make the boat go faster; even if it made the individual sailor's job more difficult.

Blake's ability to balance advocacy and inquiry skills – asking questions that probed people's hidden assumptions – enabled the crew to have the maximum freedom to experiment with their thoughts. These skills were a catalyst for TNZ's ability to design a product that was user-friendly, of outstanding quality (fast boat speed), and within the right cost and time frame.

In the Team New Zealand campaign it was the fluid interaction of the sailors with the technology design process that facilitated such rapid improvements in boat speed. In previous campaigns 'the designer was autonomous and not receptive to outside input, making it hard for team members to become involved; his decisions were *relayed* to the crew via the campaign managers'. This is akin to the conventional 'linear' design process that was prevalent before the advent of concurrent engineering. The TNZ experience proved 'that 60 brains all contributing to the campaign are better than one'.

Figure 7.3 shows the pattern of improvement in boat speed over the final six months of the race. Significant gains were made near the end where the cumulative learning effect was at its peak. This pattern contradicts the conventional learning curve model (that of the Boston Consulting Group, BCG) which asserts that learning rate diminishes with volume of activity. This pattern, however, is consistent with Analogue Device's (Stata, 1989) cumulative learning notion based on experimentation, which maintains that 'the time required for each cycle of improvement is largely a function of the complexity and bureaucracy of the organisation'. This is also consistent with research findings showing that firms may learn faster at high quality levels than at low quality levels (Fine, 1986). Initially, the learning rate for groups will be slower than that of individuals, because team members have to come to terms with one another's communication mannerisms and diffuse any personality issues that may hinder dialogue. As the team develops greater harmony and unity, its capacity to learn collectively is enhanced. In other words, collective learning is influenced largely by group dynamics rather than by the volume of activity.

Figure 7.3 Improvements in boat speed over the final six months of the campaign (used by permission of P. Mazany)

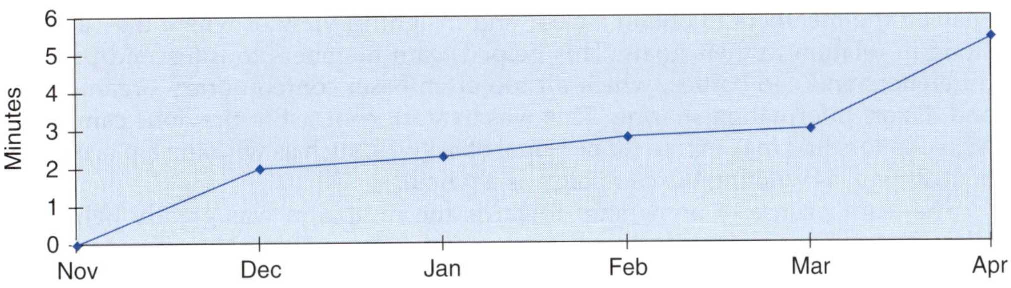

The Team New Zealand story demonstrates that the learning cycle (design, test, evaluate), assisted by simulation technology, has powerful outcomes. In order to reflect on their 'theories' and develop new hypotheses regarding boat redesigns, TNZ spent considerable time together, thinking and talking. Having two similar boats, where one could in effect be used as a 'control', catalysed the experimentation. The improvements could then be analysed with great accuracy and a particular reason for any change could be pin-pointed. Integration of simulation into the design, test and evaluation process was an effective aid to rapid group learning. Constant evaluation and reflection allowed TNZ to examine and review its assumptions and enabled managers to gain deeper insight into team dynamics.

Summary

The rapid team learning exhibited by Team New Zealand contributed substantially to the team's phenomenal success. The fluid interaction between the design process and people yielded benefits for the whole campaign. Sailors' involvement as a central part of the design process led to an exceptional product (the boat) and very quick design improvement cycle times.

Genuine dialogue enabled TNZ to improve group dynamics and team building steadily. Because team members were encouraged to contribute, and an environment existed where there was no fear of expressing 'silly' ideas, very few ideas were missed. This provides a fundamental lesson for new product development teams.

This approach helped avoid both the application of poor design decisions and the rejection of novel ideas that might have led to large performance gains. By using simulation, i.e. learning labs, TNZ allowed non-technical members of the design team, such as sailors, to experience the implications of design decisions in the context of the environment for which they were intended. TNZ employed each of the elements of the 'design, test, and evaluate' cycle in quick succession. Additionally, because of the high speed of the test phase, TNZ was afforded time to reflect and isolate those variables that truly had an impact on the boat speed. In general, compressing the test phase in product development projects will allow more time for experimentation and reflection – areas in which valuable learning occurs.

Team New Zealand's drive to continually increase boat speed came from an intrinsic sense of mission on the part of individual team members and the team itself was unified by a shared vision. A high degree of personal integrity and honesty enabled the members to obtain a clear and insightful view of where they actually stood in relation to their goals. This helped team members to transcend personal differences and ego battles, which all too often beset contemporary organisations and distort information sharing. This was in stark contrast to previous campaigns where sailors had to compete for personal objectives, such as winning a place on the boat, as well as winning the campaign as a whole.

The team's sense of ownership towards the campaign was greatly helped by allowing everyone to contribute to the process of *designing* Team New Zealand. Team members *collectively* designed the process to achieve victory in the America's Cup.

The role of the leader is central in creating a lasting shared vision. Peter Blake instilled ownership of the common vision that proved to be so critical a factor in Team New Zealand's success. In contrast, too many contemporary organisations attempt to impose visions on their staff, whilst giving them no control over the design of the process to achieve the vision.

The balance of advocacy and inquiry skills helped elicit the best contributions from people in the design process. Many managers can advocate their ideas strongly, but often this happens at the expense of the contribution of others. Blake displayed strong stewardship towards the campaign as a whole and towards the people he served. Consequently, team members felt inspired to do anything for him as they observed that he would do likewise. The early actions taken in creating a learning culture were essential prerequisites for the rapid learning manifested in the campaign.

How to introduce systems thinking in your organisation

Systems thinking works better within a group than for an individual. However, it is important to introduce systems thinking to a group with care and wisdom. Enthusiasm can help, but it should be tempered by wisdom. People often view jargon and 'latest' management fads with caution and cynicism. Therefore, it is important that people should not feel threatened by the introduction of any new tool. The cardinal rule of success is to first 'gently' educate your colleagues. This can be done in a variety of ways – some suggestions follow.

- Give your superior/colleagues interesting and thought-provoking readings about the subject. Readings are generally seen as neutral and non-threatening.

- Organise introductory systems thinking workshops in your company. Encourage senior management to attend.
- Once basic awareness has been established and initial training has been completed, start systems thinking activities or projects in your organisation. Start with small, non-controversial issues or projects. In Part II we will present a number of real-life cases, some of which have been conducted by university students. These cases demonstrate how a systems thinking study can be carried out in a step-by-step fashion, as outlined below.

Steps in conducting a systems thinking study/project

● 1 Define the problem or situation

A problem or situation can be a policy decision (e.g. hiring, credit return, etc.); a strategy (e.g. marketing/sales plan); an operational or financial problem (excessive defects or customer complaints, decline in sales); a human resource issue (e.g. high turnovers, decline in productivity and morale); or any other management, organisational or governmental issue.

● 2 Identify key variables

Variables are the key factors, conditions or decisions that affect and are affected by the dynamics of a system. The variables can be performance measures that show the 'pulse' of the system and indicate its 'health'. In group situations, identifying variables sometimes requires additional steps and facilitated group techniques such as affinity diagrams and hexagons, which are discussed in Chapter 3.

● 3 Identify behaviour over time (BOT)

Identify the BOT of the key variables to observe the pattern of change of these variables over time. In the absence of historical or numerical data, one can use interviews to obtain data for the relevant variables. This is especially useful for qualitative (or soft) variables.

● 4 Construct causal loop diagrams

Link the key variables in the most meaningful way to construct one or more CLD for the situation or question at hand. This is the most crucial part of the exercise as the group needs to reach consensus about the nature and direction of relationships amongst the variables. To this end, it is very important that the participants share their assumptions about different relationships and issues. This process will enhance group learning and will bring shared understanding and ownership to the participants.

It must be remembered that constructing the CLD itself should not be seen as the final result of this exercise. While the *process* of constructing CLDs is very beneficial, the value of the resulting CLD is not always immediately evident. Initial CLDs tend to look busy and confusing with many variables and arrows going around. These should be refined further in several iterations using group discussion for consensus building and alignment of vision. In general, detailed CLDs provide insights at the variables level. This can provide greater clarity and consensus within the group as to the nature of individual relationships. Often this clarity is missed in organisations as individuals are not invited to participate or are reluctant to discuss their mental models (i.e. assumptions). This is a major barrier to organisational learning.

● 5 Identify systems archetypes

Once a CLD has been constructed it is useful to ask 'What is going on here?' The ability to articulate a succinct answer to this question indicates proficiency and insight into systems thinking. The answer to this question provides a high-level view of the situation where one can see what is *really* going on. Systems archetypes are useful tools in this regard, as they provide a high-level picture of the story using a generic structure. Often it is possible and helpful to 'see' the archetype(s) before one has constructed a CLD. As systems thinking skills become more ingrained, the ability to see the archetypes quickly and directly increases. However, we must remember that one should not attempt to force-fit a situation or a problem into an archetype pattern.

● 6 Identify key leverage points

Once CLDs have been constructed and possible archetypes identified, the insights gained should help the group to make necessary interventions. Key leverage points are those areas in the system where adverse effects or trends can be arrested and their negative dynamics reversed. In theory, any point (or variable) in a causal loop model can be a leverage point. However, some variables are more powerful 'levers' than others in effecting change in the system. Again, the decision about which leverage points to use should be reached through group consensus in order to bring unity of thought and action to the group.

● 7 Develop intervention strategies

Once leverage points have been identified by the group, the next step is to develop appropriate strategies to deal with them. Usually, there are two possible courses of action. One is applying the short-term solution(s), and the other is employing the long-term or fundamental intervention. Generally there is room for both. While short-term solutions are 'quick-fix' in nature and will possibly have adverse consequences, it is nevertheless sometimes necessary to use them in order to protect the system from immediate collapse. Fundamental interventions are those that can stop an adverse trend or break and reverse a vicious cycle.

● 8 Implement strategy

Implementation of intervention strategies is the final step in the systems thinking exercise. Again, in order to create ownership of the process and the outcome, it is vital to make judicious use of wisdom and sound judgement. It must also be borne in mind that the systems thinking process does not end here. Regular reviews and group debriefings must be held to evaluate progress and, if necessary, to make adjustments to the implementation strategy.

Notes

1 Baha'i Faith, in existence since 1844, is one of the world's major religions.

2 An in-depth study of Team New Zealand including two interviews conducted in August 1997 provided the foundation for this study. For a full report of the study see Maani and Benton, 1999.

REFERENCES

Argyris, C. (1992) The Next Challenge for TQM: Overcoming Organisational Defences. *Journal for Quality and Participation*, March: 26–29.

Bowonder, B. and Miyake, T. (1994) Innovations and Strategic Management: A Case Study of Hitachi Ltd. *Technology Analysis and Strategic Management*, 6(1): 55–81.

Cohen, E. and Tichy, N. (1997) How Leaders Develop Leaders. *Training and Development*, May.

De Geus, A. (1997) The Living Company. *Harvard Business Review*, March–April: 51–59.

Fine, C. (1986) *Management Science*, 32(10).

Goodstein, L. and Burke, W. (1991) Creating Successful Organization Change. *Organizational Dynamics*, 19(4): 5–17. Spring.

Isaacs, W. (1993) Taking Flight: Dialogue, Collective Thinking and Organizational Learning. *Organizational Dynamics*, 22(2): 24–39.

Kolstor, J.E. (1985) Consultation – A Universal Lamp of Guidance. George Ronald, Oxford.

Leavitt, H.J. and Lipman-Blumen, J. (1995) Hot Groups. *Harvard Business Review*, 73(4).

Maani, K. and Benton, C. (1999) Rapid Team Learning. Lessons from Team New Zealand's America's Cup Campaign. *Organizational Dynamics*, 27(4). Spring.

Nadler, D.A. and Tushman, M.L. (1990) Beyond The Charismatic Leader: Leadership and Organizational Change. *California Management Review*, Winter.

Senge, P. (1990a) *The Fifth Discipline*. Random House Australia.

Senge, P. (1990b) The Leader's New Work: Building Learning Organizations. *Sloan Management Review*, Fall: 7–23.

Senge, P. (1992) Building Learning Organizations. *Journal for Quality and Participation*, March: 1–8.

Senge, P. (1998) *Systems Thinker*. 9(9): 3 (November).

Stata, R. (1989) Organisational Learning – The Key to Management Innovation. *Sloan Management Review*, Spring: 63–74.

PART II

Case studies

PREAMBLE

In Part II we present five case studies. Through these cases, we intend to demonstrate the applications of systems thinking and modelling methodology. The first three cases primarily use causal loop modelling as their core methodology. Cases 1 and 2 are based on graduate students' projects that have been recast and summarised for the purposes of this book to demonstrate the applications of qualitative systems thinking methodology in the policy arena. Case 3 is based on a consulting assignment, in which work was done with two health care groups, clinicians and policy managers. Cases 4 and 5 show applications of dynamic modelling in detail in a hypothetical and a real business environment, respectively.

Case **1**

Public health reform – the case of New Zealand[1]

BACKGROUND

In July 1993, New Zealand's health system fundamentally changed, splitting the health care provider from the purchaser, whereas previously Area Health Boards had assumed both these roles. The providers, CHEs (Crown Health Enterprises),[2] were in future to compete amongst themselves for funding from the purchasers, RHAs (Regional Health Authorities).[3] Private sector managers were brought in to run the hospitals in a business-like manner, increasing efficiency, and even returning a profit to the Government. The objectives of the reforms (Upton, 1991) were:

- to reduce hospital waiting times;

- to improve access for all New Zealanders to an effective, fair and affordable health care system;

- to emphasise health promotion and illness prevention.

However, in reality and despite increased government spending on surgery, waiting list numbers have soared. This case study uses a systems thinking approach to investigate the effects of the reform, and to determine whether the new system is consistent with government's stated objectives. The study reveals a number of inconsistencies and gaps in current policies and proposes intervention strategies for reversing the adverse trends.

Introduction

For many decades up to the 1960s, New Zealand's health system was regarded as one of the best in the world. As New Zealand's social and economic environment changed, its health system proved too rigid to cope with the changes and slowly deteriorated. Today, health care is one of the most controversial issues in New Zealand.

New Zealand's economic position has made its health system problems worse. Over the past two decades, the New Zealand economy has grown more slowly than those of most other OECD countries. As a result, New Zealand has not been able to afford the same level of improvements in health care as other countries. Prior to the 1993 reform, Area Health Boards, the members of which were elected by the community, ran hospitals. These were funded by the Department of Health, on a per-head-of-population basis, and each hospital had overall responsibility for the health services in its particular community. Primary care providers, such as GPs, were funded directly by the Government through open-ended benefits. The following were identified as being the main problems of the old system (Upton, 1991):

- public hospital waiting lists were too long;
- there was conflict in the roles of Area Health Boards;
- there were constraints on Area Health Boards;
- funding of the system was fragmented;
- there were problems of access to services;

- little assistance was available for doctors when decisions had to be made;
- there was a lack of consumer control;
- there was a lack of equity.

The main element of the reform was the replacement of the Area Health Boards by four RHAs (Regional Health Authorities) or the *purchasers*, which allocate government health spending, and 23 CHEs (Crown Health Enterprises) or the *providers*. CHEs, which were to run groups of public hospitals, were expected to compete with one another – and with private providers – for funding from the RHAs, though they would automatically have a base contract for a certain number of operations. These contracts established that a certain number of operations were to be performed, and set the price that would be paid for them – no further operations would be funded. This was expected to lead to great efficiency gains in public hospitals. There was also to be more focus on primary health care (first-line health care), usually provided by GPs as 'gatekeepers'. In the years since the reforms, government spending on health has gone up by approximately $100 million each year, yet the number of people on the waiting list has increased (by approximately 8000 people each year) rather than decreasing.

Key variables

Health care is a complex system and several dynamic forces underlie it. In addition, public expectations of the system are high. The following variables play a key role in the health care system:

- health status of the population;
- government spending on health;
- level of co-operation among CHEs;
- waiting lists (patients waiting for non-emergency surgery);
- time on waiting lists;
- proportion of people using private health care;
- prevention efforts;
- health technology.

Dynamic patterns in health care

In this section we discuss the dynamic forces underlying New Zealand health care and their effect on the system.

Government spending

Government spending is the driving force in the health care system. Although the proportion of total health expenditure from private sources has increased (from 13% in 1980 to 19% in 1995), the major portion of funds is still provided by the government.

Government spending on health has also increased each year since the reform. This has helped increase the 'gap' between CHEs' operating expenses and the funding they received from RHAs (*gap* is defined as *surplus* here, i.e. government funds minus operating expenses). As a result, the pressure on CHEs to cut costs has been eased off. Consequently, the operating expenses of the CHEs have not fallen, and the gap (surplus) between funding and expenses has been reduced. This forms a balancing dynamic, **B1** (see Case figure 1.1). Easing off on cost-cutting affords the CHEs the option to focus more on prevention, which will, over time, result in a healthier population. This leads to fewer people joining the waiting list (referrals), and helps reduce the size of the waiting list over time. In turn, this leads to higher government funds for health care; a reinforcing pattern shown as **R1** in Case figure 1.2 on the following page.

Case figure 1.1   Cost cutting loop

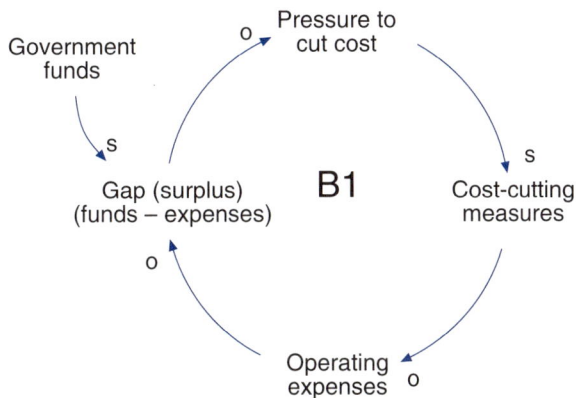

However, if the quality of public health care increases, people who would otherwise have gone to a private hospital may well wish to take advantage of the public system and, as a consequence, the waiting lists will increase again. This effect is shown as a balancing loop, **B2** (see Case figure 1.2). Furthermore, as waiting lists become longer, there will be an increase in the average waiting time and in the costs of keeping people on the waiting lists (e.g. health benefits, drugs, homecare, etc.). This, in turn, reduces both total government health care funds and the gap – hence creating the balancing dynamic (B2).

Waiting lists

Waiting lists are probably the most visible and politically sensitive aspect of the health reforms. The growing length of the waiting lists under the former Area Health Boards was one of the important factors leading to the reforms. Hence, reducing waiting lists has been one of the key aims of the reform. Despite the best of intentions, however, waiting lists have grown at an alarming rate ever since the reforms came into effect.

There are two aspects to waiting lists: length and time, which are positively correlated. That is, as the size of the waiting list increases, so does the average waiting time, and vice versa as shown by the reinforcing loop **R2** (see Case figure 1.3). As waiting lists become

Case figure 1.2 Prevention and public-private loops

excessively long, people who can afford to do so are likely to switch to the private system and the length of the waiting list will be reduced; a balancing dynamic shown as **B3**. Since the reform, the private health sector has experienced a large growth. Lengthening public waiting lists make the private system more attractive and reduce the government's burden. This 'shifting the burden' has led to a sharp rise in New Zealand's *total* health care cost due to greater proportion of health bills being absorbed by the private system. As the government has steadily reduced its funding of elective (non-emergency) surgery, the percentage of people with private health insurance has increased from 55% (in 1995) to 64% (in 1997). This has caused a rapid rise in insurance premiums. Since 1988, premiums have risen 230% for an average family and nearly 400% for older couples (*Consumer Magazine*, July 1997).

Case figure 1.3 Waiting list dynamics

The waiting list dynamic is made worse by doctors who refer patients to waiting lists in advance, even if the patient does not require the operation immediately (*New Zealand Herald*, 21 October 1997). With the introduction of a proposed booking system, doctors will not be able to book patients unless they are already at the point where they need the operation.

Co-operation amongst CHEs

The lack of co-operation amongst the CHEs can have serious repercussions for the overall effectiveness of the health care system. In the new competitive environment, co-operation has, in effect, been eliminated. Efficiency and quality gains have become 'competitive advantages' for the CHEs and are closely guarded by them. As the total government health funding is fixed, it is likely that the lack of co-operation will result in higher expenses and slower diffusion of innovation and quality, leading to a reduction in the number of people using the public system: eventually causing waiting lists to decline. This dynamic is also captured in balancing loop **B3** (Case figure 1.3).

Acute and elective surgery

Acute surgery is the surgery that is performed as a result of accidents or emergencies. Because such surgery must be performed immediately, it often displaces scheduled elective surgery. Since the CHEs' base contract with the RHAs stipulates a pre-specified number of operations, an increase in acute surgery means less elective surgery is performed and waiting lists will increase. Furthermore, as the time on waiting lists increases, the chance of a patient's condition becoming acute increases. If a patient's acute condition can be stabilised, the patient is discharged and he/she rejoins the waiting list. This 'double handling' of patients increases the operating costs of the CHEs, resulting in greater financial pressure. As the RHAs fund less than the full cost of the surgery, the net operating expenses of the CHEs will increase with the number of surgical operations performed, and this would amplify the funding gap dynamic, **B1**. At the same time, longer waiting lists bring more pressure to bear on the government to provide increased funding for operations. The additional operations thus funded by the RHAs reduce the waiting lists in the short run, temporarily relieving pressure on the government and creating a balancing dynamic, shown as **B4** in Case figure 1.4.

Case figure 1.4   Elective surgery loop

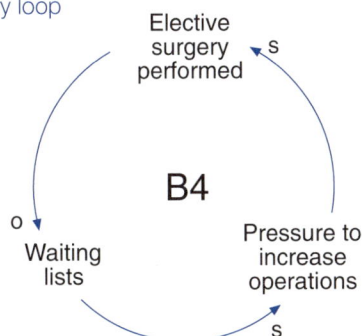

Health technology

New and advanced health technologies enable the health system to treat a wider range of illnesses. This has two opposing effects on the system. Firstly, there will be a gradual increase in the average life expectancy. As more people are treated for critical illnesses, the life expectancy of the population increases. However, this also increases the size of the population needing health care, which increases waiting lists and reduces government funds for health care. This introduces a new cycle of cost cutting, leading to less prevention measures and a poorer health status for the population, hence lower life expectancy. This dynamic is captured by the balancing loop B5 in Case figure 1.5.

The second effect of advanced health technology is the creation of new waiting lists, because of the development of treatments that previously did not exist. For example, dialysis treatment or CAT scans were not available two decades ago. Today they are considered to be routine operations and there are sizeable waiting lists for them.

Case figure 1.5 Health technology–life expectancy loop

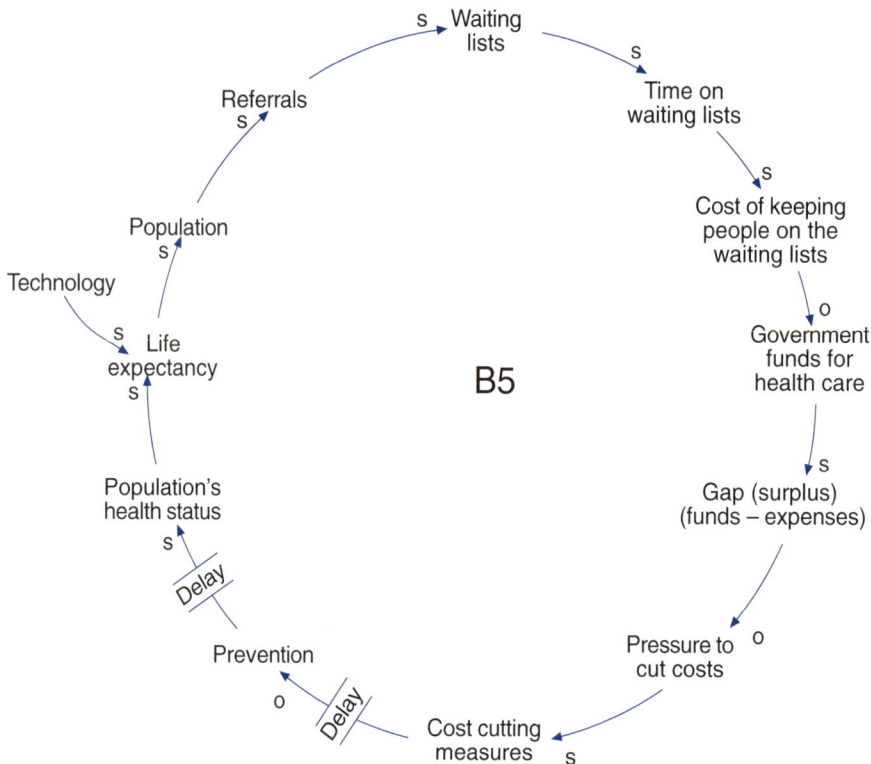

The managed care (IPA) model

The managed care model is based on the 'gatekeeper' theory. In New Zealand this operates mainly through the IPAs (Independent Practitioners Associations); a group of GPs working together. Under this system, the IPAs manage their patients' health under a capped funding scheme (budget holding). The IPAs run health promotion programs, awareness campaigns, and encourage immunisation and similar preventative measures which, in time, will result in a healthier community. This means that, in the longer term, people would visit their GPs less frequently, would need fewer prescription drugs and tests, and thus overall health expenses would be reduced. However, a potential adverse effect of the budget holding scheme is that the IPAs, in order to reduce costs, could under-serve their area by referring their patients to the CHEs. This creates a balancing dynamic, which could offset the beneficial effects of the IPAs.

Since the IPAs receive a certain amount of funding regardless of their expenses, this means that as expenses go down, more funds will be available for health prevention and promotion programs. This is a reinforcing cycle indicating that, over time, the GPs in the IPA could become wealthier as the community becomes healthier. Since this scheme has only recently been introduced in New Zealand, there is little evidence to confirm this dynamic.

Leverage points

The study of the New Zealand health reform highlights three leverage points or areas for improvements. The leverage points are identified based on their potential impact on the system. These leverage points are discussed below.

CHE co-operation

The notion that CHEs should compete is fundamentally wrong. Competition reduces the willingness of CHEs to co-operate with one another, which would otherwise lead to better practices and greater overall efficiency and effectiveness. As a result, any innovation or improvement by a CHE is viewed as a competitive advantage and is closely guarded. Furthermore, as the RHAs tend to award contracts to the lowest bidder, the CHEs' primary focus has become the need to cut costs – to the extent where CHEs can even refuse to accept patients from outside their community area.

Waiting lists

Currently, the average time that a person will spend on the waiting lists is increasing. The longer the patients have to wait, the more likely it is that their condition will deteriorate. This increases the complexity and cost of treatment, as well as reducing the chance of recovery. Further, while people wait for treatment, they may not be able to work, and will need to receive assistance from other government agencies such as social welfare, or the Accident Compensation Corporation (ACC). Therefore, shortening the waiting list could bring tremendous cost savings and higher overall health gains for the nation.

Prevention

In a competitive environment, with a focus on cost cutting, there will be no incentive for using preventative measures. This short-term view ignores the fact that preventing health problems is, in the long term, a far cheaper option than having to treat people later on. Unfortunately, governments are often trapped in short-term and quick-fix modes, which makes them reluctant to invest in fundamental and long-term strategies.

Recommended strategies

The discussion of the leverage points leads to the identification of four strategies for dealing with current weaknesses in the health system. These strategies can reverse the adverse dynamics that impede effectiveness of the reform. The implementation of any of these strategies would require a fundamental mind-shift from a short- to a long-term view, and to a 'total' system perspective.

1   Remove the need for CHEs to compete amongst themselves.[4]

2   Change the CHE incentives: instead of rewarding cost cutting, reward the provision of quality care.

3   Focus on prevention strategies.

4   Encourage GPs to operate under an integrated health care model (e.g. IPA).

As described earlier, competition amongst various stakeholders in the public health system is detrimental to the overall success of new policies. The requirement that CHEs compete with each other for contracts should be removed, and instead they should be encouraged to actively work together to solve common problems.

The short-term obsession of the CHEs to cut costs has to give way to a common goal of improving the health status of the population. To ensure responsible spending, CHEs should be given a capped budget, similar to that in the managed care model. This budget should not, however, include the cost of acute surgery, so that elective surgery would not have to be traded off against emergency cases. The capped budget for each CHE would have to take into account the differences in the health status of the areas they serve. For example, South Auckland has a high Pacific Islander population, and people in this area need to have a higher level of health care. An integrated performance management system, similar to the Balanced Scorecard approach, should be introduced to measure and monitor the performance of CHEs.

The ultimate aim of any public health system should be to enhance the health status of the population. By focusing upon short-term fixes and improvements this aim is unlikely to be achieved. There has to be greater emphasis on education, prevention and on promoting healthier lifestyles. This is the fundamental way to improve the state of the nation's health in the long run. Increasing elective surgery levels only serves to relieve the problem in the short term. Spending more on surgery without increasing prevention tends simply to increase a person's lifespan and thus the likelihood of more health care in that time. Spending money on prevention is a long-term investment. In the case of diabetes, for example, it is estimated that every dollar spent on prevention saves three to four dollars later, by reducing diabetes-related hospital cases, including strokes, heart attacks, kidney failure and blindness (*New Zealand Herald*, 22 October 1997).

Appropriate incentive structures should be put in place to reward GPs for keeping their communities healthy, instead of having GPs profit from a less healthy community. The challenge is to convince GPs to switch to a capped budget (i.e. the IPA model). This, however, could be a win-win proposition as there is potential for GPs to realise higher profits under this system.

The focus on the waiting list is a valid objective, as reducing it will reduce system bottlenecks and will save health agencies the costs associated with keeping people on the list. Shortening the waiting list is a balancing dynamic. By improving the public health system (e.g. shorter waiting lists), the proportion of people using it will increase and hence the elective (non-emergency) waiting list will rise even as the number of operations increases. Without structural improvements in the public health system and greater emphasis on prevention, this dynamic may never reach stability. There is speculation that by under-spending, government intends making the public health system unattractive to those who can afford private care – and hence reduce the burden on public health. The strategic risk is that the health system could steadily deteriorate beyond repair as a result of persistent under-investment.

Conclusion

This systems thinking case study identifies some areas in which the New Zealand health reform has not reached its desired objectives. Numbers on waiting lists have gone up and access to the system has become more limited, as there appears to be a deliberate effort to shift people to private health care. Despite increased government spending, the gap in quality and level of care between the advantaged and disadvantaged has widened. The government's emphasis on cost cutting has resulted in false economies. The higher number of operations performed is mainly due to the increases in acute surgery, and has not reduced waiting list levels, as fewer elective surgical operations are performed. At the same time, New Zealand's population is ageing, which increases the stress on the system even further. Counteracting these trends, there has been a significant shift to the private system, partly due to excessive waiting times and perceived deterioration in public health quality. A result of this shift has been much greater total national expenditure on health.

The systems thinking approach has identified a number of dynamic patterns that underlie the behaviour of the health system. These dynamics include co-operation amongst CHEs, the lengthening of the waiting list, government spending, and technological development. Underlying these dynamics are beliefs, assumptions, and agendas (i.e., mental models) of the key stakeholders in the health system. The government has insisted that the CHEs must cut costs to accommodate the extra amount of elective surgery needed. The CHEs and the public resent this and demand greater levels of funding. Yet, in order to reduce the burden on the public system, the government is implicitly encouraging people to move into the private system. Thus there is a growing perception that the public system will not adequately cater for all people. As a result, the proportion of people with private insurance has been increasing, resulting in rapid growth in the private health system and in overall health care costs.

In order to reverse the undesirable dynamics created by the reform, four intervention strategies have become evident.

1 Remove the need for CHEs to compete amongst themselves.
2 Change the incentives of CHEs, so that they do not focus on cutting costs, at the expense of providing better care.
3 Focus more on prevention.
4 Encourage GPs to work under an IPA or integrated model.

The systems thinking approach has identified critical deficiencies in the structure, policies and incentives of the present health system. This led to the identification of a number of leverage points and intervention strategies that could provide corrective mechanisms to counter the adverse effects of the reform and would allow for fuller realisation of its objectives.

Notes

1 This case is based on a study originally conducted by Alex Yeoh and Keith Wallace, graduate students in the Systems Modelling course at the University of Auckland, 1997.
2 The CHEs are now called HHSs.
3 The Government has recently consolidated RHAs under a single agency, HFA (Health Funding Authority).
4 The competition regulation was removed in 1997.

REFERENCES

Upton, S. (1991) *Your Health and the Public Health*. Ministry of Health, Wellington.

Lowering the legal drinking age[1]

BACKGROUND

Alcohol is a key feature of New Zealanders' social and sporting activities. Eighty-nine per cent of men and 85% of women consume alcohol regularly.[2] Current legislation states that '… to legally consume alcohol in New Zealand an individual must be 20 years or older. An individual can also consume alcohol if between the ages of 18–20 and consuming food or accompanied by a parent/ guardian.'[3]

At present, various members of the Parliament are pushing for changes to these laws.[4] A number of changes have been proposed, including Sunday liquor sales and permitting supermarkets to sell liquor. One proposed change that is causing considerable debate within the government and in public circles, is the idea of lowering the legal drinking age from 20 to 18 years.

The liquor industry

The liquor industry is a major revenue earner for the government. Currently the liquor industry accounts for estimated sales of more than one billion dollars annually, and of this, $500 million is raised in excise tax.[5] Liquor sales make up 2.6% of total consumer spending in New Zealand; on average, $17.60 per person is spent on alcohol each week. The amount of beer and spirits consumed between March 1996 and March 1997 declined by around 7.8% while wine consumption increased over the same time period by 7%.[6]

Key issues

One of the key issues related to alcohol consumption is drink driving and road accident fatalities. The government, police and various action groups have campaigned very hard to decrease the annual number of alcohol-related road fatalities in New Zealand.

Another key issue is the debate over the drinking habits of today's youth. Are young people responsible and mature enough for the drinking age to be lowered? Attached to this question is the call for compulsory photo identification cards which would make it easier for police and liquor retailers to enforce the drinking age laws.

Why is this issue important? As indicated above, alcohol plays a significant part in most New Zealanders' lives. It would be reasonable to say that alcohol and the liquor industry affect all New Zealanders in some way or another.

There are numerous stakeholders in this issue, including:

- the general public;
- government;
- the alcohol industry;
- the police;
- social, religious and community groups.

In this study, we examine the underlying forces that affect drinking age dynamics. The central question being asked is:

> What will the short- and long-term effects be if the legal drinking age is lowered to 18 years, and how could the transition be managed so that the negative elements are minimised?

As part of the systems approach we will first identify the key variables and their behaviour over time. Then the core causal loops and their underlying mental models will be explored. Based on this, key leverage points will be identified and possible intervention strategies will be discussed.

Key variables

Changing the legal drinking age is a complex issue. There are a number of variables that influence and are influenced by the legal drinking age. The following is a list of some of these variables (not in the order of importance):

- alcohol consumption;
- government revenue;
- government expenditure;
- number of people consuming alcohol;
- alcohol-related road deaths;
- drink driving offences;
- drink driving education;
- alcohol-related crimes;
- crime-related education;
- police workload;
- police resources;
- need for photo identification;
- excise tax;
- youth responsibility.

The list is not exhaustive. There are a number of other variables that affect and are affected by the dynamics of the legal drinking age. Some of these are listed below. For the sake of simplicity, however, these variables are not used in this study.

- teenage health problems;
- teenage crime;
- teenage pregnancy;
- teenage suicide.

Patterns of behaviour

In this section we discuss how some of the key variables behave over time. The behaviour over time (BOT) of these variables is shown in Case figure 2.1. The BOTs indicate how these variables would react if the legal drinking age were decreased to 18 years. The BOTs also foreshadow whether the changes are of a reinforcing or a balancing nature.

Case figure 2.1   Expected BOTs of key variables

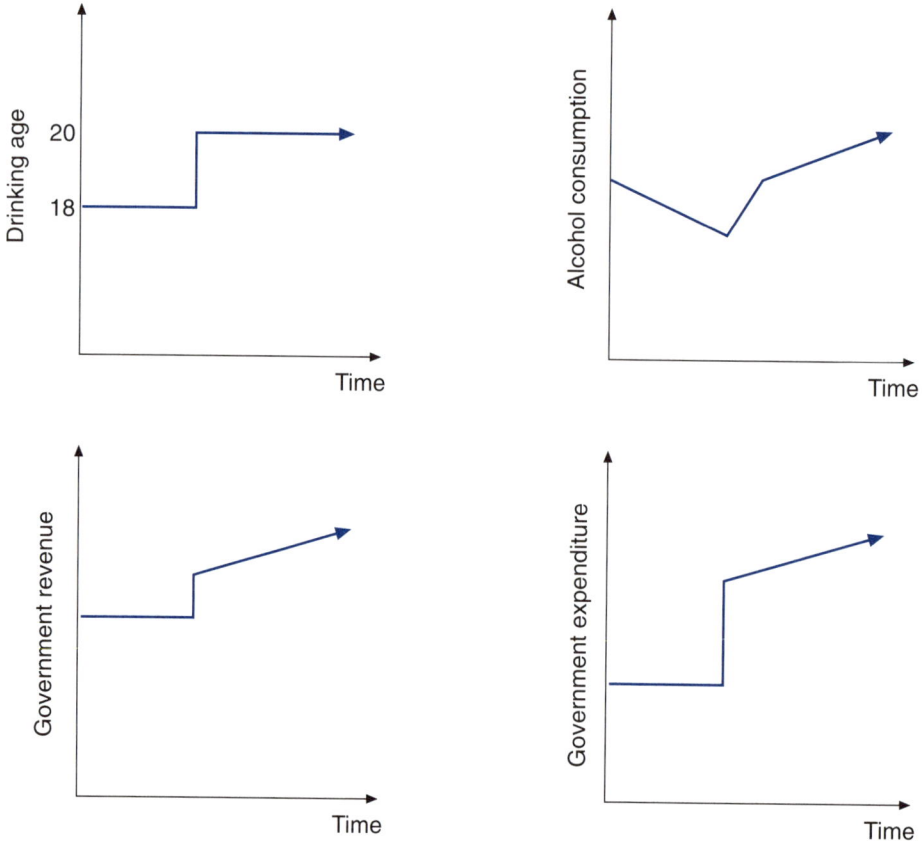

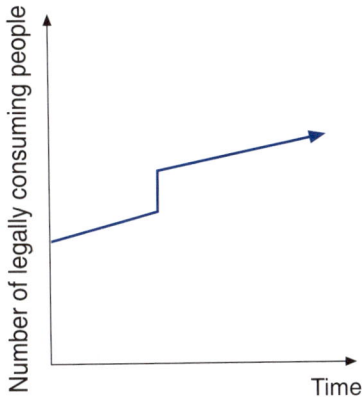

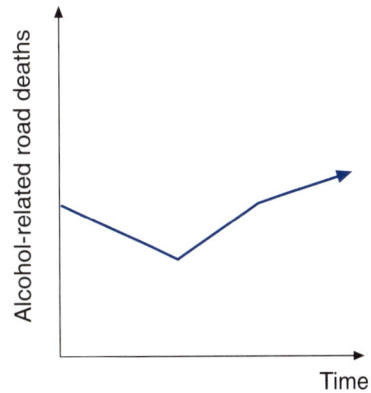

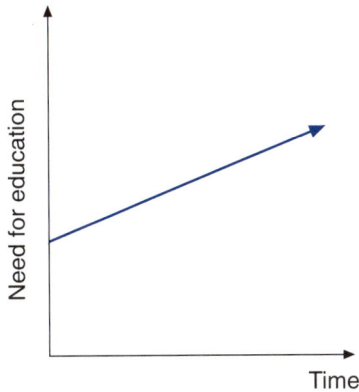

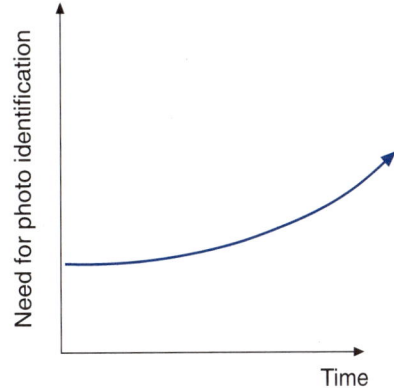

Alcohol consumption is key to the overall dynamic. Supporters of the bill to decrease the legal drinking age maintain that if the age were decreased, alcohol consumption would not increase dramatically. This is because, they believe, 18- to 20-year-olds already consume alcohol and lowering the legal age would not change current alcohol consumption patterns dramatically. Here it may be mentioned that, regardless of the legal drinking age, alcohol consumption has fallen by 25% over the past 10 years (ALAC, 1998: 2).

The opposing view argues that total alcohol consumption will in fact increase if the legal drinking age is increased, as the change will push down the threshold of drinking by two years; hence 16- and 17-year-olds will, it is believed, feel more at ease to use alcohol.

Considering the above views, we adopt the scenario that lowering the drinking age will increase alcohol consumption among 16- to 17-year-olds and hence will cause an overall increase in alcohol consumption. This will in turn increase government revenue from alcohol sales, mainly through excise taxes. But lowering the drinking age will also increase the need for a national photo identification card, and the need for awareness education, as young people are more susceptible to the dangers of alcohol abuse.

Another serious concern is that the lowering of legal drinking age would reverse the fall in road tolls of recent years. This concern is supported by experiences in the USA and Australia. In 1972, a number of US states lowered the legal drinking age from 21 to 18. Within a short time it became evident that the lower drinking age had resulted in an increase in alcohol-related road fatalities (*New Zealand Herald*, 16 June 1998: 4). Subsequently, when the drinking age was raised back to 21, road fatalities among 18- to 20-year-olds decreased by 13%. Similarly, the Australian experience has shown that 'lowering the [drinking] age to 18 saw increases in road accidents, juvenile crime, social problems and emergency hospital treatment' (*New Zealand Herald*, 23 March 1997: 3).

Another effect that the proposed change would have is the increase in government expenditure that would be necessary, i.e. costs associated with road fatalities, education and crime prevention, and the costs related to identification and law enforcement. In this regard, the Land Transport Safety Authority (LTSA) reports that 'dropping the drinking age to 18 would cost the country an extra $28.3 million with four extra crashes a year' (*New Zealand Herald*, 16 June 1998: 4).

Some argue that the above-mentioned effects would be tempered by greater responsibility on the part of young people. According to a former Governor-General, 'young people now have a more responsible attitude to drinking and driving than previous generations' (*New Zealand Herald*, 6 April 1998: 5). Others who support this view suggest that the level of responsibility taken by young people has been increasing over time and lowering of the drinking age will help increase it further. The link between alcohol and crime is also widely accepted. According to the New Zealand police, '80% of all reported crime is alcohol-related' (Orsman, 1997: 12). This rate has been fairly stable in the past. However, it is expected that if the drinking age were lowered, the number of crimes would also increase over time.

Causal loops

After examining the key variables and their behaviour over time, four key causal loops emerge in this case. They are the consumption loop, enforcement loop, road fatality loop, and crime loop.

Consumption loop (R1)

The consumption loop is shown in Case figure 2.2. As discussed on p. 163, and based on evidence from other countries, the lowering of the legal drinking age would result in an increase in the number of people who consume alcohol, and therefore in overall alcohol consumption. This, in turn, would cause an increase in government excise tax collected and therefore an increase in government revenue. The prospect of higher revenues would increase the government's tendency to lower the drinking age. In addition, the assumption that young people are becoming more responsible reinforces this tendency. Over time, these pressures increase the likelihood that the legal drinking age will be lowered, creating a reinforcing loop. However, this loop has a practical lower bound and at some point it becomes stable.

Case figure 2.2 The drinking age dynamic

Enforcement loop (B1)

If the legal drinking age is lowered, there will be a greater need for tighter law enforcement. This, in turn, increases the need for a national photo identification system. The cost associated with the introduction and implementation of photo identification cards increases government expenditure. This offsets some of the attractiveness of lowering the drinking age and hence lessens the pressure to do so. Presumably, youth responsibility would still increase over time, keeping the pressure on to lower the drinking age. However, the potential government revenue loss would decrease the effect of this pressure – hence creating a balancing dynamic.

Road fatality loop (B2)

As we discussed earlier, evidence from the USA and Australia shows that an increase in alcohol-consuming population leads to an increase in the number of drink driving offences and also in alcohol-related road deaths (*New Zealand Herald*, 1997, 23 March: 3).

Road fatalities have a significant human and social cost, which increase the government's burden. This creates a counteracting or balancing dynamic similar to the enforcement loop.

Crime loop (B3)

As the drinking population grows, the number of alcohol-related crimes also increases (Orsman, 1997: 12). This increases the police workload and creates the need for additional police resources. Public pressure could force the government to increase police resources, which will increase government expenditure and will decrease total government funds. This loop also works as a counteracting force (balancing loop) prompting the government to reconsider or reverse its policy.

Discussion

The four causal loops presented above collectively capture the key dynamics of the legal drinking age issue. The consumption loop (reinforcing), which is central to this dynamic, results in an increase in government revenue while the other loops (balancing) capture the direct and indirect drinking-related costs to government and society.

The consumption loop illustrates the underlying mental model of the government on the issue. It shows the revenue side of the picture, since lowering the drinking age would result in increased revenue for the government through higher taxes. This is a reinforcing loop, with lower and upper bounds on the 'reasonable' legal drinking age, perhaps between 17 and 22 years of age.

The enforcement loop illustrates one way in which the negative effects of the policy change could be minimised. This loop illustrates the counteracting effect of the costs of photo identification and law enforcement, costs that will reduce or even outweigh the additional tax revenue.

The road fatality loop illustrates one of the most critical side-effects of the proposed policy. If this loop is left unchecked, the social, psychological and financial burden to the country and the government can be substantial.

System archetypes

The dynamics of the legal drinking age issue discussed above lend themselves to a number of systems archetypes. In particular, the fixes-that-fail and shifting-the-burden archetypes provide a clearer insight into some of the dynamics and help identify key leverage points.

Fixes that fail

There are two fixes-that-fail or 'backfire' archetypes that are at work here. The first illustrates the government's (hidden) interest in the revenue-generating potential of the proposed law change. This archetype shows that the need for revenue increases government's tendency to lower the drinking age. As discussed earlier, this leads to greater alcohol consumption and hence government revenue is substantially increased as a result of additional taxes (i.e. excise and income taxes). This is illustrated by loop **B1** in Case figure 2.3. However, an 'unintended' consequence follows this action. With a lower drinking age and higher alcohol consumption, social problems – including crime, road fatalities and family violence – increase correspondingly. This will have a detrimental effect on government revenue, creating a greater need for revenue as illustrated by the reinforcing loop **R1**.

Case figure 2.3   Social costs backfire

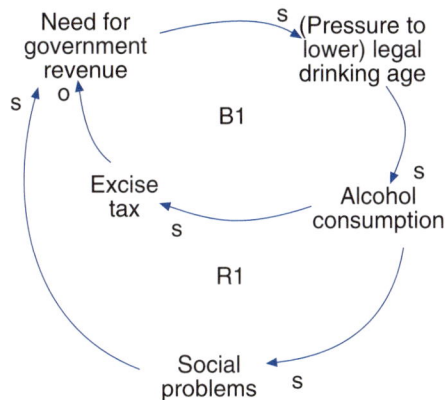

The second fixes-that-fail archetype shows the (side) effect of the proposed policy on underage drinkers, i.e. on those under the legal drinking age who are nonetheless able to obtain and consume alcohol illegally. A critical assumption of the proposed policy change is that as the legal drinking age is lowered, the number of underage drinkers will decrease, relieving the pressure to lower the drinking age. This is shown as **B1** in Case figure 2.4.

However, the unintended consequence of this policy is that it will create a new 'grey' age group (the 16- and 17-year-olds) who will feel more at ease about drinking as they will be closer to the legal age limit. Effectively, by lowering the legal drinking age, the age of the population who can obtain alcohol 'illegally' will be pushed down to 16 and 17 years. This will exacerbate the initial problem of underage drinking. This dynamic is illustrated by **R1** in Case figure 2.4 below.

Case figure 2.4   Under-age drinking backfires

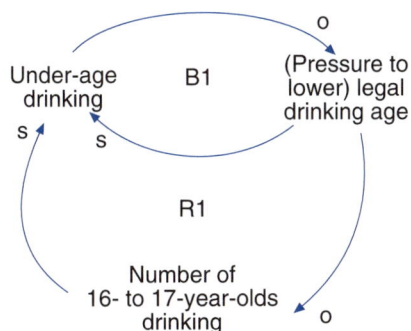

Shifting the burden

As alcohol-related crimes increase, the need for law enforcement and tighter controls increases correspondingly. Such increases in law enforcement are 'symptomatic' solutions requiring ever-increasing fines and intensified policing. This would initially decrease the level of drinking offences and crime as shown by balancing loop **B1** in Case figure 2.5. As a result, government's (as well as society's) reliance on the use of legislation and enforcement at the expense of more fundamental solutions to the problem would be increased (reinforcing loop **R1**). A fundamental solution is education of the public on the effects of alcohol. As alcohol-related crime increases, the level of public education must be increased to counter the negative effects of alcohol consumption. In the long run, education and other awareness programmes should have a moderating effect on the level of alcohol-related crime, as shown by the balancing loop **B2**.

Case figure 2.5.   Shifting the burden

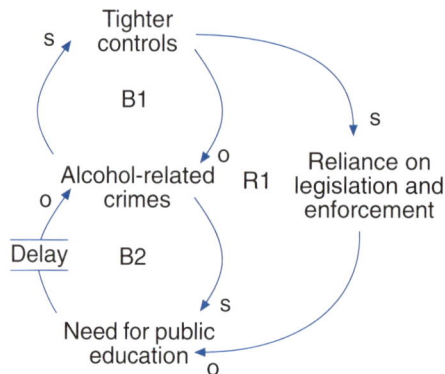

Intervention strategies

Ultimately, the best strategy is to not lower the drinking age. This will essentially remove all of the negative effects discussed in this study, since drink driving, crime and underage drinking are shown to be adversely affected by an increase in the level of alcohol consumption.

However, if the proposed policy is adopted then public education and awareness are key intervention strategies to mitigate the effect of alcohol consumption. The causal loop models illustrated in this study point to two areas for enhanced public education: crime prevention and drink driving. As recent drink driving campaigns have convincingly shown, aggressive and persistent public education can dramatically affect the level of drink driving offences, and especially of alcohol-related road deaths. This should reduce government's overall financial burden and would reduce public pressure on government. Similarly, crime education could reduce the level of alcohol-related crime and reduce the need to recruit further police resources.

Conclusion

The use of systems thinking has enabled us to reach a much clearer understanding of the complex issue of lowering the legal drinking age and its effects, implications, and unintended consequences. The systems thinking approach demonstrates that the drinking age should not be lowered to 18 years of age. This is supported by evidence relating to the *total* long-term costs of policy change. The social and economic costs of increased road deaths, police resources and crime can outweigh the anticipated tax-based benefits. If the policy change does occur, however, education of the public and the introduction of a universal photo identification system would be key factors in limiting the negative effects of the policy change.

The cost of four extra alcohol-related road crashes per year is estimated at $28.3 million (*New Zealand Herald,* 1998, 16 June: 4). Given this scale of cost, a systems perspective to help reveal the 'total costs' of the change may alter the government's view of lowering the legal drinking age.

Research process hint

The use of the cognitive mapping technique for interview data collection is very valuable. This technique helps with the extraction of unsolicited information. It also allows the interviewer to alter the direction of the interview and take the discussion where he/she wants. Cognitive mapping also assists in identification and discussion of causal relationships. The instant feedback that can be obtained by the use of this technique is an added advantage.

Mental models

Public view: 'Lowering the drinking age would be seen by society as a government endorsement of the value of drinking alcohol…'
(*New Zealand Herald*, 30 July 1998: 3)

Minister of Youth Affairs: '… people [are] drinking in unsafe environments, on the street and in parks … it would be much better if young people could drink in a controlled environment,' and '[lowering the age], coupled with a highly effective education campaign … could ensure that young people were getting the right education they required to make safe decisions about alcohol consumption.' (*New Zealand Herald*, 16 January 1997: 12)

Member of Parliament: [Young people today have] 'a more sophisticated and mature approach to liquor and also have a more responsible attitude to drinking and driving.' (*The Evening Post*, 6 April 1998: 12)

Another MP: 'Better educational programmes on the consequences of alcohol consumption are needed, as well as a more effective system of law enforcement...' (*Waikato Times*, 13 April 1998:2)

Opposing view: '... there was little evidence that people, particularly heavy drinkers, could be educated to drink responsibly.' (*New Zealand Herald*, 23 March 1997: 3)

Automobile Association (AA): 'Lowering the drinking age will cause more young drivers to crash.' (*New Zealand Herald*, 16 June 1998: 4)

Another view: 'Under 20-year-olds already frequent bars, so lowering the age won't change anything.' (Student, University of Auckland, interviewed August 1998)

Youth: 'Everyone I know drinks now, but it would be good to not have to worry about getting caught in a pub or at the liquor store.' (Youth, interviewed 20 September 1998)

Notes

1 This case is based on a project prepared by David Todd for the graduate course in systems modelling at the University of Auckland.

2 Data obtained from a nationwide telephone survey of 4232 people aged 14–65 (Wyllie et al., 1996).

3 The Sale of Liquor Act 1989. Subsequent to this study, the Act was revised in July 1999, and the legal drinking age was lowered to 18.

4 Paul East, the former Attorney-General; Deborah Morris, Minister of Youth Affairs; Doug Graham, Minister of Justice.

5 Beer Wine and Spirits Council 1996.

6 Statistics New Zealand, 1997.

REFERENCES

ALAC. (1998) Information pack, www.alac.co.nz

The Evening Post. (1998, 6 April) East seeks to lower drinking age, p. 12.

New Zealand Herald. (1997, 16 January) Youth minister advocates lower drinking age, p. 12.

– (1997, 23 March) Higher road toll tipped if drinking age lowered, p. 3.

– (1998, 6 April) Drop drinking age says East, p. 5.

– (1998, 16 June) AA slams plan to lower drink age, p. 4.

– (1998, 30 July) Lower drinking age opposed, p. 3.

Orsman, B. (1997, 16 January) Youth minister advocates lower drinking age. *New Zealand Herald*, p. 12.

Waikato Times (1998, 13 April) Labour opposes drinking age proposal, p. 2.

Wyllie, A., Millard, M. and Zhang, J. (1996) *Drinking in New Zealand: A National Survey 1995*. Alcohol and Public Health Research Unit, Auckland.

Case **3**

Drivers of quality in health services[1]

OVERVIEW

This case describes how an exploratory project at the New Zealand Ministry of Health, using a qualitative system dynamics approach in order to identify the factors that interact to drive quality in the health and disability sector, revealed sound evidence for the much-cited different world views of medical/health clinicians and policy managers.

Genesis of the project

New Zealand health and disability services have undergone radical reshaping since 1991, in an attempt to improve access, quality, safety, effectiveness, efficiency and equity. The cornerstone of the new structure is a funder–provider split, where the national Health Funding Authority (HFA) contracts with a range of publicly and privately owned services to provide specified services to a specified quality standard (Upton, 1991; MOH, 1997). As in other countries, the changes are driven by rising consumer expectations, developing technology, concerns about access and equity, and the perennial search for ways to get more health care for the tax payers' dollar.

Most New Zealanders receive high-quality care from skilled practitioners. However, there remains continuing evidence of sub-standard care for some. Quality problems include avoidable errors, under-use of necessary services, over-use of services, and variations in services.[2]

Following an enquiry into seven deaths at Christchurch Hospital, the Ministry of Health (MOH) brought together a group of its own senior policy managers and clinical advisers in an attempt to understand the issues that interact to drive quality at a systems level. It commissioned the New Zealand Organisational Learning Centre to facilitate a programme of system dynamics workshops to help address the behavioural, structural, communication and relationship issues that together determine the quality of services delivered.

The system dynamics approach offered a way to make sense of the complex relationships and information flows through the sector. This pilot project was to be a trial of the utility of the system dynamics methods, rather than rigorous policy analysis based on empirical evidence. The Ministry would develop a more considered project should the initial explorations appear to have potential.

Overview of the workshops

MOH staff wishing to participate in the workshops were not available as one group for the time required to work through the system dynamics process. The eleven staff members were placed in two groups, one of five and one of six. Each of the groups were to meet for four hours on one day, in consecutive weeks. There was to be third and final joint session to compare the CLDs and the insights those brought to the organising question:

> What are the factors that interact to drive quality in the health and disability sector?

Staff self-selected into the two groups on the basis of availability, and the consultants from New Zealand Organisational Learning Centre worked with each group for the planned sessions. All participants were Ministry of Health staff. Clinicians employed in the Ministry are expected to maintain strong professional ties, and many continue to practise part-time.

- **Group 1** consisted of four policy staff and one clinician. Policy staff included two economists and two senior policy managers. Group 1 is referred to as the policy managers group.

- **Group 2** consisted of four clinicians, one environmental scientist and one senior policy manager. Group 2 is referred to as the clinicians group.

The consultants used coloured hexagons (see p. 174 and Kreutzer's FASTbreak™ process (Kreutzer, 1995)) as a facilitation tool to construct a causal loop diagram (CLD) of the factors that the participants identified as the factors which interact to drive quality.

An account of the utility of hexagons (*idons*) at the preliminary issue-conceptualisation stage of modelling can be found in Hodgson (1994). The general approach used for workshops described below was based on the qualitative aspects of the system dynamics methodology.[3]

The following process was followed with each group.

1 Hexagons were generated for each issue, opportunity or obstacle and placed on a whiteboard.

2 These hexagons were then grouped into clusters and given a 'descriptive' name.

3 A small number of variables were identified for each cluster (see Case figures 3.1 and 3.3 for examples of a cluster of issues from each group with variables generated).

4 These variables were then separated from the clusters, so that links between the variables could be established.

5 A directed arrow was provided for each pair of related variables.

6 An initial version of the causal loop diagrams was developed.

Care was taken to record the 'discourse' of each group, thus the terms used in the clusters and CLDs that follow are the terms agreed to and used by the group.

The coloured hexagons used for issue generation and identification of variables in the workshops are represented in Case figures 3.1 and 3.3 as follows:

'Yellow' hexagons	issues, opportunities, obstacles – text in a clear frame
'Pink' hexagons	strongly held/felt – are lightly shaded with capitalised text and bold border
'Blue' hexagons	variables – are shaded and in italics with a double-line border

Revealed mental model of policy managers group

The following diagram illustrates one cluster produced by the policy managers group (Group 1). It illustrates Steps (1) to (3) described above. This cluster has one 'pink' hexagon and three variables. The variables are used to build the CLD in Case figure 3.2 on p. 175.

Case figure 3.1   Example of a cluster of issues from Group 1 (policy managers)

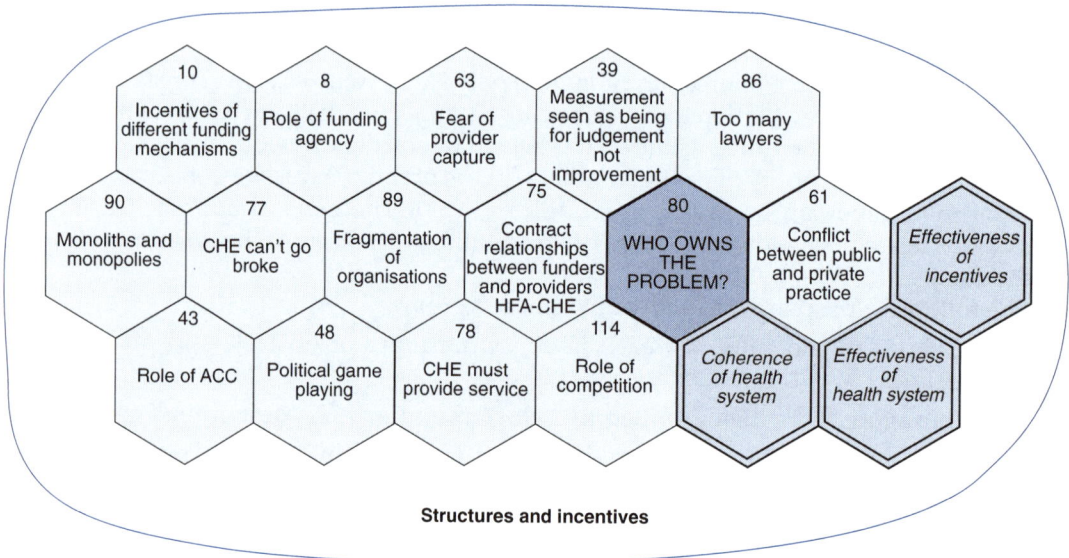

Structures and incentives

The issues generated by Group 1 (policy managers) in the 16 clusters included 'incentives of different funding mechanisms', 'economies of scale', 'scarce resources', 'choices and opportunity costs', 'monoliths and monopolies' and 'providers don't bear the cost of rework', 'funder has fixed budget' and 'quality inflation'. The clusters produced 26 variables, examples of which are: 'desire for choice', 'effectiveness of incentives', 'provider exposure to consequences', 'extent of collectivism', 'fit with public goals/fit with private goals', 'ability to measure quality' and 'GDP growth per capita'.

Following Steps (4) to (6) of the process described above, the causal loop diagram in Case figure 3.2 was developed by the policy managers group. It represents their shared mental model, addressing the organising question stated earlier: 'What are the factors that interact to drive quality in the health and disability sector?'

Case figure 3.2   Initial causal loop diagram built by Group 1 (policy managers)

The key to help interpret the causal loop diagrams is provided below:

Key:

B1	=	Balancing (or control) loop no. 1
R1	=	Reinforcing (or growth/decay) loop no. 1
o	=	Variable at the head of an arrow changes in the opposite direction to the variable at the tail
s	=	Variable at the head of an arrow changes in the same direction as the variable at the tail
||	=	Indicates a significant time delay

Revealed mental model of clinicians group

The following diagram (Case figure 3.3) illustrates one cluster produced by the clinicians group (Group 2). It illustrates Steps (1) to (3) described on p. 173. This cluster has five 'pink' hexagons and four variables. The variables are used to build the CLD.

Case figure 3.3   Example of a cluster of issues from Group 2 (clinicians)

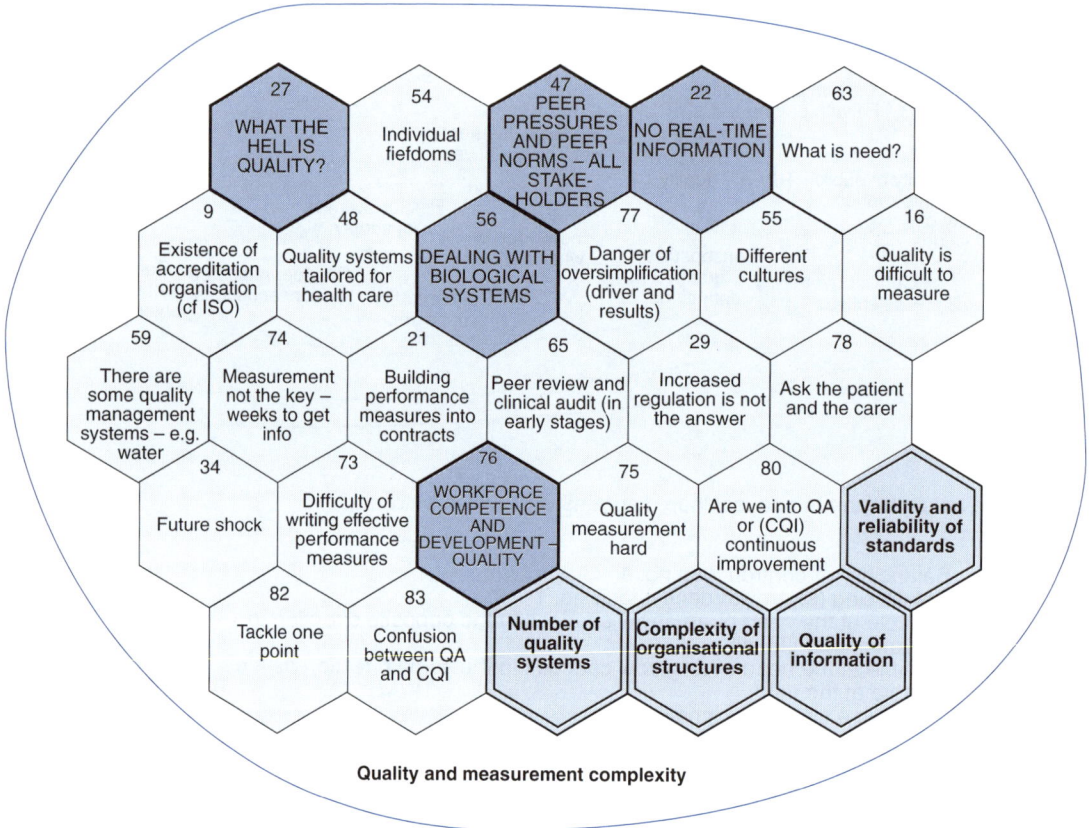

Quality and measurement complexity

The issues generated by Group 2 (clinicians) in the 11 clusters included: 'commitment (positive) workforce and public', 'peer pressures and peer norms – all stakeholders', 'trust/confidence', 'peer review and clinical audit'. The clusters produced 28 variables, including 'validity and reliability of standards', 'number of quality systems', 'health worker participation', 'health worker confidence', 'task diversity', 'adverse events' and 'ownership of quality'. The variables led to the following initial causal loop diagram (revealing the mental model of the clinicians group).

Case figure 3.4   Initial causal loop diagram built by Group 2 (clinicians)

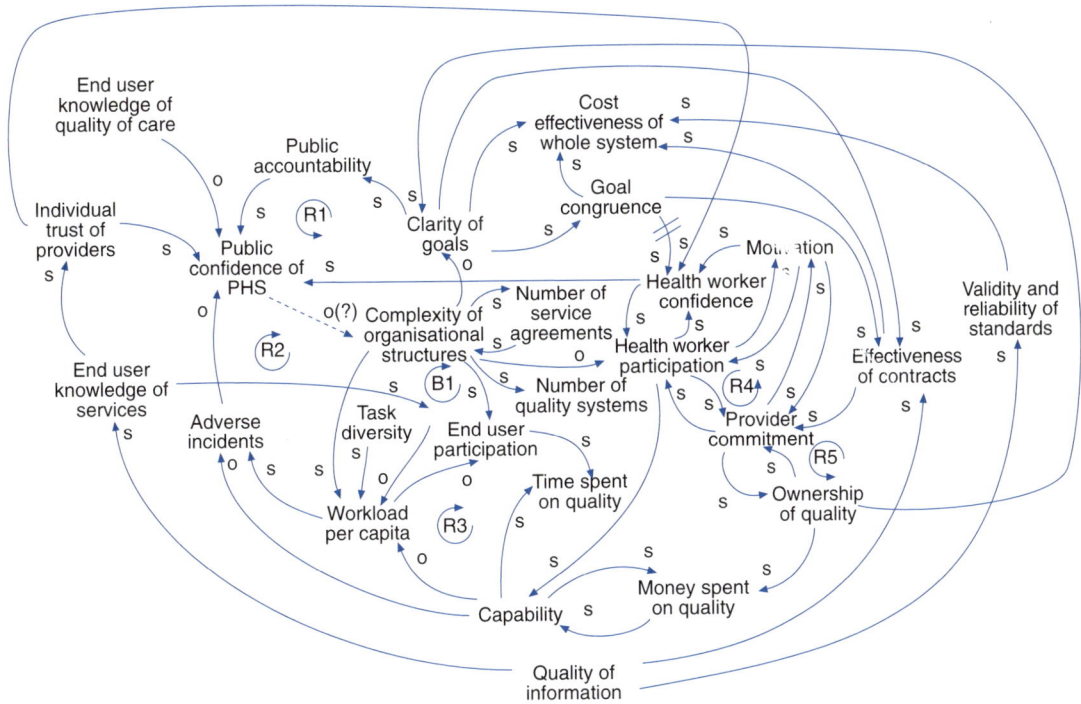

Comparison of world views

The causal loop diagrams generated by each group have sharply different characteristics yet the eleven people in the two groups work together to prepare policy advice. The vocabulary and conceptual terms of the policy group CLD are characterised by abstract concepts such as choice, competing priorities and macro-economic concerns, whereas those generated by the clinical group are markedly more concrete, including, for example, adverse incidents, workload, and individual trust of provider.

The CLD for the policy group suggests that the 'quality of public information' is a key influence upon 'public confidence' which influences the politics of health through funding (Vote: Health) and 'system stability'.

The CLD for the clinical groups also identifies 'public confidence' as being significant. But how 'public confidence' exerts its influence is not mapped. The key influence on 'public confidence' is 'health worker confidence': the professionals and their mission.

The CLDs illustrate the differences in the two groups' understanding of their scope of responsibility and the tasks for which they are accountable. The policy group looks to the effectiveness of the whole sector, while the clinicians look to the delivery of a service.

Raelin (1986) suggests that professionalism is a set of task-oriented behaviours with associated social behaviours, which include a high level of expertise, autonomy or the freedom to control the management of each task, commitment to the task, identification with peers, a system of ethics and a means of maintaining standards.

Managers and policy analysts are accountable for the overall effectiveness of a system, and this accountability includes balancing competing objectives such as quality and cost, allocating and rationing resources, and designing organisational and production systems. Note that patients are not present in the CLD of the policy group. For them the effectiveness of the health system is influenced by the effectiveness of incentives, the effectiveness of quality leadership and system stability.

Although imperfectly developed in terms of clear loops and relationships, the CLDs are useful in illustrating the roots of different world views: of a micro- and macro-, small-picture and big-picture understanding, of looking into the organisational and professional environment versus looking outward to the wider context of the broader social and economic environment. There is no doubt that a rich discussion of the differences, the missing parts, the complementarities and the incomprehensible links would come from the two groups contemplating their CLDs. For example, it may be that the clinicians' term 'cost effectiveness of the whole system' is a collapsed expression of the policy managers' loop around 'vote health expenditure'.

Comments by participants

Feedback on this early stage of development indicates a split between participants from an economic or analytical background, who generally perceived the workshops and CLDs as potentially powerful policy tools, and practitioners, who by and large perceived them as having little practical use. The early feedback included the following comments.

- 'Helped create deeper understanding and a bigger picture. Has the potential to help us be much more strategic. Policy analysis as we usually do it requires us to reduce everything to simple two- or three-variable causal relationships – we fix one to make the other move in a particular direction without thinking about what the other effects might be – the classic unintended consequences.' (Economist.)

- 'Clearly much more work is needed to get the model to the point where it can be used to model behaviour. Despite this, the process has already shown its power in that those people who participated have a mental model of the health sector which is more overt and shared – the rudiments of a common understanding. There's also a new wariness about our customary responses to policy questions – even at this early stage of development it is apparent that much of the work we do is irrelevant to the real drivers which are embedded in the deep and enduring relationships and traditions of the professional groups themselves, and between professionals and their patients.' (Policy manager.)

- 'I wouldn't say it has advanced my understanding at all. It was a fun way of getting a disparate group of people working though – that might be half the battle.' (Environmental scientist.)

- 'The output on paper was not useful and has not altered any way I would approach a problem.' (Medical practitioner.)

Concluding comments

System dynamics tools are often used to develop an explicit shared mental model of a complex system amongst a group. In this case the happenstance of group self-selection enabled strongly divergent mental models to emerge.

On the one hand, dividing the groups usefully illustrated the different perspectives of the two groups of health workers (i.e. medical/health practitioners and policy managers). On the other hand, it did not immediately help move the debate forward. While it may have obscured the underlying issue, mixing the groups would probably have produced a shared model, thus beginning the process of bridging the divide between the two world views and building a common mental model incorporating both perspectives. Doing so must be a priority for moving forward in terms of a public policy that reduces quality problems and brings benefits for health consumers.

Nevertheless, this exploratory project in the New Zealand Ministry of Health has provided sound evidence for the much-cited strong and enduring tension between clinicians, health managers and policy managers that has been illuminated in the literature (see Mintzberg, 1979; Raelin, 1986; and for more recent discussions in the context of New Zealand and Australian health reforms respectively, Barnett et al., 1998 and Southon and Braithwaite, 1998). The revealed mental models of these two groups presented here could be used to help understand the differences in their world views.

All countries with developed health systems are confronting the issue of providing equitable, quality health services within limited health resources. Achieving this requires the co-operation of policy makers and clinicians in order to bridge the divide between their two world views. Qualitative system dynamics methods offer a way of accomplishing this. However, the difficulty of doing so must not be underestimated, as evidenced by some of the comments after the workshops from participants in the clinicians group.

Notes

1   This case is reproduced from a paper by Cavana, R.Y., Davies, P.K., Robson, R.M. and Wilson, K.J. (1999) Drivers of quality in health services: different worldviews of clinicians and policy managers revealed. *System Dynamics Review*, 13(3).

2   See, for example, MOH (1996); MOH (1998); Mason, Johnston and Crowe (1996); Health and Disability Commissions (1998).

3   See Chapter 3 of this book; see also Coyle (1996); Forrester (1961); Morecroft and Sterman (1994); and Wolstenholme and Coyle (1983).

REFERENCES

Barnett, J.R., Barnett, P. and Kearns, R. (1998) Declining Professional Dominance?: Trends in the Proletarianisation of Primary Care in New Zealand. *Social Science and Medicine*, 46(2): 193–207.

Cavana, R.Y., Davies, P.K., Robson, R.M. and Wilson, K.J. (1999) Drivers of quality in health services: different worldviews of clinicians and policy managers revealed. *System Dynamics Review*, 15(3): 331–340.

Coyle, R.G. (1996) *System Dynamics Modelling: A Practical Approach.* Chapman and Hall, London.

Forrester, J.W. (1961) *Industrial Dynamics.* MIT Press, Cambridge, Mass.

Health and Disability Commissioner. (1998) *Canterbury Health Ltd: A Report by the Health and Disability Commissioner.* Health and Disability Commission, Wellington, New Zealand.

Hodgson, A.M. (1994) Hexagons for Systems Thinking. In Morecroft, J.D.W. and Sterman, J.D. (eds). *Modeling for Learning Organisations.* Productivity Press, Portland, OR.

Kreutzer, D.P. (1995) FASTBreak™: A Facilitation Approach to Systems Thinking Breakthroughs. In Chawla, S. and Renesch, J. (eds). *Learning Organisations: Developing Cultures for Tomorrow's Workplace*, pp. 229–241. Productivity Press, Portland, OR.

Mason, K., Johnston J. and Crowe, J. (1996, May) *Inquiry under section 47 of the Health and Disability Services Act 1993 in respect of certain mental health services: Report of the Ministerial Inquiry to the Minister of Health Hon. Jenny Shipley.* Wellington, New Zealand.

Ministry of Health. (1996, March) *Risk-Adjusted Measurements of Hospital Safety: Mortality, Readmissions, Complications.* Ministry of Health, Wellington, New Zealand.

Ministry of Health. (1997, May) *Implementing the Coalition Agreement on Health: The report of the Steering Group to oversee Health and Disability Changes to the Minister of Health and the Associate Minister of Health.* Ministry of Health, Wellington, New Zealand.

Ministry of Health. (1998, March) *Purchasing for Your Health 1996/97: A performance report on the fourth year of the regional health authorities.* Performance Management Unit. Ministry of Health, Wellington, New Zealand.

Mintzberg, H. (1979) *The Structuring of Organizations.* Prentice Hall, Englewood Cliffs, NJ.

MOH *see* Ministry of Health.

Morecroft, J.D.W. and Sterman, J.D. (eds). (1994) *Modeling for Learning Organisations.* Productivity Press, Portland, OR.

Raelin, J.A. (1986) *The Clash of Cultures: Managers and Professionals.* Harvard Business School Press, Boston.

Southon, G. and Braithwaite, J. (1998) The end of Professionalism? *Social Science and Medicine*, 46(1): 23–28.

Upton, S. (1991) *Your Health and the Public Health: a Statement of Government Health Policy.* Ministry of Health, Wellington, New Zealand.

Wolstenholme, E.F. and Coyle R.G. (1983) The development of system dynamics as a methodology for system description and qualitative analysis. *Journal of the Operational Research Society*, 34(7): 569–581.

Case **4**

Mainland Beer distribution model[1]

This case illustrates model conceptualisation, model construction, and provides an introduction to policy analysis. It is based on the famous beer game first developed in the 1960s at the Massachusetts Institute of Technology's Sloan School of Management (Senge, 1990: 27). The version of the beer distribution system presented here is derived from Clark (1988: 106).

OVERVIEW

The distribution system for Mainland Beer consists of a retail store (distributor) and brewery; each managed independently under a centralised inventory policy. The retail manager has been told to keep her inventory at about a thousand cases. She has no experience in inventory control, and tries to keep 1000 cases in stock by sending an order every day to the brewery for one-half as many cases as she is short of 1000. Each order takes five working days to arrive at the brewery. The brewery manager, on receiving an order from the retailer immediately sends the beer (assuming he has it), from brewery inventory. It takes ten working days for the beer to arrive at the retail store. The brewery manager tries to keep 1000 cases in inventory and each day orders the brewery to produce one-fourth as much beer as the brewery warehouse is short of 1000 cases. The brewery takes 15 days to produce beer once it is ordered to do so.

Each of the two inventories (retail and brewery) starts at 950, and retail sales average 50 cases per day. There are 750 cases in production at the brewery and there are 500 cases of beer in transit to the retail store. Orders for 250 cases are in the mail *en route* from retailer to brewer, and orders for 50 cases have been received by the brewer, but not filled.

The requirements for this case are:

1 develop a high-level 'systems diagram';

2 construct a stock flow diagram for the base case;

3 formulate a set of equations using the data provided for initialising stocks and parameters for other relationships between variables;

4 produce graphical and tabular output for the base case and discuss the behaviour of the model;

5 undertake a set of policy experiments with the model;

6 test the robustness of these policies.

A high-level systems diagram

The managerial issue of concern in this case is how to manage the inventory ordering system so that inventories are held at stable levels, while maintaining continuity of supply to the retail store to ensure that demand for beer is met. Although there is a centralised inventory policy, at this stage both the retail store manager and the brewery manager manage their operations independently. They both follow the 'centralised' inventory policy of attempting to maintain their stocks of beer at 1000 cases.

Although we could consider this as a single-sector model under centralised control, it is possibly better to conceptualise this system as a two-sector model: a brewery sector and a retail sector, in different locations. (We could actually consider a third sector as orders are 'in the mail' and cases of beer are 'in transit'. However, to simplify matters we will treat the system as consisting of two sectors.) We also recognise two material stocks (main variables) in the system, i.e. 'cases of beer' and 'orders for beer'. Beer flows from the brewery sector to the retail sector, and orders flow in the opposite direction. This can be represented by the *ithink* systems map in Case figure 4.1.

Case figure 4.1   A systems map of the Mainland Beer distribution model

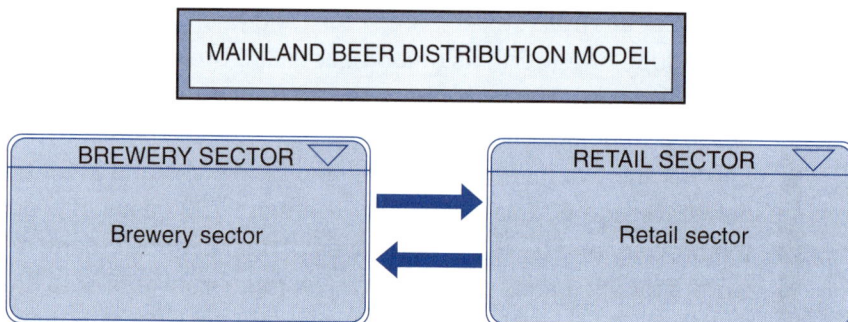

A stock flow diagram for the base case

The two material stocks (i.e. accumulations) in the system are 'cases of beer' and 'orders for beer'. These stocks are in different states and in different locations, hence these overall stocks can be disaggregated. For example, we can follow the supply line of beer from 'production', to the 'brewery inventory', then as it is shipped out 'in transit' to the retail outlet, until it is finally in the 'retail inventory' before being sold to customers, and consumed in – we hope – a very amicable environment! Similarly we recognise that orders for beer can be measured in two different states, i.e. 'in the mail' or in a 'backlog at the brewery'. These stocks and the physical flows between them, are illustrated in Case figure 4.2 on p. 184. We have allocated the physical stocks and flows to the two sectors we identified in the systems map in Case figure 4.1.

However, although Case figure 4.2 illustrates the stocks and flows in the system (i.e. the basic 'physics' of the system), it does not capture the policy and information links that control changes to these stocks and flows over time. In the language of *ithink*, we have to overlay this physical stock flow diagram with the relevant connectors and converters. Now we need to identify the remaining variables, graphical variables and constants (called 'converters' in *ithink*). These variables and their linkages are shown in Case figure 4.3 on p. 185.

Case figure 4.2   Stocks and flows in the beer distribution model

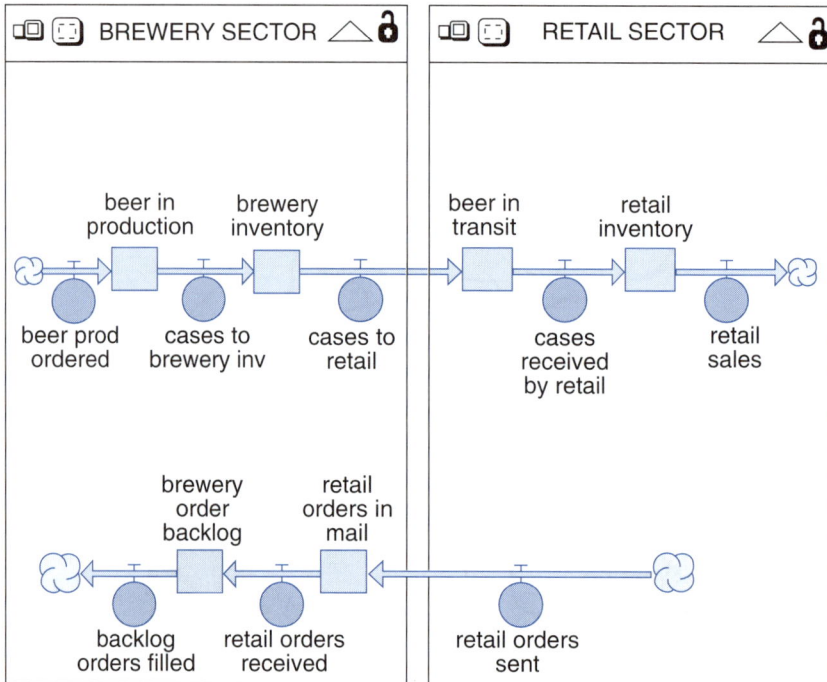

To avoid 'cluttering up' this stock flow diagram, we have not shown the delays as separate converters; instead we have included them in the equations (provided in the next section). For example, we have the included the five-day delay until the retail orders are received as a number in the equation as follows:

$$\text{retail\_orders\_received} = \text{retail\_orders\_in\_mail}/5 \ \{\text{cases/day}\}$$

rather than as a converter incorporated into that equation as:

$$\text{retail\_orders\_received} = \text{retail\_orders\_in\_mail}/\text{delay\_in\_mail} \ \{\text{cases/day}\}$$

$$\text{delay\_in\_mail} = 5 \ \{\text{days}\}$$

The second alternative is 'technically' more correct, as it facilitates parameter sensitivity analysis by allowing the number of days to be varied during model sensitivity tests and scenario analyses. However, for this case we have modelled these 'delay' times in the equations to restrict the size of the model for illustrative purposes.

Case figure 4.3   Stock flow diagram of the beer distribution model (base case)

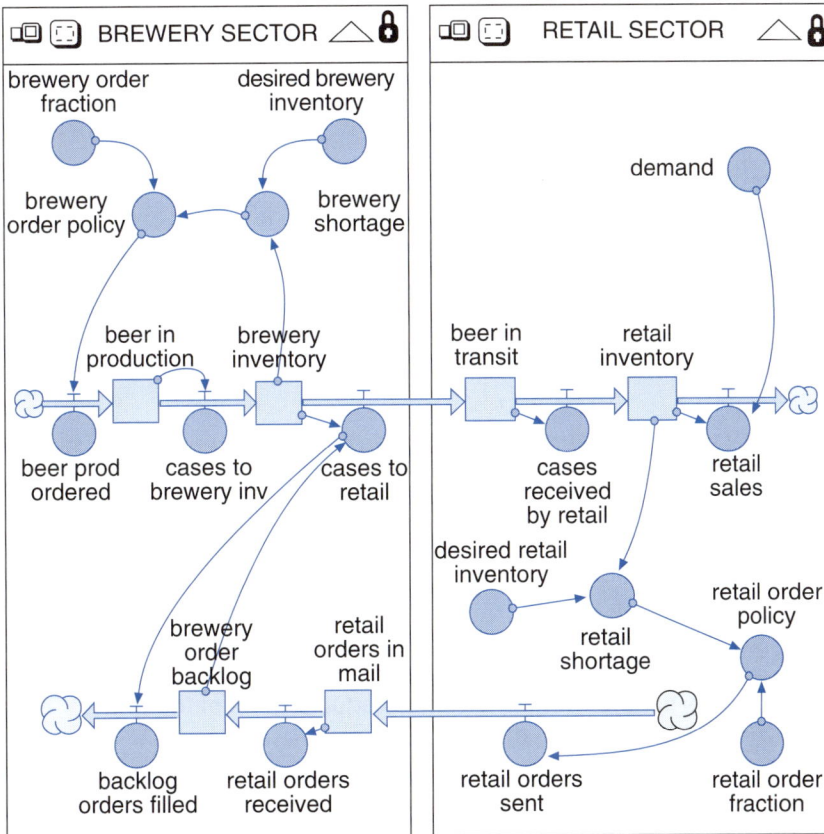

Equations for the base case of the beer distribution model

The *ithink* equations for the base case for this model are provided in Case figure 4.4 (on pp. 186–189). These are the documented versions of the equations. Generally, each equation should be fully documented, including explanations for the assumptions contained within the equation and the sources of any relationships, or parameter values. However, in this model, all the assumptions and parameter values have been derived from the case overview. We have provided the dimensions for each variable in brackets at the end of each equation.

In Case figure 4.4, the equations are separated into the two sectors, brewery and retail. The first group of equations shows the equation for the stock (e.g. beer in production) followed by the initial value for that stock. The remaining equations associated with each stock are flows in (beer production ordered) and flows out (cases to brewery inventory) of the stock. After all the stocks and associated inflows and outflows are presented, the converters are provided (i.e. constants, auxiliary variables and graphical relationships).

BREWERY SECTOR

beer_in_production(t) = beer_in_production(t - dt) + (beer_production_ord - cases_to_brewery_inv) * dt

INIT beer_in_production = 750 {cases}

DOCUMENT: Initially there are 750 cases of beer in production at the brewery.

INFLOWS:

beer_production_ord = max(brewery_order_policy,0) {cases/day}

DOCUMENT: The beer ordered from the brewery is determined by the brewery order policy, set by the brewery manager.

OUTFLOWS:

cases_to_brewery_inv = beer_in_production/15 {cases/day}

DOCUMENT: It takes about 15 days to produce beer once it has been ordered. The simplifying assumption made in this equation is that the cases sent to brewery inventory equals $1/15$th of the total cases of beer in production each day.

brewery_inventory(t) = brewery_inventory(t - dt) + (cases_to_brewery_inv - cases_to_retail) * dt

INIT brewery_inventory = 950 {cases}

DOCUMENT: Initially there are 950 cases of beer in the brewery inventory.

INFLOWS:

cases_to_brewery_inv = beer_in_production/15 {cases/day}

DOCUMENT: It takes about 15 days to produce beer once it has been ordered. The simplifying assumption made in this equation is that the cases sent to brewery inventory equals $1/15$th of the total cases of beer in production each day.

OUTFLOWS:

cases_to_retail = MIN(brewery_inventory,brewery_order_backlog) {cases/day}

DOCUMENT: Once the brewery manager receives an order, cases of beer are sent immediately as long as they are available in the brewery inventory.

brewery_order_backlog(t) = brewery_order_backlog(t - dt) + (retail_orders_received - backlog_orders_filled) * dt

INIT brewery_order_backlog = 50 {cases}

DOCUMENT: Initially there are orders for 50 cases of beer received by the brewery but not filled.

INFLOWS:

retail_orders_received = retail_orders_in_mail/5 {cases/day}

DOCUMENT: It is assumed that the brewery receives $1/5$th of the total stock of orders in the mail each day.

OUTFLOWS:

backlog_orders_filled = cases_to_retail {cases/day}

DOCUMENT: Backlog orders filled each day equals the number of cases sent to the retail store each day.

retail_orders_in_mail(t) = retail_orders_in_mail(t - dt) + (retail_orders_sent - retail_orders_received) * dt

INIT retail_orders_in_mail = 250 {cases}

DOCUMENT: Initially there are orders for 250 cases of beer in the mail from the retail store.

INFLOWS:

retail_orders_sent   (IN SECTOR: RETAIL SECTOR)

OUTFLOWS:

retail_orders_received = retail_orders_in_mail/5 {cases/day}

DOCUMENT: It is assumed that the brewery receives $1/5$th of the total stock of orders in the mail each day.

brewery_order_fraction = 0.25 {fraction/day}

DOCUMENT: This policy parameter, represents the percentage of the shortage of beer at the brewery inventory, that the brewery manager orders each day. The initial fraction of 0.25 or $1/4$, is equivalent to the brewery manager ordering the entire beer shortage in four days. Hence a larger fraction (e.g. 0.5 or $1/2$) represents the manager's desire to meet the beer shortage more quickly (i.e. over 2 days), and conversely, a smaller fraction (e.g. 0.125 or ¹/₈th) represents the brewery manager's policy of closing the beer shortage (or gap) more slowly (e.g. over 8 days).

brewery_order_policy = brewery_shortage*brewery_order_fraction {cases/day}

DOCUMENT: The brewery order policy is to order a percentage (fraction) of the inventory beer shortage each day.

brewery_shortage = desired_brewery_inventory-brewery_inventory {cases}

DOCUMENT: The brewery shortage is the difference between the desired brewery inventory less the actual number of cases of beer in the brewery inventory.

desired_brewery_inventory = 1000 {cases}

DOCUMENT: The desired brewery inventory is initially set at the 'centralised inventory policy' target of 1000 cases.

RETAIL SECTOR

beer_in_transit(t) = beer_in_transit(t - dt) + (cases_to_retail - cases_received_by_retail) * dt

INIT beer_in_transit = 500 {cases}

DOCUMENT: Initially there are 500 cases of beer in transit to the retail store.

INFLOWS:

cases_to_retail   (IN SECTOR: BREWERY SECTOR)

OUTFLOWS:

cases_received_by_retail = beer_in_transit/10 {cases/day}

DOCUMENT: Since it takes 10 days for the cases of beer to arrive from the brewery, it is assumed that the retail store receives ¹/₁₀th of the total number of cases in transit per day.

retail_inventory(t) = retail_inventory(t - dt) + (cases_received_by_retail - retail_sales) * dt

INIT retail_inventory = 950 {cases}

DOCUMENT: Initially there are 950 cases of beer in the retail inventory.

INFLOWS:

cases_received_by_retail = beer_in_transit/10 {cases/day}

DOCUMENT: Since it takes 10 days for the cases of beer to arrive from the brewery, it is assumed that the retail store receives $1/10$th of the total number of cases in transit per day.

OUTFLOWS:

retail_sales = MIN(retail_inventory_demand) {cases/day}

DOCUMENT: It is assumed that demand for beer is met each day as long as there is sufficient beer in the retail inventory.

retail_orders_sent = max(retail_order_policy,0) {cases/day}

DOCUMENT: The number of orders sent by the retail store each day is determined by the retail manager's order policy.

INFLOW TO: retail_orders_in_mail   (IN SECTOR: BREWERY SECTOR)

demand = 50 {cases/day}

DOCUMENT: This is the daily demand for cases of beer from customers, assumed to be exogenous to the system.

desired_retail_inventory = 1000 {cases}

DOCUMENT: The desired retail inventory level is set by the 'centralised' inventory policy.

retail_order_fraction = 0.5 {fraction/day}

DOCUMENT: This policy parameter represents the percentage of the shortage of beer in the retail inventory that the retail manager orders each day. The initial fraction of 0.5 or $1/2$, is equivalent to the retail manager ordering the entire beer shortage in 2 days.

retail_order_policy = retail_shortage*retail_order_fraction {cases/day}

DOCUMENT: The retail order policy is to order a percentage (fraction) of the inventory beer shortage each day.

retail_shortage = desired_retail_inventory-retail_inventory {cases}

DOCUMENT: The retail shortage is the difference between the desired retail inventory less the actual number of cases of beer in the retail inventory.

![icon] Model behaviour for the base case

The model is simulated over a 100-day period, and the simulation interval (DT) is set at 0.25 days.[2] The unit of time for this model is days. The graphical output for the main variables for the base case is provided in Case figure 4.6 and these results are also summarised in Case table 4.1, for every fifth day of the model simulation.

In Case figure 4.6(a), some of the main stocks are shown, i.e. retail inventory, brewery inventory and brewery order backlog. The desired retail inventory is also provided, as this provides a visual reference point, for comparison with the actual retail and brewery inventory stocks. In the base case the target (desired) inventories for both the brewery and the retail store have been set, by the centralised inventory policy, at 1000 cases. Case figure 4.6(b) contains some of the main flows, i.e. retail sales, retail orders sent, beer production ordered, and cases sent to the retail store.

Case figure 4.5   A simplified causal loop diagram for the beer distribution model

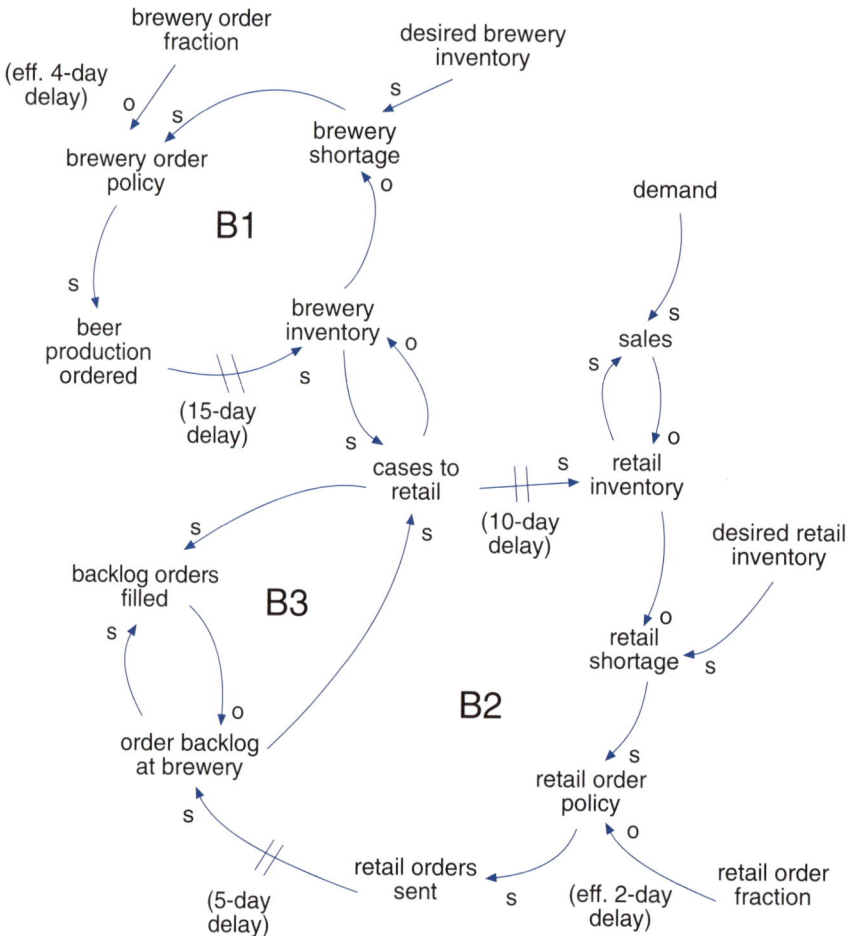

Case figure 4.6   Base case behaviour for the beer distribution model

(a)

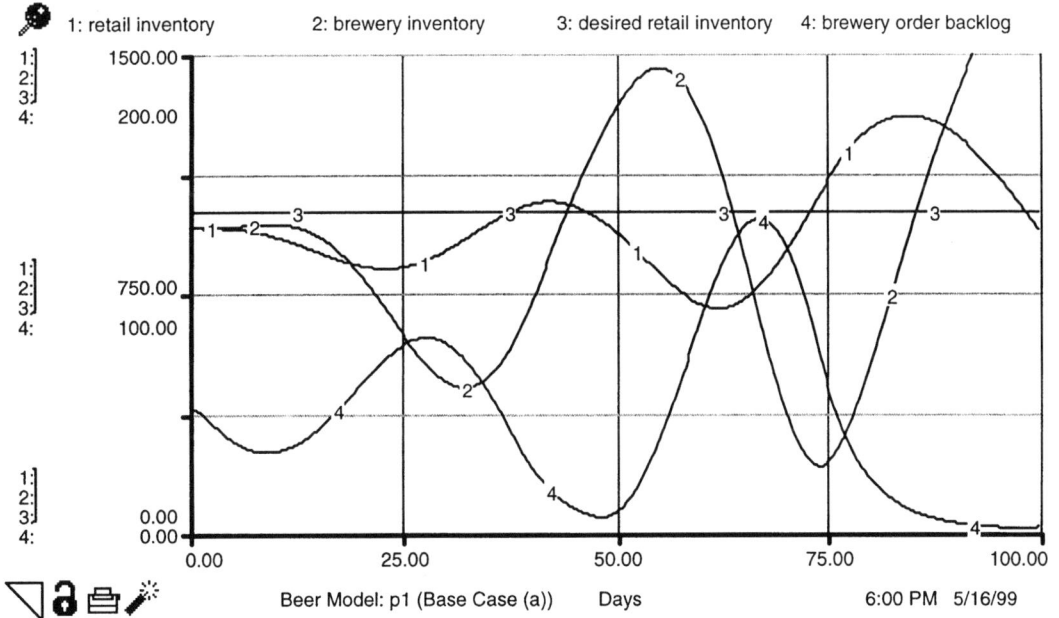

Beer Model: p1 (Base Case (a))   Days   6:00 PM 5/16/99

(b)

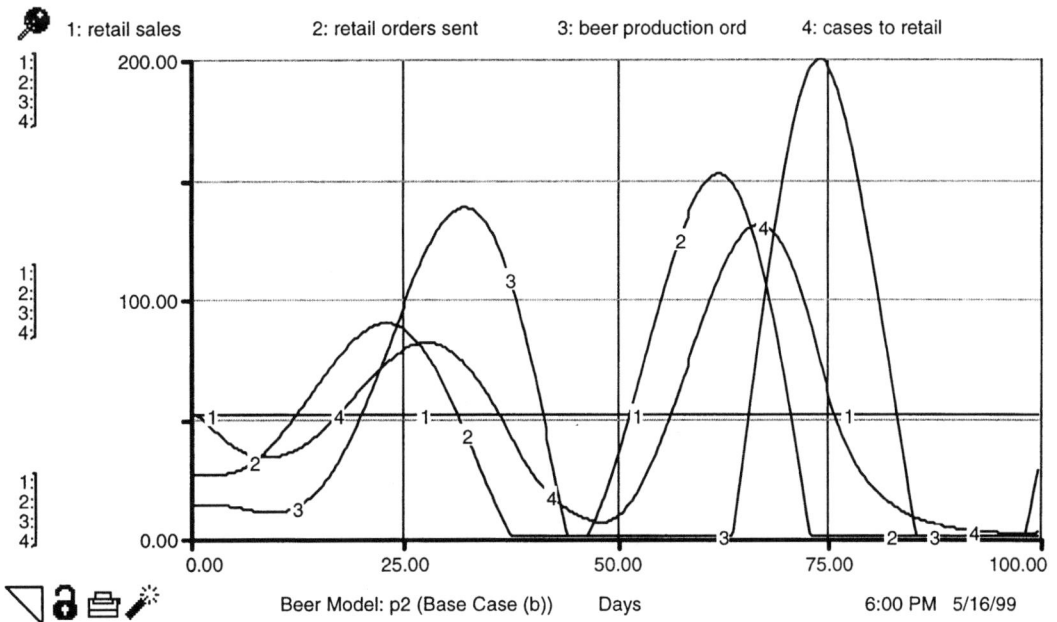

Beer Model: p2 (Base Case (b))   Days   6:00 PM 5/16/99

Case table 4.1   Base case output for the beer distribution model

Day	Retail inventory	Brewery inventory	Retail orders in mail	Retail sales	Retail orders sent	Beer production ordered	Cases sent to retail
0	950	950	250	50	25	13	50
5	946	954	171	50	27	11	36
10	919	962	168	50	40	9	33
15	871	919	232	50	65	20	43
20	830	791	331	50	85	52	62
25	828	607	400	50	86	98	78
30	880	465	379	50	60	134	78
35	964	487	254	50	18	128	57
40	1027	721	101	50	0	70	25
45	1019	1055	36	50	0	0	9
50	935	1331	53	50	33	0	8
55	806	1454	238	50	97	0	38
60	707	1301	496	50	146	0	89
65	723	865	652	50	138	34	127
70	877	366	556	50	61	159	119
75	1098	211	242	50	0	197	60
80	1258	509	87	50	0	123	22
85	1302	964	31	50	0	9	8
90	1246	1350	11	50	0	0	3
95	1119	1635	4	50	0	0	1
100	946	1841	17	50	27	0	1

To analyse the base case behaviour of the model, it may be useful to construct a simplified causal loop diagram for the model. This is provided in Case figure 4.5 (p. 190), where the major delays are shown with parallel lines crossing the links. There are two major balancing loops: loop **B1** which controls the brewery manager's actual inventory to his desired inventory level; and loop **B2** which controls the retail shop manager's actual inventory to her desired inventory level.

In loop **B1**, the response time for a change in inventories is about 19 days (a 15-day delay for production delivery, and a 4-day equivalent delay for the brewery order fraction), whereas the response time is about 17 days in loop **B2** (there is a 10-day delay for beer in transit, a 5-day delay for orders in the mail, and a 2-day equivalent delay for the retail order fraction). However, if there is not sufficient stocks at the brewery inventory, then the effective delay for loop **B2** could be as high as about 36 days (adding total delays for loops **B1** and **B2**), with backlog orders accumulating at the brewery.

The minor loop **B3** controls the order backlog once cases of beer have been dispatched to the retail store.

Initially the system is in equilibrium with all inflows equal to outflows from each stock, at 50 cases each. However, as soon as the simulation commences, the system immediately moves out of equilibrium. The principal reason for this is that neither the retail manager nor the brewery manager is ordering 50 cases of beer in the first day from the brewery inventory or the brewery production department respectively.

Their ordering policies are both based on the shortages between their desired and actual inventories corrected over a number of days (rather than immediately). Hence the retail manager corrects her beer shortage over two days (i.e. a retail fraction = 0.5 or 1/2), and the brewery manager corrects his shortage over four days (i.e. the brewery order fraction = 0.25 or 1/4).

Initially the retail shop manager is ordering 25 cases per day, compared with about 13 cases being ordered from production by the brewery manager. This is well under the 50 cases per day being sold to consumers. Hence both retail and brewery inventories are being depleted, thus increasing the gap to the desired 1000 cases in each inventory. This results in an increasing quantity of retail orders being sent, which, after a 5-day delay, results in an increase in backlog orders at the brewery. This precipitates an increasing number of cases being sent to the retail shop, arriving there about 10 days later. Meanwhile, the rapidly depleting brewery inventory results in increased production orders, which are delayed by about four days due to the brewery manager's ordering policy, and a further 15 days are spent in production, before the brewery inventories start increasing again.

After about 25 days, the number of cases of beer being received by the retail manager exceeds the quantity being sold (50 cases per day), and retail inventories start rising again until they reach 1000 cases (at about day 40). At that point, the retail manager ceases to place any more orders for beer, until her inventory again drops below 1000 cases, after day 48. Meanwhile, in response to the rapidly decreasing brewery inventories reaching their lowest point in the cycle at about day 32, beer production ordered in response to this situation reaches a peak a short while after this time. However, the order backlog in the brewery has started to decrease, and the number of cases of beer being sent to the retail shop is dropping during the period in which there is a rapidly increasing quantity of beer being produced, pushing up stocks at the brewery past the target brewery inventory level of 1000 cases (reached about day 42). Although the brewery inventory is still increasing, the brewery manager ceases to order any more beer from production for a period of about 20 days, thus ensuring further shortages of beer at subsequent stages, when the inventory stockpiles have been eroded! Thus the cycle of over-ordering, inventory surpluses, under-ordering and inventory shortages, is perpetuated at ever-increasing rates. In other words, the system is well and truly out of control!

The next stage of this analysis is to design and test policies which might help both the retail and the brewery managers to overcome the problems associated with this violently fluctuating behaviour of their beer inventories, while at the same time satisfying the consumers' demand for beer.

Policy experiments with the beer distribution model

Policy experiments refer to how a manager uses information about the system in the formulation and design of policies. These policies can then be tested in a laboratory setting, removed from the 'real' world. We shall consider two types of policy experiments with this model:

1 changes to the policy parameters in the model; and
2 changes to the policy structure in the model by the addition of new variables and/or new linkages between variables.

The idea behind policy analysis with a dynamic simulation model is to develop the structure of the policies gradually, testing the model at each stage of policy development. Once the policies in the model are behaving 'correctly', the policies should be subjected to exogenous shocks (or scenario tests) to see if they are 'robust' with respect to reasonable variations in the external parameters.

In this model we will subject the policies to a 20% (or 10 cases per day) step increase in the demand for beer after day 20 and hold it at that new level for the remainder of the simulation run, i.e. until day 100. If the policies perform satisfactorily under these scenario tests (that is, satisfactory to the managers concerned), then the policies are said to be 'robust'.

We will now consider a range of policy and robustness tests with the beer distribution model.

Policy parameter changes

● Policy experiment 1 (Retail order fraction = 1)

Firstly we shall consider changes to the policy parameters. As we discussed in the previous section when analysing the behaviour of the base case simulation of the beer distribution model, one of the initial problems is that retail orders sent and beer production ordered are both well below 50 cases (the average daily sales). As previously discussed, this sets up the oscillating inventory cycles that appear in Case figure 4.6 and in Case table 4.1. A closer examination of these policies is appropriate here.

The retail manager's retail order policy is defined in the base case by the equations:

retail_orders_sent = retail_order_policy {cases/day}

retail_order_policy = retail_shortage*retail_order_fraction {cases/day}

retail_order_fraction = 0.5 {fraction/day}

retail_shortage = desired_retail_inventory-retail_inventory {cases}

desired_retail_inventory = 1000 {cases}

Now initially the retail inventory is 950 cases, hence the retail shortage is 1000 less 950 cases = 50 cases. However, the retail order policy is to multiply this retail shortage by 0.5 or 1/2 (i.e. to correct this shortage over two days). This results in the retail order policy, and the retail orders sent were initially set at: 50 * 0.5 = 25 cases per day. An initial experiment might suggest that we try a retail order fraction of 1.0, thus correcting the gap immediately. Case figure 4.7 shows the results of this experiment, and although the retail inventory is now stable throughout the simulation (at 50 cases per day below the desired inventory level), there are still some fluctuations in the brewery inventory.

Case figure 4.7   Model behaviour for policy experiment 1 (retail order fraction = 1)

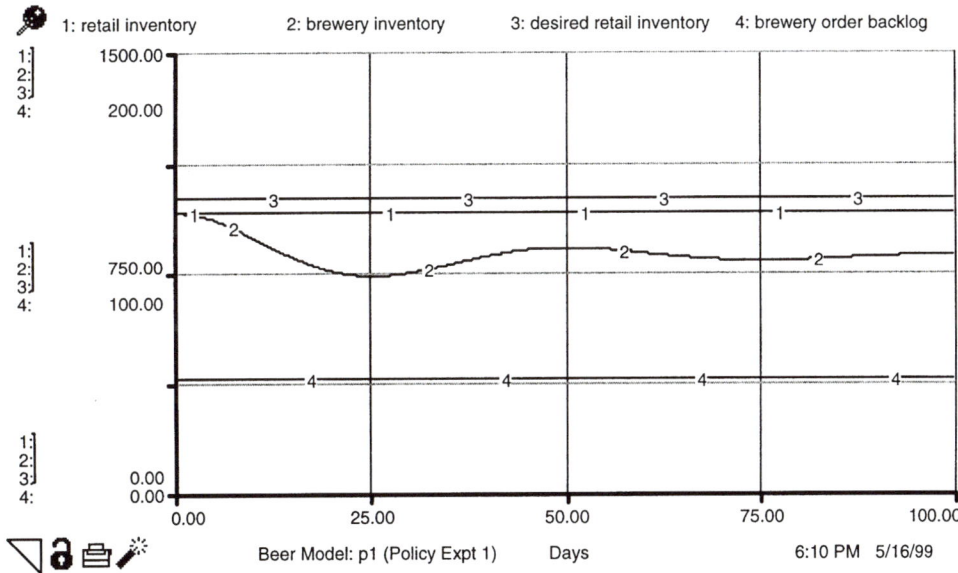

● Policy experiment 2 (both order fractions = 1)

Since this beer distribution system has a centralised inventory control system, we now set the brewery order fraction equal to 1, using the same logic as above for the retail order fraction. However, for this policy experiment we set both order fractions equal to 1, and the simulation results for the main variables are summarised in Case figure 4.8 on the following page.

Case figure 4.8   Model behaviour for policy experiment 2 (both order fractions = 1)

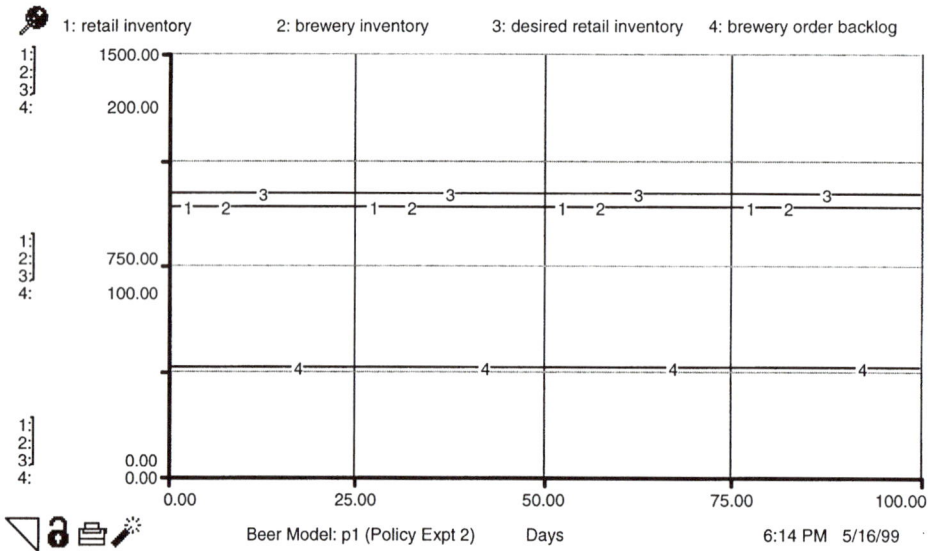

Case figure 4.9   Model behaviour for robustness test on policy experiment 2

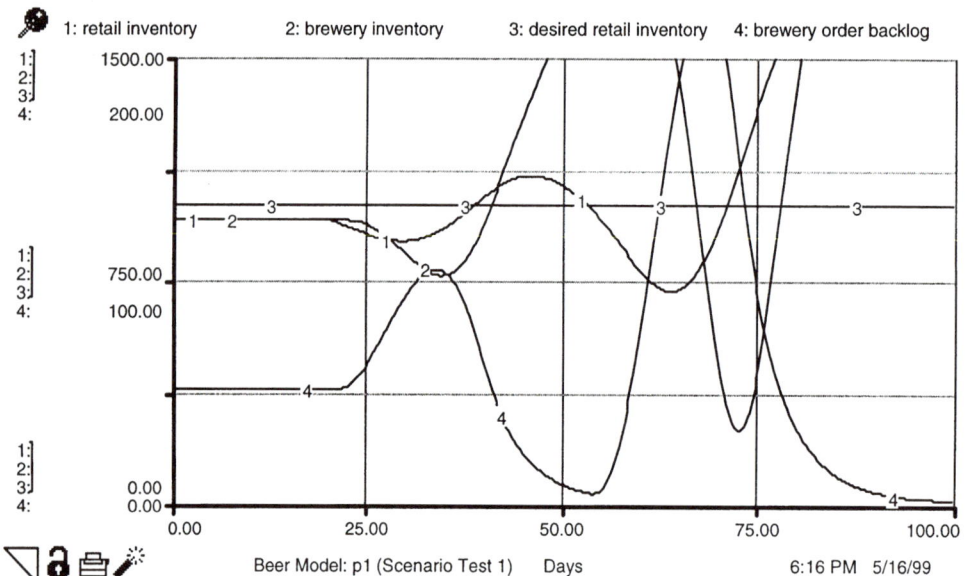

At this stage we may feel inclined to start congratulating ourselves, since we have now achieved a perfect equilibrium in both the retail and brewery inventory levels, although the levels are 50 cases per day below the desired inventory levels. However, we now have to ask ourselves the question: 'How robust are these policies?' We can perform a number of checks on the exogenous parameters and variables to test for robustness, but one very useful test is to incorporate a STEP function[3] into the main exogenous variable, which is the demand for beer in this model. This will involve increasing the demand for beer by 20% (10 cases per day) from day 20 for the remainder of the simulation run. The new demand equations[4] in the model are:

demand = 50+STEP(step_change_in_demand, 20) {cases/day}

step_change_in_demand = 10 {cases/day}

The results of this robustness test are presented in Case figure 4.9, and unfortunately this shows that the system is out of control again.

As an additional policy experiment, we set the desired inventories equal to the initial inventories (i.e. 950 cases) and the result was much the same as the results for policy experiment 2.

These experiments suggest that changes to the policy parameters only are unlikely to be enough to ensure that inventory management policies remain sufficiently robust to withstand reasonable changes in the external variables (e.g. the demand for beer). Hence we will now consider variations to the structure of the retail and brewery inventory control policies.

Structural changes to policies

● Policy experiment 3 (variable desired inventories)

We indicated at the end of the previous experiment that we had undertaken another policy parameter experiment, namely by setting the desired inventory levels equal to the initial inventory levels. With demand for beer constant at 50 cases per day, these policies generated stable inventory levels throughout the simulation. Unfortunately, when the model was exposed to a 20% step increase in demand at day 20, the inventories began to oscillate out of control again. This suggests that the fixed target for each inventory is perhaps contributing to these periods of under- and over-supply, and that desired inventory should possibly be held at a level to cover a number of days' sales or orders, to maintain a buffer, rather than having a fixed inventory level irrespective of the external conditions.

The original 'central inventory policy' specified a target of 1000 cases of beer in both the retail inventory and brewery inventories. This is equivalent to 20 days' supply for both the retail store and the brewery. Now we will try this experiment assuming 20 days' worth of cover is required by both the retail and brewery managers. We also include in these policies averaged or smoothed information about beer sales and orders for beer, rather than the instantaneous flows, to smooth out the 'noise' or random variations in these flows. We also set both the retail and brewery order fractions equal to 1, as is the case for policy experiment 2. The restructured equations for the desired retail and brewery inventories are:

retail_order_policy = retail_shortage*retail_order_fraction {cases/day}

desired_retail_inventory = retail_cover*ave_retail_sales {cases}

retail_cover = 20 {days}

ave_retail_sales = SMTH1(retail_sales,7) {cases/day}

retail_order_fraction = 1 {fraction/day}

brewery_order_policy = brewery_shortage*brewery_order_fraction {cases/day}

desired_brewery_inventory = brewery_cover*ave_orders_filled {cases}

brewery_cover = 20 (days)

ave_orders_filled = SMTH1(backlog_orders_filled,7) {cases/day}

brewery_order_fraction = 1 {fraction/day}

Note that the dimensions for these equations should also be checked. For example, the dimension of the 'desired retail inventory' variable is checked as follows:

desired_retail_inventory = retail_cover*ave_retail_sales

The right hand side dimensions = days * cases / day

now 'days' can be removed from the numerator and denominator:

~~days~~ * cases / ~~day~~ = cases

= dimensions of the 'desired retail inventory'.

Hence the dimensions on the right-hand side of the equation have been reduced to the dimensions on the left-hand side of the equation, so the equation is 'dimensionally consistent'. The results of this policy experiment are summarised in Case figure 4.10.

Unfortunately, when we subject this policy experiment to the 20% step increase in demand, the inventory levels also becomes highly unstable after day 20, and the model behaviour is very similar to that shown in Case figure 4.9.

Case figure 4.10 Model behaviour with policy experiment 3 (variable desired inventories)

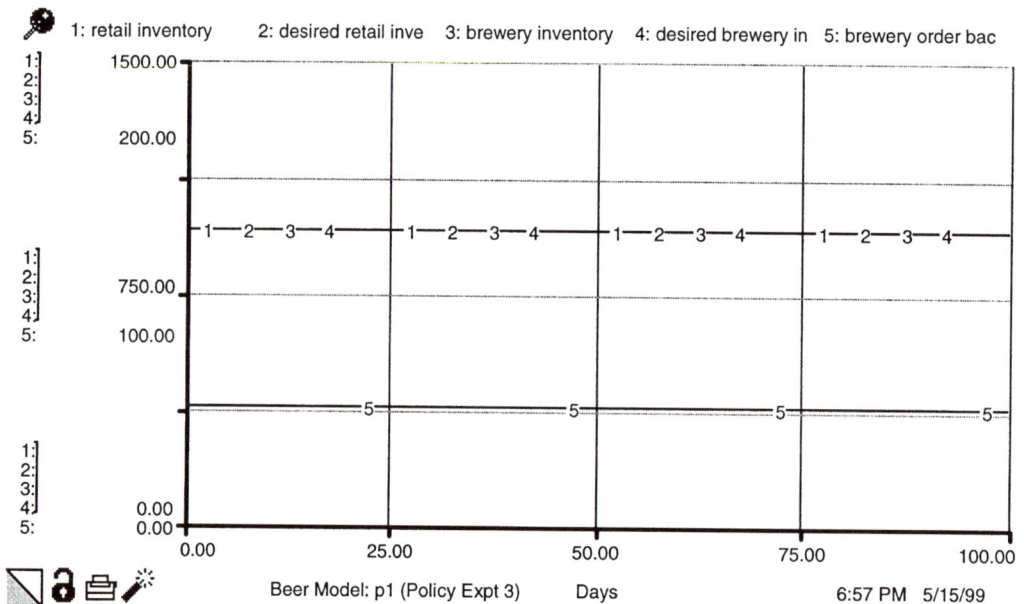

1: retail inventory   2: desired retail inve   3: brewery inventory   4: desired brewery in   5: brewery order bac

Beer Model: p1 (Policy Expt 3)   Days   6:57 PM 5/15/99

● Policy experiment 4 (average sales and orders)

In the previous experiment, the revised retail and brewery order policies were performing well until demand was altered, thus disturbing the equilibrium state and pushing the actual inventories out of alignment with the desired inventories (essentially the same sort of behaviour as in Case figure 4.9). This suggests that we should perhaps experiment with a different type of order policy experiment, by ignoring the shortages in the desired inventories, and basing the order policies on the average daily sales and the average daily orders filled by the brewery. This can be achieved, in our model, either by removing the linkages from the inventory shortages to the order policies or by setting the order fractions equal to zero. We shall use the former approach in this experiment. In addition we need to 'connect' the average sales and orders filled to the retail and brewery order policies. The restructured equations are:

retail_order_policy = ave_retail_sales {cases/day}

ave_retail_sales = SMTH1(retail_sales,7) {cases/day}

brewery_order_policy = ave_orders_filled {cases/day}

ave_orders_filled = SMTH1(backlog_orders_filled,7) {cases/day}

The model behaviour for this experiment is the same as that shown in Case figure 4.10 (i.e. all the variables remain in equilibrium). We will now subject these policies to a 20% step increase in demand from day 20 onwards, to test the robustness of these policies. The demand equations are:

demand = 50+STEP(step_change_in_demand, 20) {cases/day}

step_change_in_demand = 10 {cases/day}

Although these policies (shown in Case figure 4.11 on the following page) appear to be robust for the 20% step increase in demand after day 20, inventories are now held at a lower level – about 750 cases each after the steady-state levels have been reached (i.e. about 60 days after the step increase in demand). However, to help support the retail and brewery managers' confidence that these policies are now robust with respect to demand, we shall subject the consumer demand for beer to a series of sharp increases (i.e. pulse increases using a PULSE function[5]). We shall consider an experiment where the demand for beer increases by 50% (or 25 cases per day) every 30 days starting at day 20. This experiment resembles the situation in New Zealand when there is a rugby test on, particularly against old rivals like Australia and South Africa!

The final demand equations are:

demand = 50+STEP(step_change_in_demand, 20)+PULSE(size_of_pulse, 20, 30) {cases/day}

size_of_pulse = 25 {cases/day}

step_change_in_demand = 0 {cases/day}

Case figure 4.11   Model behaviour with a STEP test on policy experiment 4

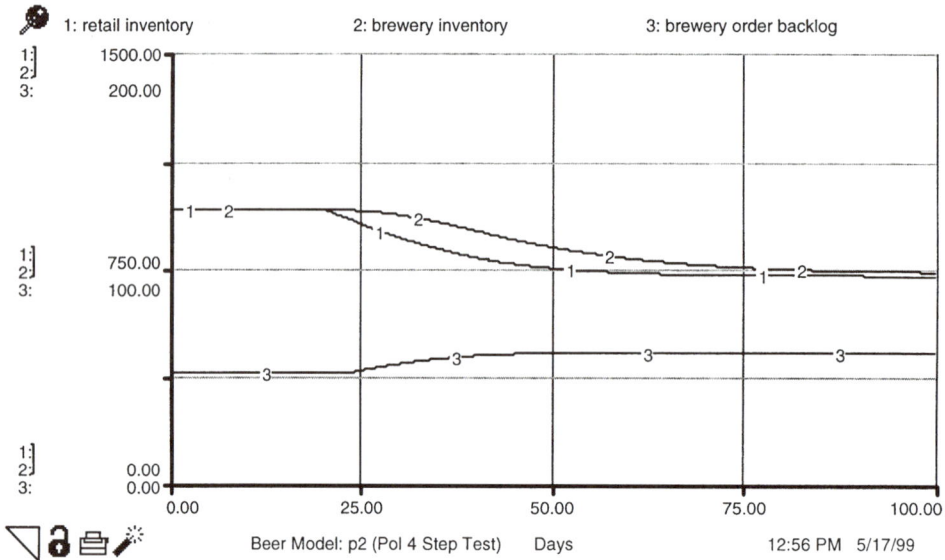

The results of this PULSE test are shown in Case figure 4.12 on the following page, and we can see that the policies remain robust when subjected to these sharp 'shocks', and equilibrium is restored to the inventory control system. Based on these two tests of robustness (shown in Case figures 4.11 and 4.12), we can be reasonably confident that these retail and brewery order policies will remain robust in respect of reasonable variations in demand, and that they would be suitable for implementation by the retail shop and brewery managers.

● Policy experiment 5 (modified Rolf Clark policy)

Finally, in this policy experiment[6] we shall incorporate more information about previous order decisions in the retail and brewery order policies. One of the problems with the previous policy experiments is that we have not been including information about previous orders placed by the retail and brewery managers. In this experiment we will base the retail order policy on the current shortage – i.e. the differences between desired and actual retail inventories, orders in the mail and the order backlog at the brewery. In addition, we include the average daily sales in the reorder policy, to ensure a smoother response to recent demand trends. We also impose the constraint that a retail order for more cases of beer is to be sent out only if the estimated order quantity is positive. (That is, we don't 'call back' or cancel orders previously sent!) We have also retained the restructured equation for a variable 'desired retail inventory' from policy experiment 2, which includes 20 days' average sales cover for the desired inventory. The only other change to the base case is that we have now excluded the 'retail order fraction' (although this parameter could have been retained and 'neutralised' by setting its value equal to 1).

The equations for this restructured retail order policy are:

retail_order_policy = max(0, retail_shortage-
    (retail_orders_in_mail+brewery_order_backlog)+ave_retail_sales) {cases/day}

Case figure 4.12 Model behaviour with a PULSE test on policy experiment 4

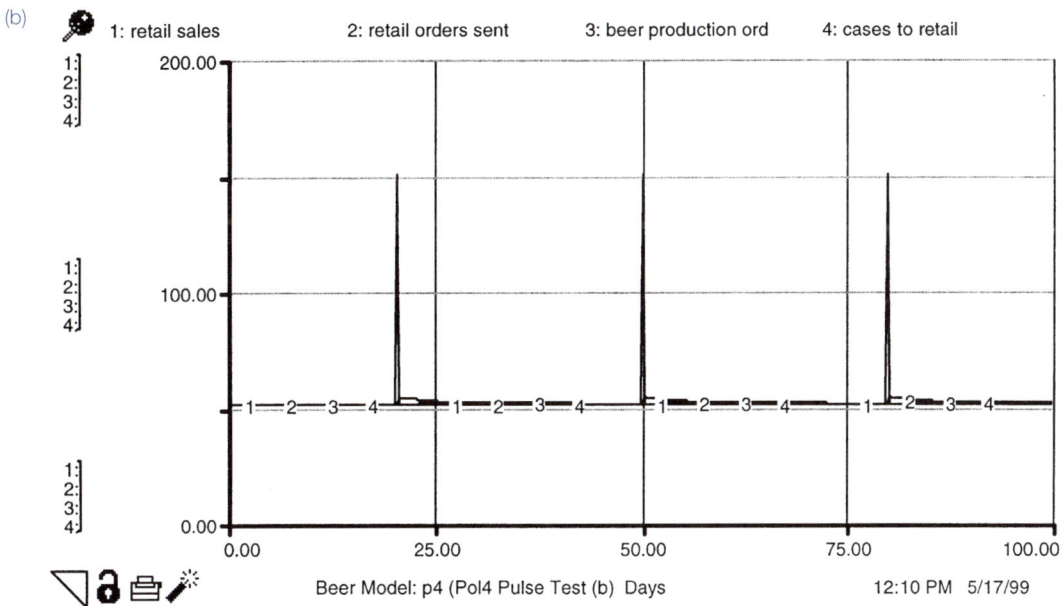

(a) 1: retail inventory   2: brewery inventory   3: brewery order backlog

Beer Model: p3 (Pol4 Pulse Test (a) Days   12:10 PM 5/17/99

(b) 1: retail sales   2: retail orders sent   3: beer production ord   4: cases to retail

Beer Model: p4 (Pol4 Pulse Test (b) Days   12:10 PM 5/17/99

retail_shortage = desired_retail_inventory-retail_inventory {cases}

desired_retail_inventory = retail_cover*ave_retail_sales {cases}

ave_retail_sales = SMTH1(retail_sales,7) {cases/day}

retail_cover = 20 {days}

Similarly, we have restructured the brewery order policy by including information about the current shortage between desired and actual retail inventories, beer in production (representing the brewery's previous orders) and the average orders filled. The restructured equations for the brewery order policies are:

brewery_order_policy = max(0, brewery_shortage-beer_in_production+ave_orders_filled) {cases/day}

brewery_shortage = desired_brewery_inventory-brewery_inventory {cases}

desired_brewery_inventory = brewery_cover*ave_orders_filled {cases}

ave_orders_filled = SMTH1(backlog_orders_filled,7) {cases/day}

brewery_cover = 20 {days}

Case figure 4.13   Stock flow diagram for the beer distribution model (policy experiment 5)

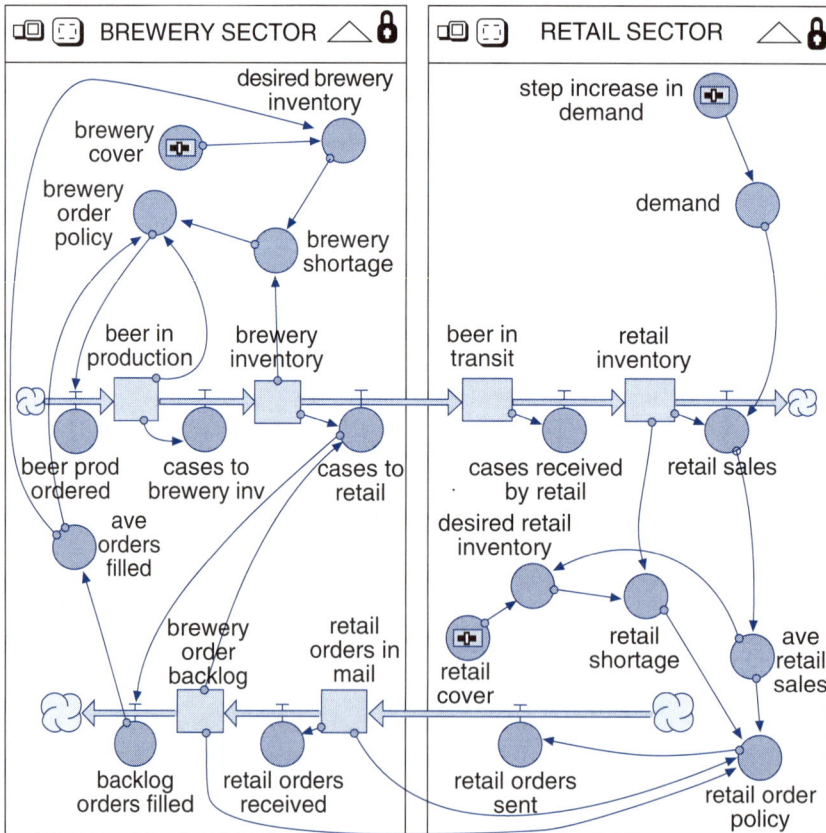

Case figure 4.14 Model behaviour with policy experiment 5

(a)

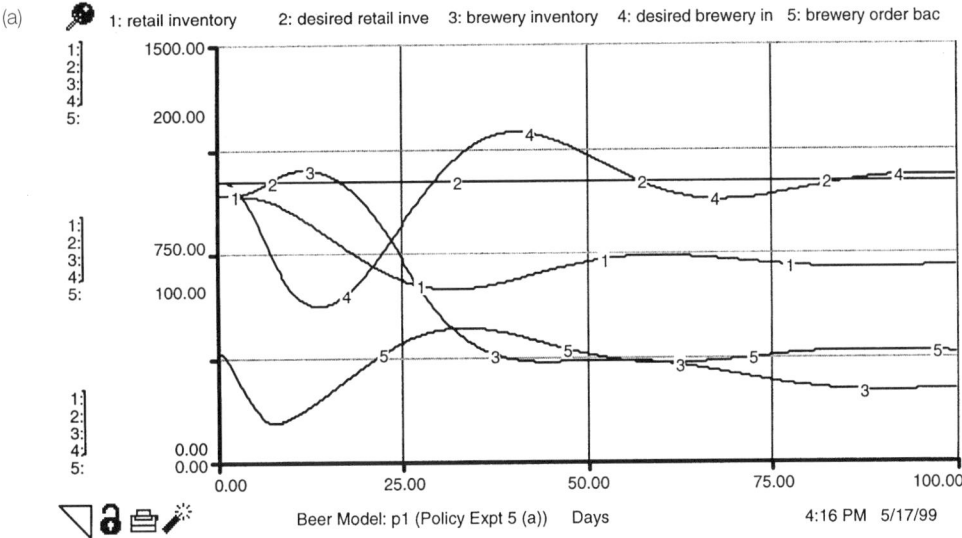

Beer Model: p1 (Policy Expt 5 (a))   Days   4:16 PM 5/17/99

(b)

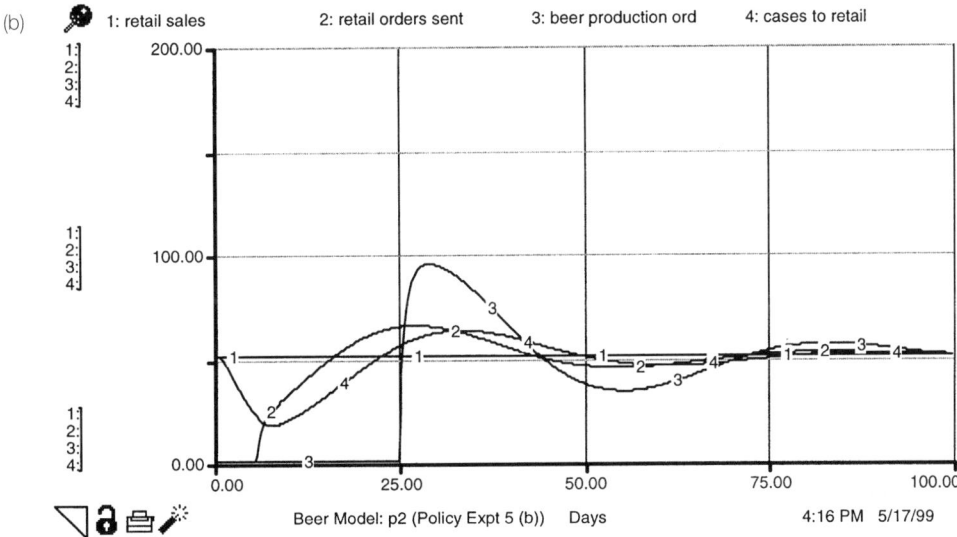

Beer Model: p2 (Policy Expt 5 (b))   Days   4:16 PM 5/17/99

The stock flow diagram for the beer distribution model including the restructured retail and brewery order policies is provided in Case figure 4.13 (with the new variables and linkages shown in bold).

The model output for the main variables for this policy experiment is provided in Case figure 4.14 above and in Case table 4.2 on pages 204–205. Both the retail and the brewery managers can run down their inventories of beer with this restructured policy. The brewery manager is now effectively holding stocks of beer in the production system,

Case table 4.2   Model output for main variables for policy experiment 5

Day	Retail order policy	Average retail sales	Retail orders in mail	Brewery order backlog	Retail shortage	Retail inventory	Desired retail inventory
0	0	50	250	50	50	950	1000
5	0	50	90	22	58	942	1000
10	33	50	109	20	112	888	1000
15	48	50	172	32	202	798	1000
20	60	50	238	45	293	707	1000
25	65	50	287	56	358	642	1000
30	64	50	311	62	387	613	1000
35	60	50	310	62	382	618	1000
40	54	50	292	59	355	645	1000
45	49	50	268	55	321	679	1000
50	45	50	246	50	291	709	1000
55	45	50	232	47	273	727	1000
60	45	50	227	46	268	732	1000
65	47	50	231	46	274	726	1000
70	49	50	239	47	285	715	1000
75	51	50	247	49	298	703	1000
80	52	50	254	51	307	693	1000
85	52	50	258	51	311	689	1000
90	51	50	258	52	311	689	1000
95	51	50	256	51	308	692	1000
100	50	50	253	51	303	697	1000

rather than in final form in the brewery inventory (i.e. he is employing a JIT (just-in-time) policy!). With the high level of stock in the production line and in the inventories, the brewery manager does not order any new production of beer for nearly 20 days; however, because of the delays in the system, he then over-orders for a period of about 10–15 days and his inventory levels start to stabilise after about 35 days. Meanwhile, the retail manager

Brewery order policy	Average orders filled	Beer in production	Brewery shortage	Brewery inventory	Desired brewery inventory
0	50	750	50	950	1000
0	43	536	-123	976	853
0	30	383	-438	1038	600
0	28	274	-463	1021	558
0	34	195	-236	908	672
41	43	145	143	711	854
94	51	471	513	513	1027
81	57	715	739	401	1140
64	59	821	826	355	1180
47	58	822	811	346	1157
37	55	764	746	350	1096
33	51	693	675	352	1027
35	49	640	627	344	971
41	47	621	615	325	940
48	47	635	635	301	936
53	48	670	675	277	952
56	49	712	719	257	976
56	50	749	755	245	1000
54	51	772	775	241	1016
52	51	780	781	246	1023
50	51	775	774	247	1021

ceases ordering from the brewery manager for the first 6 or 7 days, in response to higher inventories than she needs and also based on previous orders she has placed. However, the retail manager's inventories settle down quite quickly after about 20 days.

As can be seen from Case figure 4.14 on p. 203, these retail and brewery order policies do result in stability of inventories and reliability of supply to consumers, compared with

Case figure 4.15   Model behaviour with a STEP test on policy experiment 5

(a)

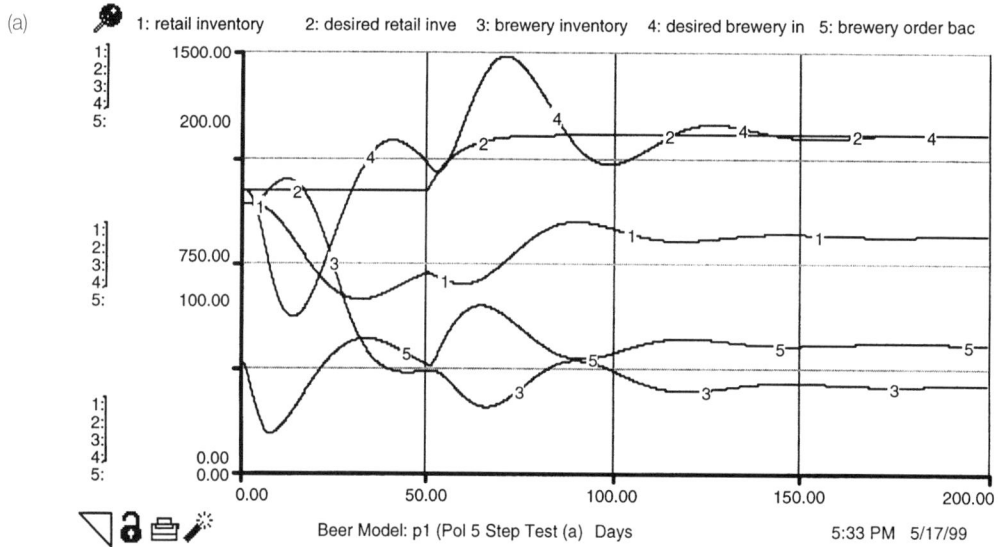

1: retail inventory   2: desired retail inve   3: brewery inventory   4: desired brewery in   5: brewery order bac

Beer Model: p1 (Pol 5 Step Test (a) Days   5:33 PM 5/17/99

(b)

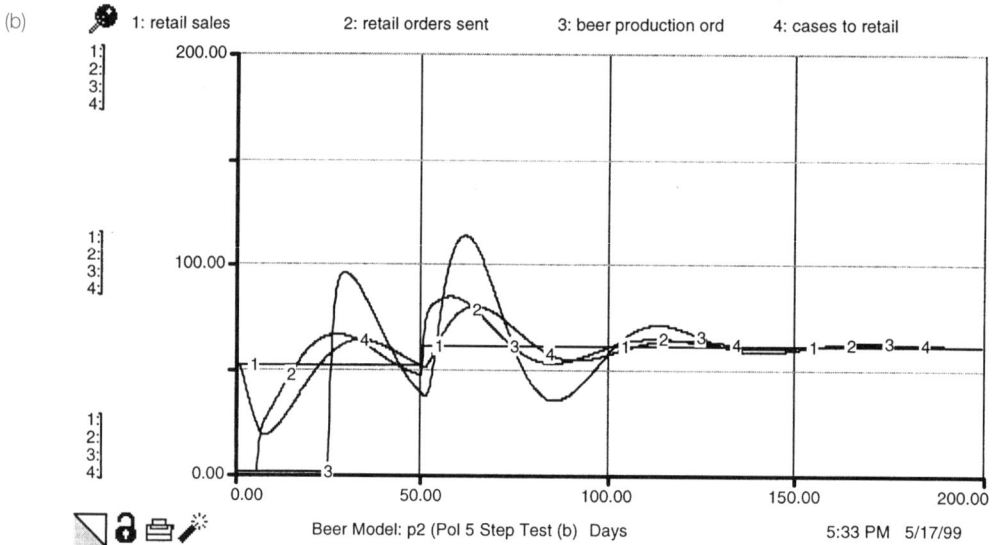

1: retail sales   2: retail orders sent   3: beer production ord   4: cases to retail

Beer Model: p2 (Pol 5 Step Test (b) Days   5:33 PM 5/17/99

the base case, as shown in Case figure 4.6. We now test the robustness of these policies by increasing demand for beer by 20% (or 10 cases per day) from day 50 onwards. We delay the step increase in demand until the system is clearly stable, to see how the system will respond to this shock. Also, we have extended the length of the simulation run to 150 days, so we can observe how long the model behaviour takes to settle down. The results of this scenario test are presented in Case figure 4.15. It is clear that these policies are 'moderately robust' but it does take some 60–70 days before the system settles down again.

Concluding comments

We have undertaken five policy experiments for this beer distribution model, with the last two experiments producing reasonably robust retail and brewery order policies. However, in addition to the primarily graphical analysis we have undertaken here, it is often valuable to provide numerical measures of the overall performance of the system for the purpose of comparing the different policies; e.g. some cost measure including inventory holding costs and stock costs, or some measure reflecting the instability costs in the system.

However, we would also like to emphasise that policies should be designed in conjunction with the actual managers in the system, to utilise information that they regard as relevant to the policy issues or decisions being examined. However, these policies can then be tested with a dynamic simulation model to determine their robustness to reasonable variations in external parameters and variables. More is said in Chapter 5 and Case 5, on scenario planning and modelling, about subjecting policies or strategies to systematic possible changes in the external environment.

Finally, we would like to offer a cautionary note here. One should not underestimate the time it takes to design and test managerial policies. For example, in a recent paper based on a consulting report, Jim Lyneis[7] has indicated that it took three months for the conceptualisation and construction of a small policy model for a major association of credit card users in the USA, then a further six months to calibrate the model, develop it further and undertake rigorous policy and strategy analysis using the model!

However, we would like to reiterate that the model provides a laboratory tool for policy experimentation, safe from the consequences of the 'real' world. This creates an ideal environment in which to learn.

Notes

1 Adapted from Clark (1998). Reprinted by permission, the Operations Research Society of America (currently INFORMS), 901 Elkridge Landing Road, Suite 400, Linthicum, Maryland 21090–2909 USA.

2 The value of the simulation interval is set at less than $1/4$ of the smallest delay in the model. In this model the smallest delay is 2 days (or the reciprocal of the retail order fraction). Hence DT is selected as a smaller amount. The value of 0.25 is the default setting for most system dynamics simulation software.

3 The STEP function is discussed further in Richmond and Petersen (1997).

4 The height of the step increase in the STEP function is modelled as a converter, rather than as a numerical value. This facilitates sensitivity analysis, particularly when this converter is placed on the upper level control panel of the model.

5 The PULSE function is outlined fully in Richmond and Petersen (1997).

6 This experiment is based on the policies suggested by Rolf Clark, 1988: 44.

7 See Lyneis, 1999: 56.

REFERENCES

Clark, R. (1988) *System dynamics and modelling*. Operations Research Society of America, Arlington.

Lyneis, J.M. (1999) System dynamics for business strategy: a phased approach. *System Dynamics Review*, 15(1): 37–70.

Richmond, B. and Petersen, S. (1997). *An Introduction to Systems Thinking*. High Performance Systems, Hanover.

Senge, P. (1990) *The Fifth Discipline: The Art and Practice of the Learning Organization*. Doubleday/Currency, New York.

Case 5

Strategy development for a telecommunications business unit[1]

OVERVIEW

This case demonstrates the approaches to simulation and scenario modelling outlined in Chapters 4 and 5. In particular, it is based on a consultancy project for a business unit in the telecommunications industry in New Zealand. However, the issues, data and names have been changed to preserve client confidentiality. The major issues dealt with in this case are how to design policies, and strategies to help managers turn around a business unit that is experiencing a declining market share and eroded profitability.

A dynamic simulation model is developed using the *ithink* computer simulation software.[2] The model contains four sectors:

- a market sector which includes variables for price, quality, market share, and the total market;

- an operations sector that deals with the processing of the services provided by the business unit, and relative productivity factors;

- a human resources sector that incorporates natural attrition, replacement and hiring decisions; and

- a finance sector that calculates costs, revenues, profit margins, cash flow and net present value for the business unit over a five-year period.

The initial managerial problems and issues are identified, following the strategic thinking and modelling process that is outlined in this book, and this is followed by the behaviour over time chart for the main variables in the case (i.e. the reference mode). Then a systems map is drawn of the main sectors and linkages between these sectors, and an overview is obtained of the main assumptions in the case. A simplified causal loop diagram for the system is presented with a brief discussion of the main feedback loops that, it is hypothesised, drive the observed behaviour of interest to the managers. The stock flow diagrams for the model are provided next, together with a brief overview of the main relationships in each sector. This is followed by a discussion of the base case behaviour of the model, and then the model is subjected to a series of rigorous validation tests. A systematic range of sensitivity tests is undertaken to determine the sensitive parameters in the model and the high leverage points. These provide the basis for the development of some alternative operations and human resource policies, and then ranges of consistent policies are combined to form strategic alternatives. Finally, some scenarios of possible future business environments that the business unit might operate in are presented, and the developed strategies are evaluated for robustness against these scenarios. The documented equations are provided in the technical appendix to this chapter.

Introduction

This case is based on a business unit of a telecommunications company operating in a small city in New Zealand. The operations of the telecommunications business unit (called TBU for the purposes of this case) include replacing, maintaining and installing telecommunications lines and connections to commercial and residential sites in the small city in which it works. The processes involve the design and planning of these connections, as well as undertaking the work to deliver the services. These are known as 'jobs' in the industry and we will refer to the whole process from design to delivery as a 'job' in this case. The case is based an actual consulting project for a New Zealand company, although, as mentioned above, the issues, data and names have been changed.

The particular problems that this business unit (TBU) had been experiencing were that although there had been a steady growth in the overall market for the services offered by the TBU (i.e. jobs), the TBU's market share had been steadily declining in preceding years (its share had dropped from nearly 30% in 1990 to below 25% by 1995). Also, the real prices (i.e. after inflation) had been declining and were now below the industry average for comparable jobs completed by competitor firms (the TBU was receiving about $9800 per average job compared with the industry average of about $10 000 per job of similar size). However, over the same period the average time taken to complete an 'average' job had been steadily increasing and was currently about 17% above the industry average (2.92 months per job compared with an average of 2.5 months per job for the industry in general). The recent historical behaviour of these variables is summarised in the behaviour over time (BOT) charts in Case figure 5.1. This became the reference mode for this case.

Case figure 5.1   Behaviour over time chart for the TBU strategy case

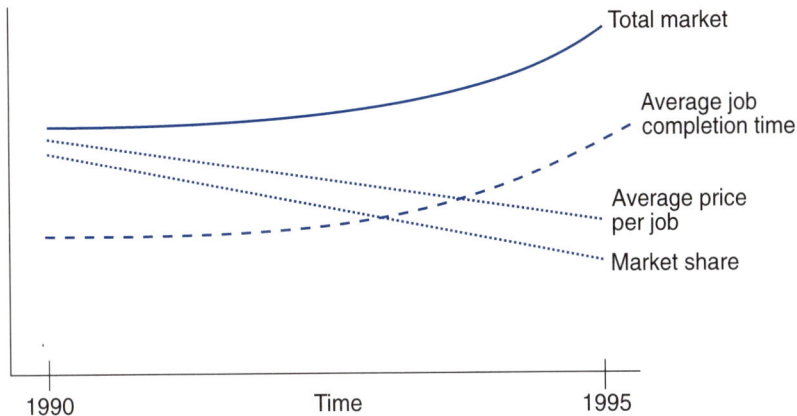

Management of the TBU was becoming increasingly concerned about this situation, as there were indications that it was going to persist. At this stage, a systems thinking and modelling (ST&M) intervention was commissioned

1   to help management understand why this behaviour was taking place; and

2   to suggest policies and strategies that might turn this deteriorating performance around and improve the TBU's performance relative to that of its competitors.

This case summarises the approach taken towards addressing these objectives.

System overview

The next stage of the ST&M intervention involved developing a systems map and causal loop diagrams to explain the behaviour of the main variables displayed in the BOT chart in Case figure 5.1. Discussions were held with senior management of the TBU as well as strategy support staff from the Head Office of the TBU's holding (parent) company. These discussions helped identify the initial set of variables to be included in the analysis, the main sectors of a potential model, and the boundaries to the problem area.

It was agreed that it would be necessary to include marketing, operations, finance and human resource information and data in order to explain the behaviour over time of the TBU, discussed in the introduction above. Since data for these variables were available from different functional parts of the TBU, it was agreed that these areas would form the 'sectors' for the initial model (these could be extended later if necessary to explain dynamic behaviour or to add 'structure' in the design of new policies and strategies). The emerging systems map or system overview diagram is summarised in Case figure 5.2. The arrows indicate connections (material and information linkages) between the sectors. Note that these linkages do not necessarily include all the flows of materials, people, information, etc. that would appear in the final model. However, we will comment briefly on the main flows here. The bold arrow between the market sector and the operations sector represents the physical flow of orders, whereas the bold arrow in the opposite direction represents the flow of completed jobs, with revenue flowing in return to the finance sector. The lighter arrows represent the information linkages between the sectors, e.g. prices from the market sector to calculate revenues in the finance sector, information about staff numbers used to calculate capacities in the operations sector, information about relative quality factors in the operations sector used to influence orders in the market sector, etc.

Case figure 5.2 Systems (high level) map of main sectors in TBU strategy model

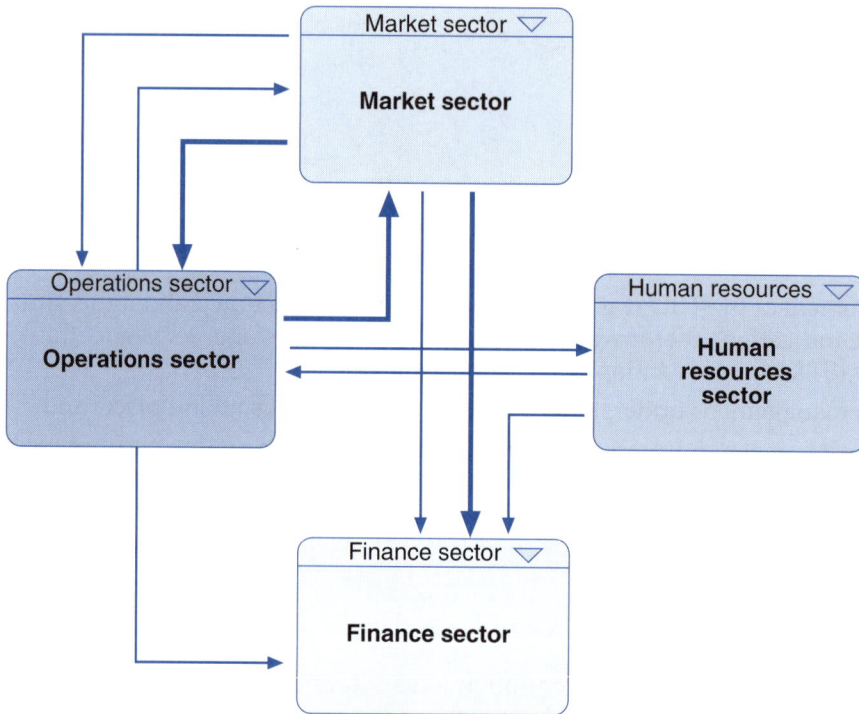

At this stage, a number of major assumptions were made limiting the boundaries of the potential model. For example, a major simplifying assumption was made in that it was assumed that capital equipment, plant and vehicles were available in the market or from the holding company at a rental price, and that the land and buildings the TBU occupied were also leased on a monthly basis but on a long-term lease.

Also, since there had been considerable downsizing of staff numbers in the telecommunications industry over the period of structural reforms in New Zealand since 1984, it was assumed that there was an available pool of skilled people that the TBU could employ without having to undertake extensive training programmes, and that training and developing newly employed staff would not take up the time of existing TBU staff.

Also, it was assumed that we could deal with an average 'job' size for the purposes of this project. Although jobs did vary in terms of their size and complexity, a sufficient proportion of them did take around the mean or average length of time to complete, so this simplifying assumption was regarded as quite realistic. In any case, this could be varied by sensitivity analysis when the simulation model had been completed.

Causal loop model

After a number of meetings with the project team (two consultants, the finance manager and CEO of the TBU, and two members of the HO strategy support staff), the causal loop diagram (CLD) appearing in Case figure 5.3 (p. 214) was developed. This development was iterative, and a whiteboard was used. This CLD became the basis for the development of the telecommunications business unit (TBU) strategy model.

A brief description of the main feedback loops in the model follows.

The quality–market loop (B1)

This is a major balancing loop in the system. We can start the qualitative analysis by assuming that there has been some positive growth in the total market size, leading to an increase in TBU's potential market. This makes an increase in TBU's job arrivals and hence an increase in the backlog of jobs awaiting start possible. This causes an increase in the average time jobs are in the backlog and a corresponding increase in total completion time for the jobs. In turn, this leads to an increase in the relative time it takes TBU to complete jobs compared with the industry average, thus diminishing the market's perception of TBU's quality performance and thus subsequently decreasing TBU's market share and potential market, hence closing the balancing loop.

Case figure 5.3 A simplified causal loop diagram for the TBU strategy model

The quality–price loop (R1)

To some extent this reinforcing loop offsets the effects of the balancing loop **B1**. Assuming also that there has been an increase in TBU's potential market, this loop follows the same path as the balancing loop **B1**, except that the decrease in perceived quality following on from TBU's increased completion times for jobs results in a decrease in the prices received by TBU, which stimulates demand and results in a slightly higher market share and potential market for TBU, hence closing the reinforcing loop.

The staff–quality loop (R2)

This is an important but slower-reacting reinforcing (or growth producing) loop in the model. Once again, we can start the analysis by assuming that there has been some increase in TBU's potential market size. This leads to an increase in TBU's job arrivals and the desired number of operations staff to cope with this increased workload. After a hiring delay, the staff numbers and staff workload capacity increase, thus making an increase in job starts and a reduction in the average time jobs remain in the backlog possible. This causes a reduction in the relative time TBU takes to complete the jobs compared with the industry average, thus improving the market's perception of TBU's quality performance and thus further increasing TBU's market share and potential market.

The staff–price loop (B2)

This loop is also a slower-reacting balancing loop that follows a very similar path to the reinforcing loop **R2**, except that, as a result of a perceived increase in quality by the market, management can increase the prices received for jobs completed, which has a dampening effect on TBU's market share, thus closing the balancing loop.

The staffing loops (B3, B4 and R3)

These are minor loops that control the number of operations staff working on TBU's jobs. For example, in the balancing loop **B3**, an increase in the desired number of staff, will cause an increase in the gap between desired and actual number of operations staff. After a hiring delay, this results in an increase in staff numbers, hence reducing the gap in staff numbers and closing the balancing loop. However, if this gap is negative this will result in the firing of staff. The effect of the balancing loop **B4** is to reduce the operations staff due to natural attrition or to staff leaving voluntarily. The effect of the reinforcing loop **R3** is to incorporate the replacement of these staff members into the decision to hire new staff.

    The qualitative analysis of these loops supports the historical pattern of the behaviour of the main variables of concern identified in the BOT chart in Case figure 5.1. That is, the causal loop analysis provides a plausible explanation of the reasons why, despite the steady increase in the total market for TBU services (i.e. jobs) in recent years, TBU's market share and real prices received for their jobs had been steadily declining, and the average time for completing their jobs had been increasing relative to the industry average. This BOT chart would now form the reference mode to be reproduced by an initial dynamic simulation model. Such a model would also support the qualitative causal loop analysis, and could be used to address TBU's first management concern – identified in the introduction to this case, namely 'to help management understand why this behaviour was taking place'.

A more in-depth analysis is required here, hence we proceed to developing a dynamic simulation model.[3]

Model development

Several of the main assumptions underlying the development of the model have been outlined in the previous sections. In this section, the detailed assumptions regarding the initial values for the stocks, the specific relationships controlling the flows in and out of the stocks, and the parameter values and structure of the remaining converters (auxiliary variables, constants and graphical relationships) will be provided for each sector (i.e. marketing, operations, human resources and finance sectors)

However, we also need to make some additional modelling assumptions about the simulation parameters for the model. These are that the analysis will be done on a monthly basis as records and data are available on that basis, and that the planning horizon (or length of the simulation run) will be five years (60 months). This was TBU's usual planning horizon for strategic analysis and planning. Data were collected from interviews with TBU and HO staff, and where data were not readily available, estimates were made – typically in collaboration with, and with the endorsement and/or approval of, the financial manager and CEO of TBU. The simulation interval (DT) was set at the default value of 0.25 months, i.e. the *ithink* computer simulation package would estimate the values for the stocks, flows and converters every 1/4 of a month for the entire simulation run of 60 months.

For each of the sectors in the model we will provide the stock flow diagram and the documented form of the equations, with full explanations about the assumptions, the relationships between the variables, and the dimensions (units of measure) of each of the variables. An overview is provided in this section and the documented equations are provided in the technical appendix to this case.

Market sector

The market sector shows the variables and relationships between the total market size, TBU's market share, and the effects of relative price and quality[4] on TBU's market share. Since the relative job completion time compared with the industry average is the proxy measure for quality in this model, it is assumed to have a direct effect on TBU's market share and also on the average price TBU receives on completion of work (i.e. jobs completed). Market size is assumed to be driven by an exogenous growth rate, which can be negative or positive. TBU's target market share is the percentage of the total market that TBU would attract if its quality and price were perceived to be at the same levels as the corresponding averages for the industry.

Case figure 5.4   Stock flow diagram for the TBU market sector

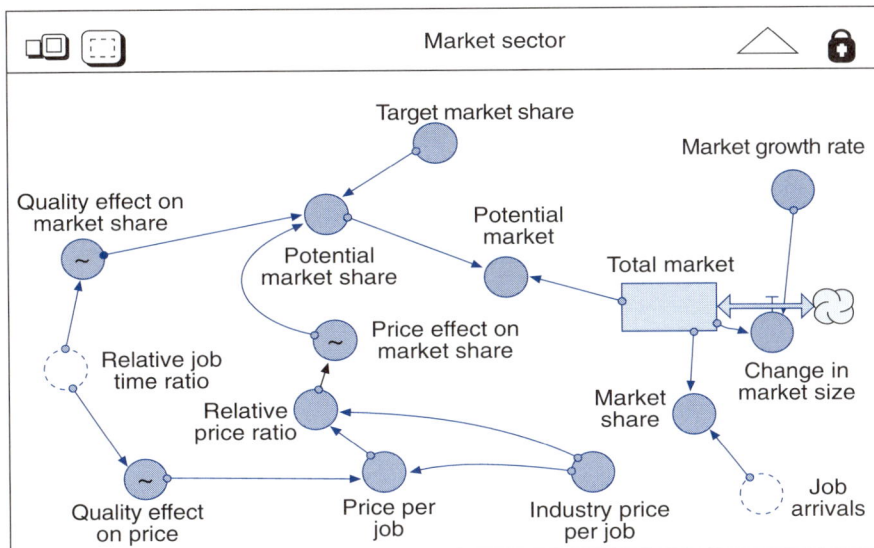

Operations sector

The operations sector summarises the service delivery aspects of TBU's business. It is assumed that jobs remain in a queue until there are sufficient staff resources to process them. However, once jobs have been started, they are subjected to a number of delays, including the normal time to process a job, plus the regulatory delays associated with getting approval for work to commence from the local council (i.e. local government). In addition, there are other delays before jobs can be completed, including logistical and supply delays, plus delays associated with staff down time. Productivity per person is a key variable in this sector, and relative completion time compared with the industry average is assumed to be the main means of assessing the relative quality of TBU's service delivery process.

Human resources sector

The human resources sector shows the structure of the hiring and staff replacement decisions, as well as the natural attrition of operations staff after a period of time in the organisation. This is a very 'simplistic' human resources sector; the reason being that we made the simplifying assumption much earlier (see p. 212), that skilled workers would be available without any further training throughout the period of the simulation run with the model. A more elaborate model could include variables and relationships that include trained and untrained workers with differing productivity levels.

Case figure 5.5   Stock flow diagram for the TBU operations sector

Case figure 5.6   Stock flow diagram for the TBU human resources sector

Finance sector

In the base case of the model, this sector is used only to measure the financial performance of TBU's service delivery processes. There are no feedback effects assumed from the financial variables to the other sectors of the model. For example, since we have made the assumption earlier that capital equipment can be leased from the market or from TBU's parent company, there is no capital investment sector in the model, which might depend on the profitability or the cash flow generated by the system. Nor is there any direct feedback connection linking salary or bonus payments with productivity. These variables and relationships can be added later, if they are necessary to meet management's objectives for the model. All prices and costs in the model are expressed in constant dollars.

Material costs are assumed to be paid for when the jobs start, labour costs and equipment rentals are assumed to depend on the number of operations staff. Some parts of the process are subcontracted out, and other overheads are allocated on a monthly basis. Cash revenue is assumed to be received when the jobs are completed. A pre-tax gross margin is calculated, and tax is deducted from this amount to provide the net cash flow which is discounted over the simulation run at a real rate of 10% p.a. to produce the net present value (NPV) for TBU.[5]

Case figure 5.7   Stock flow diagram for the TBU finance sector

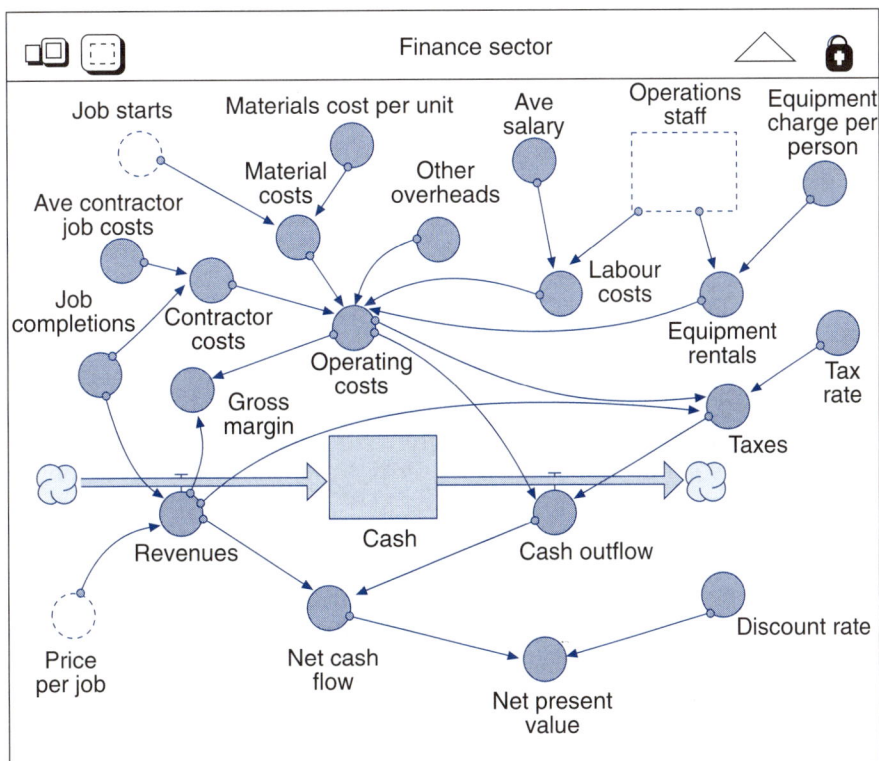

Base case behaviour

The model outlined in the previous section was built up gradually in a step-by-step fashion, with the graphical and tabular output being checked at each stage so that the project team (i.e. modellers and clients) could understand the development and behaviour of the model. However, only the base case and some preliminary model validation runs will be presented in this section.

Once the initial model (base case) had been developed, all the growth factors (i.e. market growth rate) and behavioural graphical relationships (e.g. price and quality effects on market share, quality effects on price) were neutralised (i.e. by setting the market growth rate to zero, and all the values in the graphical input relationships to one). The purpose of this was to examine the behaviour of the base case in equilibrium. The graphical results of this run for some of the main variables are shown in Case figure 5.8. This is called validation run 1, and it can be seen that all the output values are constant, except the cumulated net present value (NPV) of the operating net cash flows after tax. However, this is accumulating at a constant rate each year (before being discounted to the present value by TBU's weighted average cost of capital (10%)).

The next run of the model included relaxing the assumption of zero market growth, and replacing it with TBU management's 'best' estimate of 5% p.a. market growth. In addition, we replaced the assumption of constant values of the quality and price behavioural relationships with the graphical relationships outlined in the equations in the market sector (i.e. with the assumptions that the market would react against poor quality and higher prices by placing orders for less jobs to be undertaken by TBU). We called this run the base case and the model behaviour of the main variables is summarised in Case figure 5.9.

The base case can be directly compared with the reference mode behaviour, identified in the BOT charts in Case figure 5.1. As can be seen, the average completion time for jobs continues to track upwards over the next 5 years, and the market share and average price per job continue to decline, although the total market expands by 5% p.a. These results suggests that TBU's performance will continue to deteriorate unless some changes are made to its policies or strategies.

However, some additional comments should be provided about the short-term behaviour of some of the variables in Case figure 5.9. This includes a brief explanation of why the 'gross margin' (effectively the ratio of the gross profit (net cash flow before tax) to revenue) and the 'net cash flow' in Case figure 5.9(b) increase in the first few months of the simulation before settling in to a longer-term downward trend over the simulation run. Although the market is growing by 5% p.a., TBU's average time for completing jobs is about 17% higher than the average time in the industry. This causes an initial further reduction in market share and market potential. Hence job arrivals are lower, causing a small reduction in the job start rates. Since material unit costs are linked to jobs starts and all the other costs are linked either to operations staff, job completions, or overheads, there is an initial increase in the gross margin and after-tax net cash flow, since more jobs are being completed than started. After a few months, job completions begin to lag behind job starts as the effects on the growing market are felt throughout the TBU business unit, and the average time to complete the jobs increases since jobs are building up in TBU's backlog.

Case figure 5.8   Validation run 1 (in equilibrium) of the TBU strategy model

(a)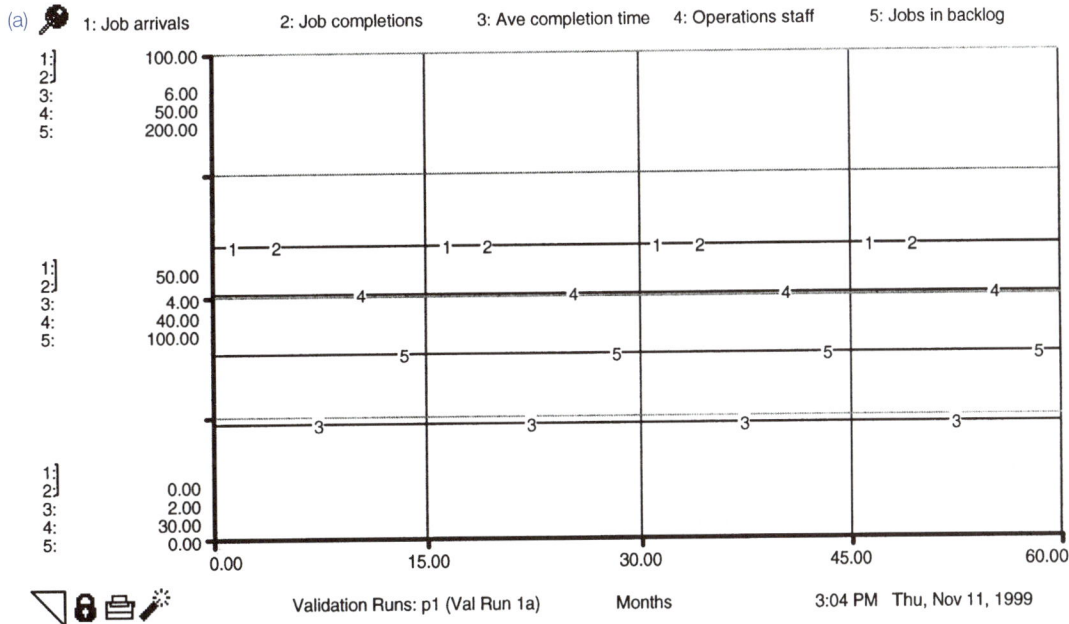

(b)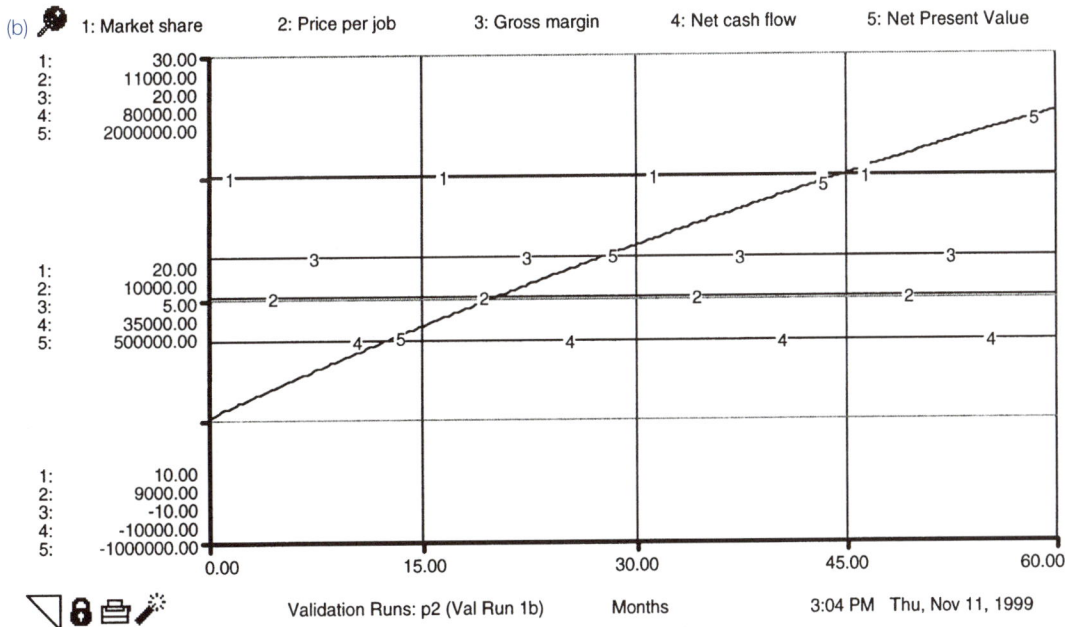

Case figure 5.9 Base case behaviour of the TBU strategy model

(a)

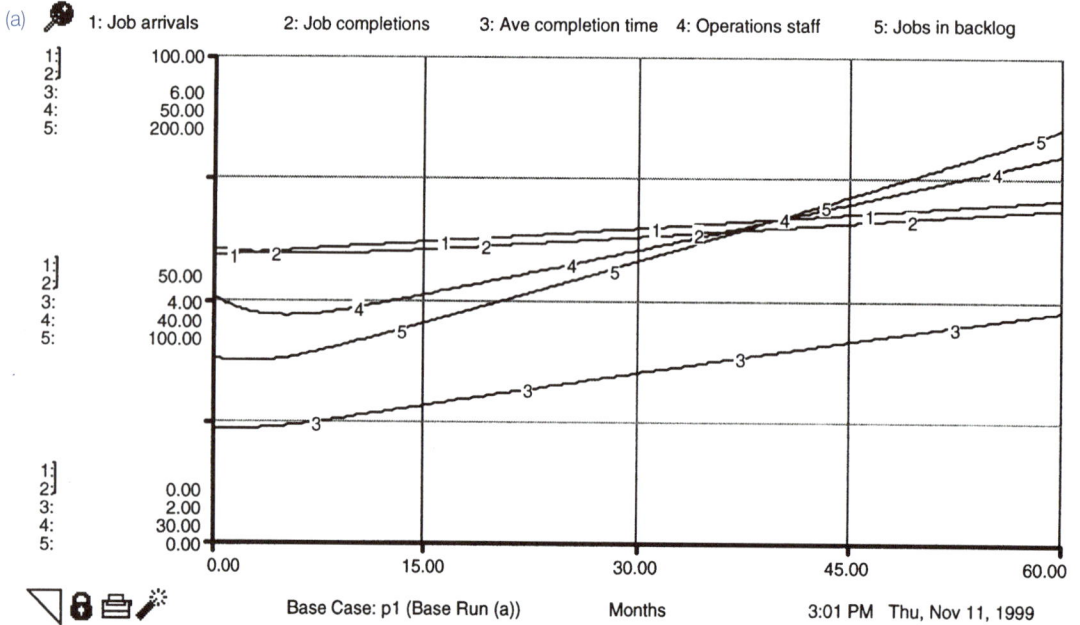

1: Job arrivals   2: Job completions   3: Ave completion time   4: Operations staff   5: Jobs in backlog

Base Case: p1 (Base Run (a))   Months   3:01 PM Thu, Nov 11, 1999

(b)

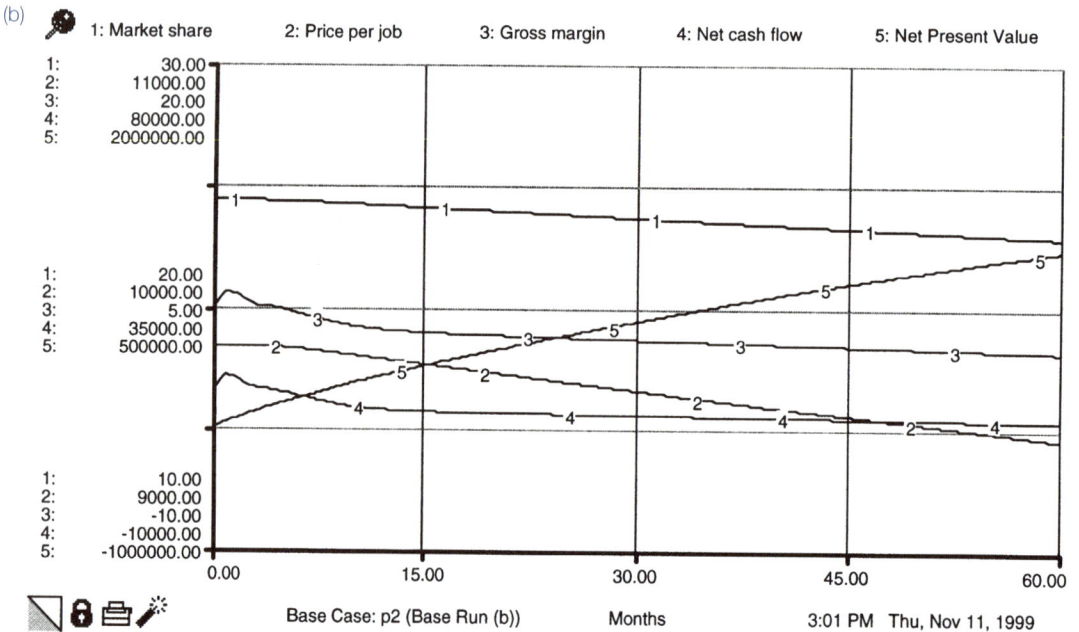

1: Market share   2: Price per job   3: Gross margin   4: Net cash flow   5: Net Present Value

Base Case: p2 (Base Run (b))   Months   3:01 PM Thu, Nov 11, 1999

Model validation

The base case version of the model was then subjected to a range of the validation and verification tests suggested by Coyle[6] (1996: 96–97) that are outlined in Chapter 4. (One of these validation tests has been demonstrated in the previous section.) The purpose of these tests was to give the project team more confidence in the model, so that it could be used for policy analysis and strategy development to help management and so to meet both the objectives outlined in the introduction to this case (p. 211).

The model has been subjected to the following tests, which are briefly summarised below.

- **The causal loop diagram must correspond to the statement of the problem**.

The causal loop diagram for the TBU strategy model provided in Case figure 5.3 does correspond to the problem statement outlined in the introduction to this case and illustrated in the behaviour over time (BOT) charts in Case figure 5.1. Confirmation that the causal loop diagram does correspond to the problem statement is also reinforced by the qualitative analysis of the feedback loops in the causal loop model section.

- **The equations must correspond to the causal loop diagram; in particular the 's' and 'o' signs in the equations must match the signs in the causal loop diagram.**

A close inspection of the model equations contained in model development section revealed that the direction of the relationships in the causal loop diagram (Case figure 5.3) matched the direction of the relationships in the computer model. However, it must be mentioned that the causal loop diagram contains less variables and details than the stock flow diagrams (Case figures 5.4 to 5.7), which form the basis for the detailed model equations.

Nevertheless, this process did reveal one or two very important linkages that were incorrectly placed in the market sector. These errors were corrected, and finally correspondence was confirmed between the causal loop diagram and the model equations.

- **The model must be dimensionally valid, i.e. it should be possible to convert the dimensions (or units of measure) of the variables on the right-hand side of the equation to the dimensions of the variable on the left-hand side of the equation. (Has each equation in the model been checked for dimensional consistency?)**

For example, let us consider the dimensions of the following equation used to calculate the stock 'Jobs_in_backlog':

Jobs_in_backlog(t) = Jobs_in_backlog(t – dt) + (Job_arrivals – Job_starts) * dt

INIT Jobs_in_backlog = 60 {jobs}

Job_arrivals = Potential_market {jobs / month}

Job_starts = MIN(Staff_capacity,Jobs_in_backlog) {jobs / month}

The dimension of the variable 'Jobs_in_backlog' (at the current point in time i.e. at 't') on the left-hand side of the equation is 'jobs'. The dimensions of the right-hand side variables are 'jobs' for 'Jobs_in_backlog' (at the previous time point 't-dt'); 'jobs/month' (i.e. jobs per month) for the flow variables 'Job_arrivals' and 'Job_starts'; and 'months' for the simulation time period 'dt'. Hence the dimensions of the variables on the right-hand side can be expressed as:

$$= \text{Jobs} + (\text{Jobs}/\text{month} - \text{Jobs}/\text{month}) * \text{month}$$

By the ordinary laws of algebra this equation can be reduced to:

$$= \text{Jobs} + (\text{Jobs}/\text{month}) * \text{month}$$

(now 'month' can be deleted from the numerator and denominator of the second term)

$$= \text{Jobs} + \text{Jobs}$$
$$= \text{Jobs}$$

Hence the dimensions of the variables on the right-hand side of the equation have been reduced to the dimensions of the variable on the left-hand side, namely 'Jobs'.

All the equations in the TBU strategy model were subjected to dimensional analysis. Although the base case run of the model (Case figure 5.9) reproduced the reference mode behaviour of the main variables shown in the behaviour over time charts in Case figure 5.1, the dimensional analysis revealed that a number of dimensions had been left off the descriptions of some variables and equations (e.g. 'cash', 'revenues', 'cash outflow', 'other overheads', 'staff replacements') and a number of variables and relationships had incorrect dimensions (e.g. 'average salary' had dimensions of '$/month' rather than '$/person/ month'; and 'net present value' had dimensions of '$/month' rather than '$'). These were corrected for the final simulation runs.

Also, a correct understanding of the dimensions of an equation can help when preparing the model for sensitivity tests, policy experiments or scenario analysis (which will be discussed later in this case).

- **Has each equation in the model been adequately documented?**

Each equation in the TBU strategy model shown in the model development section has been documented. This has involved explaining in 'managerial terms' the nature of the relationships for each equation and the assumptions underlying them. Since all the data for the case were gathered with the TBU project team and much of it came from internal company sources, sources for each parameter and relationship have not been identified separately in the model documentation, to preserve client confidentiality.

- **The model does not produce any unrealistic values.**

Generally, the way to check this is to print out a graph of the main variables in the system over the simulation run and also to print out all the variables in a table (or all the variables in each sector separately). However, it is usually very useful to print out the variables for each simulation interval (DT) for the first few periods of the model. For the TBU strategy model we printed out all the variables for time periods 0, 0.25, 0.5, 0.75 and 1.0. This allowed us to check the 'arithmetic and logic' of the model for each variable. The model was set up with 'month' units of time, and the simulation interval, DT, was set at 0.25.

We also recommend that all the variables be printed out for selected time periods over the entire simulation length (planning horizon). The simulation length for the TBU strategy model was 60 months (5 years) so we printed out all the variable values in table form at 12-monthly intervals for periods 0, 12, 24, 36, 48 and 60.

For the initial validation runs, this process revealed a number of errors. For example, the output revealed a negative cash flow for each period, and declining operations staff numbers, resulting in dramatically increasing numbers of jobs awaiting work in a backlog. Some arithmetic errors with the cost input parameters in the model were responsible for the negative cash flow in each period, and a mistake in the formulation of the hiring and firing policies was responsible for the declining staff numbers. We had omitted to take voluntary departures into consideration when determining the hiring and firing of operations staff. After correcting these errors we were able to proceed to the steady-state 'equilibrium' validation run (displayed in Case figure 5.8).

- **The behaviour of the model should be plausible – what it does should be what we expect it to do – and the values at which it stabilises can be confirmed by simple arithmetic.**

The base case run of the model discussed in the previous section and the preliminary validation runs demonstrate the stability of the system (see Case figures 5.8 and 5.9).

- **The model should maintain 'conservation of flow'. This means that the total quantity of a variable, which has entered and left the system, together with what is still there, should be accounted for.**

This involved a thorough check on the stocks and flows in the system, and a careful analysis of all the graphs and tables of the stocks and flows generated by the model.

- **Does each equation make sense when its inputs take on extreme values?**

The TBU strategy model was subjected to a number of shocks, including pulse and step[7] functions. However, only one extreme behaviour test will be reported here. This involved a 40% increase in the normal (target) market share, peaking in month 24 as illustrated in Case figure 5.10.

In this model experiment, we assumed that the target market share increased to 40% at the beginning of month 24 (i.e. at the beginning of year 3 of the simulation run). (This means that the target market share stays at 25% for the first 12 months, climbs to 40% at the end of the second year, then declines back to 25% by the end of the third year and remains there until the end of the fifth year, as illustrated in the graph pad in Case figure 5.10). This situation could occur if a major competitor left the market, if TBU entered new domestic or international markets, or if aggressive advertising for a period resulted in a sharp increase in TBU's target market share. The behaviour of this extreme behaviour test is shown in Case figure 5.11 on p. 227.

Although the target market share increases to 40% by month 24, this is moderated by the price and quality effects on the market share. Since the extra work has put considerable pressure on the staff to undertake the additional jobs, this has resulted in a dramatic increase in the average time to complete jobs (up to 4.8 months compared with the industry average of 2.5 months). This dampens the demand for jobs as existing customers of TBU are becoming dissatisfied with having to wait longer for their jobs to be completed. Hence TBU's actual market share only rises to 34% compared with the target share of 40%. The increase in other jobs arriving results in an increase of operations staff after a delay, and this helps TBU cope with the additional work and the average completion time drops back. However, as the additional work and the average completion time drop back to the

Case figure 5.10 Graphical input to extreme behaviour test

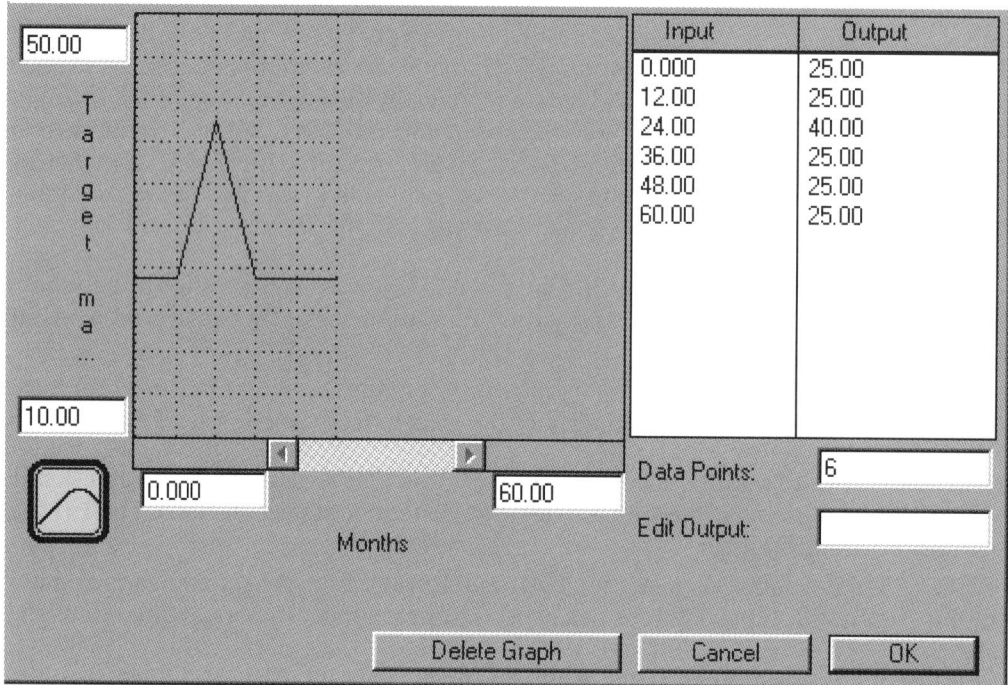

longer-term trend level, TBU lays off staff and all the major variables return to their medium-term growth pattern (see Case figure 5.11 on the following page), which is very similar to that of the base case (see Case figure 5.9).

However, this extreme conditions test does demonstrate the ability of the model to return to the path identified in the base case (hence demonstrating that the balancing and reinforcing loops in the model are working well). Although the model is working well, it does raise a question about the realism of some of the policies, especially the assumption regarding the hiring and firing of operations staff. The model assumes that TBU will be able to recruit an additional 16 operations staff by the point of 'peak staff members' (i.e. at month 30). This represents an increase of 40% in staff members over the beginning of the simulation run. This suggests that the hiring and firing policies may have to be re-examined, or that the extreme test may be too unrealistic – expecting an additional 40% in the target market for jobs by month 24.

Other extreme conditions tests were undertaken but each demonstrated the model's ability to return to the medium-term path illustrated in the base case. Hence the fundamental problem of the TBU still remains: declining market share, declining relative real prices, and longer average completion times for jobs compared with TBU's competitors.

We will now subject the model to a range of sensitivity tests to identify the parameters that have the most impact on the behaviour and performance of the model. This will help TBU management identify which variables to monitor more closely. We shall undertake a systematic analysis of the parameters by increasing and decreasing them by 10% and examining the impact of these changes on selected indicators of performance.

Case figure 5.11   TBU model behaviour for the extreme value test

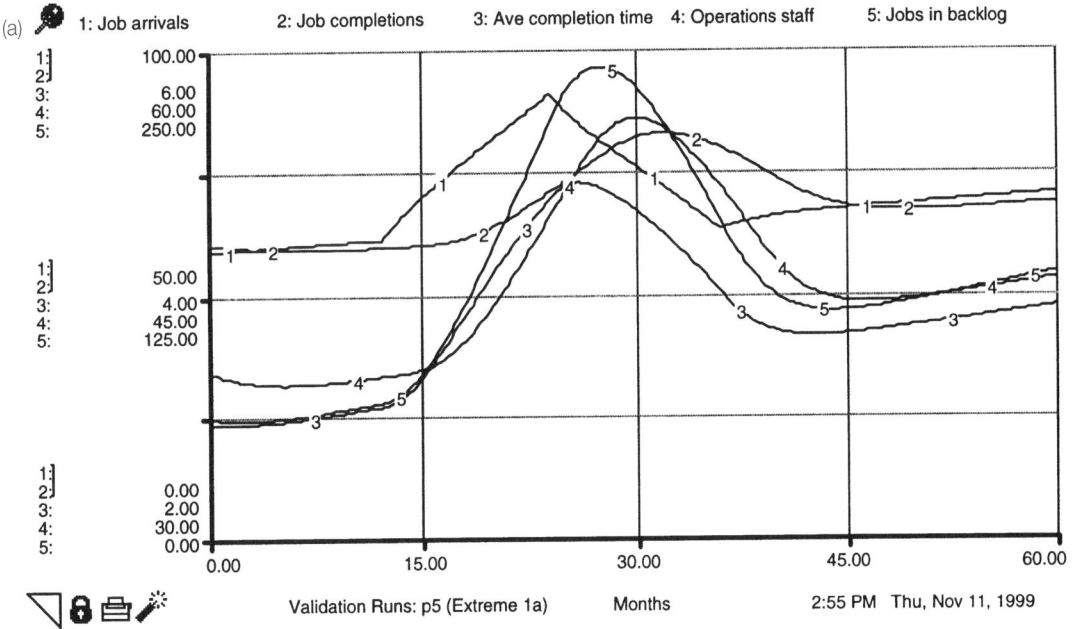

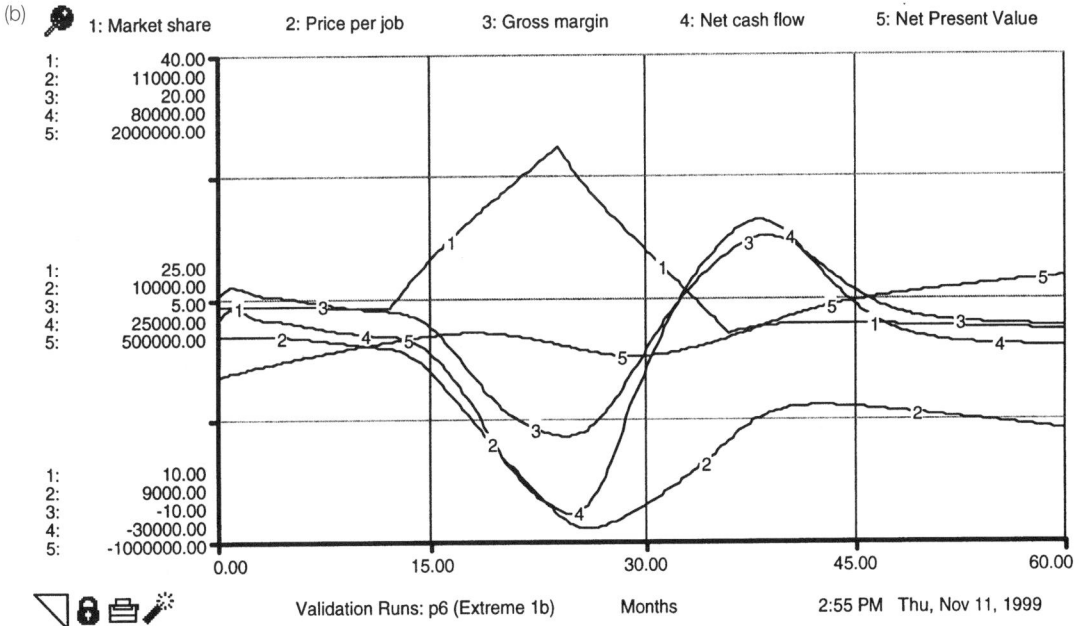

(a)

1: Job arrivals   2: Job completions   3: Ave completion time   4: Operations staff   5: Jobs in backlog

Validation Runs: p5 (Extreme 1a)   Months   2:55 PM   Thu, Nov 11, 1999

(b)

1: Market share   2: Price per job   3: Gross margin   4: Net cash flow   5: Net Present Value

Validation Runs: p6 (Extreme 1b)   Months   2:55 PM   Thu, Nov 11, 1999

Following this we will undertake some policy experiments and identify some strategy alternatives for TBU management. Then we will analyse some scenarios for the future and examine the behaviour of these policies and strategies under different possible scenarios, that is, we will check the robustness of these policies and strategies.

Also of importance to the validation process are sensitivity analysis, policy experiments, and scenario analysis, which will be undertaken in subsequent sections. These all help to demonstrate the validity of the model so that it can be used with confidence to address the issues.

Sensitivity analysis

Setting up the sensitivity experiments

The sensitivity analysis involved varying all the model parameters and graphical relationships by plus or minus 10%. This means multiplying each parameter by a factor of 1.1 and 0.9 to give, respectively, an increase and decrease of 10%. For example, the value of the sensitivity experiment giving a 10% increase in the base value of 'industry price per job' of $10 000 is 1.1 * $10 000 = $11 000.

The sensitivity experiments are summarised in Case table 5.1. For the sensitivity tests on the graphical relationships (price and quality effect multipliers), the differences between 1 and each value on the graph are multiplied by 1.1 and 0.9 to give a 10% increase and decrease respectively. Since these 'soft' relationships are used to modify market share in a multiplicative relationship, '1' or unity is the 'no effect' value. Hence the effects of changes are measured by the gap between the value provided (i.e. the elements) and 1. This is the value we are subjecting to sensitivity analysis, to see what impact small changes in this value will make on the performance of the model. For example, the sensitivity test on the graphical relationship 'price effect on market share' involving a 10% increase in the values includes the following steps:

Base case values = 1.5 / 1.25 / 1.0 / 0.6 / 0.1

Differences to 1   = (1.5-1) / (1.25-1) / (1.0-1) / (0.6-1) / (0.1-1)

             = 0.5 / 0.25 / 0 / -0.4 / -0.9

Multiply differences by 1.1

             = 1.1*0.5 / 1.1*0.25 / 1.1*0 / 1.1*(-0.4) / 1.1*(-0.9)

             = 0.55 / 0.275 / 0 / -0.44 / -0.99

Add differences to 1 for each element

             = 1+0.55 / 1+0.275 / 1+0 / 1-0.44 / 1-0.99

             = 1.55 / 1.275 / 1 / 0.56 / 0.01

This is the sensitivity test of a 10% increase in the graphical relationship 'price effect on market share'.

Note that for graphical relationships which are not 'multipliers' with 'no effect' values of '1' (e.g. 'target market share'), it is appropriate to multiply all the elements in the relationship by 1.1 to give a 10% increase for sensitivity testing.

Case table 5.1   Sensitivity experiments for testing parameters in the TBU strategy model

	Base case values	10% increase	10% decrease
Market sector			
Industry price per job	$10 000	$11 000	$9000
Market growth rate	5%	5.5%	4.5%
Target market share*	25%	27.5%	22.5%
Price effect on market share	1.5/1.25/1.0/0.6/0.1	1.55/1.275/1.0/0.56/0.01	1.45/1.225/1.0/0.64/0.19
Quality effect on market share	1.2/1.1/1.0/0.9/0.8	1.22/1.11/1.0/0.89/0.78	1.18/1.09/1.0/0.91/0.82
Quality effect on price	1.1/1.05/1.0/0.95/0.9	1.11/1.055/1.0/0.945/0.89	1.09/1.045/1.0/0.955/0.91
Operations sector			
Hours available per person	150 hrs	165 hrs	135 hrs
Industry job completion time	3 mths	2.75 mths	2.25 mths
Other delays	1.25 mths	1.375 mths	1.125 mths
Work intensity	80%	88%	72%
Standard processing time per job	80 hrs	88 hrs	72 hrs
Human resources sector			
Hiring delay	3 mths	3.3 mths	2.7 mths
Job arrival smoothing time	4 mths	4.4 mths	3.6 mths
Staff replacement delay	4 mths	4.4 mths	3.6 mths
Time in organisation	36 mths	39.6 mths	32.4 mths
Finance sector			
Average contractor job costs	$900	$990	$810
Average salary	$3750	$4125	$3375
Discount rate	10%	11%	9%
Equipment charge per person	$500	$550	$450
Materials cost per unit	$3800	$4180	$3420
Other overheads	$108 250	$119 075	$97 425
Tax rate	33%	36.3%	29.7%

*The 'target market share' is inputted as a graph with all elements constant for these runs. The elements are shown as percentages in this table, but they are inputted in decimal form in the model.

Case table 5.2 Selected results of the sensitivity tests with the TBU strategy model

	Relative job time (ratio) (% ch.)		Relative price ratio (ratio)(% ch.)		Market share (%) (% ch.)		Operations staff (no.) (% ch.)		Gross margin (%) (% ch.)		Net present value ($000) (% ch.)	
Base case	1.55		0.94		22.8		46		3.1		728	
				10% increase in parameter input values									
Market sector												
Industry price per job	1.55	0	0.94	0	22.8	0	46	0	11.9	284	2,640	263
Market growth rate	1.59	3	0.94	0	22.7	(0)	47	2	2.9	(6)	713	(2)
Target market share	1.60	3	0.94	0	24.9	9	50	9	4.0	29	916	26
Price effect on market share	1.56	1	0.94	0	22.9	0	46	0	3.1	0	729	0
Quality effect on market share	1.54	(1)	0.95	1	22.6	(1)	45	(2)	3.1	0	724	(1)
Quality effect on price	1.56	1	0.94	0	22.9	0	46	0	2.5	(19)	662	(9)
Operations sector												
Hours available per person	1.51	(3)	0.95	1	23.0	1	42	(9)	6.4	106	1,333	83
Industry job completion time	1.41	(9)	0.96	2	23.4	3	47	2	5.0	61	1,061	46
Other delays	1.60	3	0.94	0	22.7	(0)	46	0	2.4	(23)	605	(17)
Work intensity	1.51	(3)	0.95	1	23.0	1	42	(9)	6.4	106	1,333	83
Standard processing time per job	1.66	7	0.93	(1)	22.4	(2)	50	9	(1.4)	(145)	1	(100)
Human resources sector												
Hiring delay	1.57	1	0.94	0	22.8	0	46	0	2.9	(6)	716	(2)
Job arrival smoothing time	1.57	1	0.94	0	22.8	0	46	0	2.9	(6)	707	(3)
Staff replacement delay	1.56	1	0.94	0	22.8	0	46	0	3.1	0	727	0
Time in organisation	1.55	0	0.94	0	22.8	0	46	0	3.1	0	729	0
Finance sector												
Average contractor job costs	1.55	0	0.94	0	22.8	0	46	0	2.1	(32)	550	(24)
Average salary	1.55	0	0.94	0	22.8	0	46	0	0.4	(87)	231	(68)
Discount rate	1.55	0	0.94	0	22.8	0	46	0	3.1	0	713	(2)
Equipment charge per person	1.55	0	0.94	0	22.8	0	46	0	2.7	(13)	662	(9)
Materials cost per unit	1.55	0	0.94	0	22.8	0	46	0	(1.2)	(139)	4	(99)
Other overheads	1.55	0	0.94	0	22.8	0	46	0	1.4	(55)	385	(47)
Tax rate	1.55	0	0.94	0	22.8	0	46	0	3.1	0	696	(4)

Results from the sensitivity tests

The usual way to perform sensitivity tests with system dynamics models is to simulate the model with each altered parameter or graphical relationship changed one at a time, then to examine the graphical behaviour and the numerical results for the main variables of interest. We have selected a number of key variables to monitor for the purposes of the sensitivity tests. These variables are: 'relative job time', 'relative price ratio', 'market share',

Case figure 5.12   Model behaviour for main performance measures in the base case

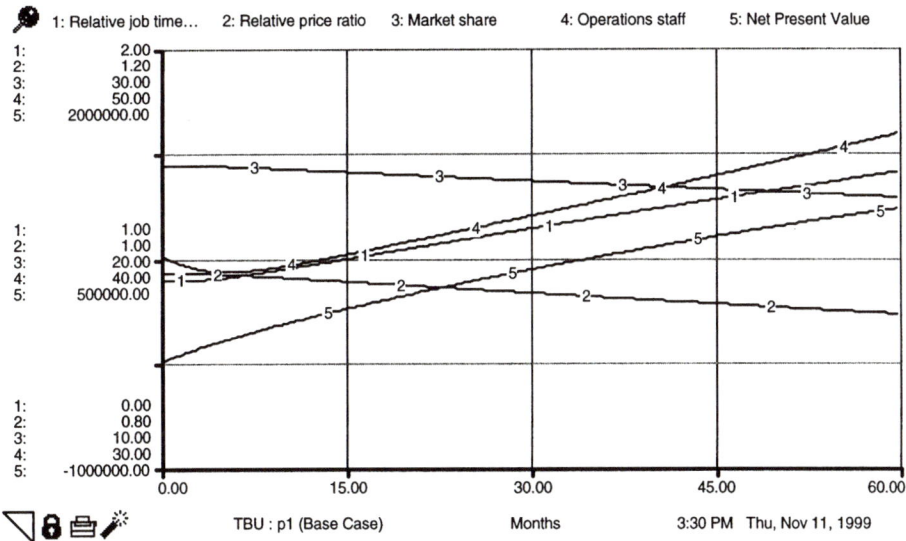

TBU : p1 (Base Case)   Months   3:30 PM Thu, Nov 11, 1999

Case figure 5.13   Model behaviour for main performance measures in a sensitivity case

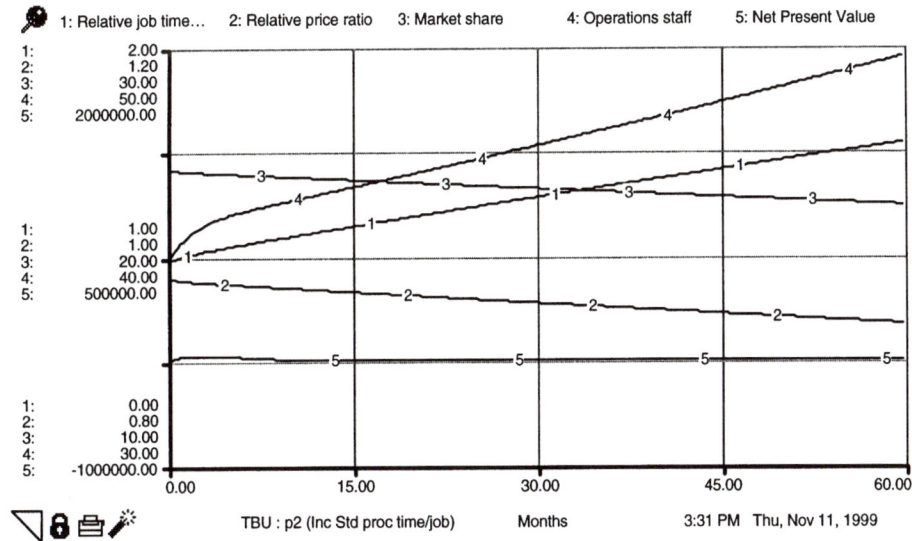

TBU : p2 (Inc Std proc time/job)   Months   3:31 PM Thu, Nov 11, 1999

'operations staff', and 'net present value'. The graphical behaviour for the base case and one sensitivity test (10% increase in the 'standard processing time per job') are presented in Case figures 5.12 and 5.13 respectively. The final values at the end of the simulation run (i.e. in month 60) for these variables are presented in Case table 5.2,[8] together with the final values for the variable 'gross margin'. The selected variables represent key relative performance measures from each of the model sectors – marketing, operations, human resources and finance sectors.

The graphical behaviour for the sensitivity test shown in Figure 5.13 indicates that the overall behaviour of the variables is similar to that of the base case. However, since TBU's standard processing times of operations staff actually working on the jobs is assumed to have increased (up to 88 hours per job, compared with 80 hours per job in the base case), TBU's total time for completing jobs has increased relative to the industry average. TBU has compensated for this by increasing staff levels to cope with the lower staff productivity. The extra staff costs result in a reduction in net cash flow and hence virtually no increase in the net present value added by the business unit over the simulation run (60 months). However, the overall behavioural pattern of the variables has not changed significantly with this sensitivity test.

The summarised results for the final values of all the sensitivity tests are provided in Case table 5.2. As can be seen from this table, the most sensitive parameters are:

- industry price per job
- target market share
- quality effect on price
- hours available per person
- industry job completion time
- work intensity
- standard processing time per job
- average contractor job costs
- average salary
- materials cost per unit
- other overheads.

Management of TBU was advised to pay very close attention to these parameters and to monitor them very carefully. (Note that, by and large, the model behaviour did not appear to be overly sensitive to some of the 'soft' variables, such as the price and quality effects on market share.) However, there are a number of uncertainties related to these relationships, and we shall be discussing them more closely later in the section on scenario analysis. Relatively small changes (of plus or minus 10%) in the finance parameters generally resulted in very large changes in the financial performance of TBU (measured in terms of the gross margin and net present value). In addition, changes in the sensitive operations sector parameters generally had a significant impact on changes in the 'relative job time' and 'operations staff numbers'. As expected, changes to the 'target market share' had a fairly similar impact on the actual 'market share' achieved by TBU.

It is interesting to note that the model performance was not particularly sensitive to small changes in the parameters in the human resources sector. This does not suggest that these parameters are unimportant, but rather that small changes to the base values do not produce any significant changes to the model's overall performance. However, changes to combinations of these parameters, perhaps with other structural changes to HR policies within TBU, may in actual fact result in considerable changes to the model's (and TBU's) overall behaviour. We shall examine this more closely in the next section, on policy analysis.

The sensitivity analysis was facilitated by the objects available on the 'high-level mapping' layer of the *ithink* software used. In particular, we found the 'slider' objects for the parameters, and the 'graphical input device' for changing the values of the graphical relationships, to be particularly efficient ways of performing sensitivity analysis. These objects avoided the need to go into the 'equation' layer of the model to change the parameter and graphical inputs. In addition, the 'numeric displays' provided final values of the overall performance measures of the model that we were monitoring. An example of a simple control panel containing the high-level objects for varying the marketing sector input parameters and graphs is provided in Case figure 5.14. Once a sensitivity test has been performed, the parameter or graphical values can be restored instantly to their base case (original) values by clicking on the 'undo' button on the slider or graphical input device. Finally, the results from each of the sensitivity tests were entered into a Microsoft Excel™ spreadsheet, to enable percentage changes to the base case values to be performed efficiently. The results of these calculations are displayed in Case table 5.2.

Case figure 5.14   A simple control panel for the market sector of the TBU strategy model

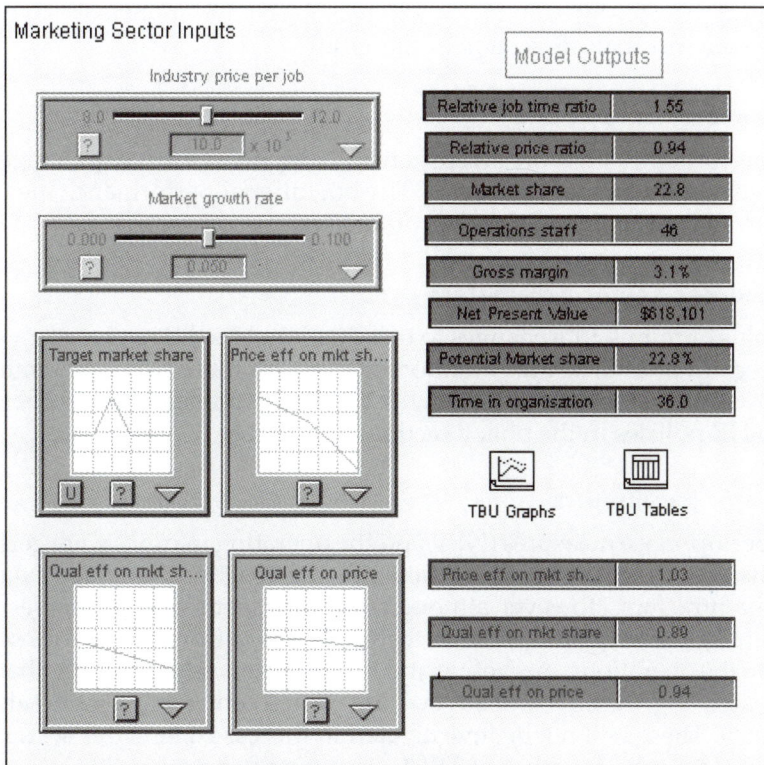

Comments on sensitivity tests

A summary of the sensitivity tests and their general impact on the overall performance measures from each of the marketing, operating, human resources and financial sectors of the model is provided in Case table 5.3. The high leverage points for management can be readily observed in this table. This table also contains a classification of the parameters and graphical relationships within the model, depending on whether they are generally controlled by management (internal), outside management's direct control (external), or influenced by both management and external factors (both). We will provide a few comments on the sensitivity of the parameters within each sector of the model.

● Market sector parameters

Most performance measures were sensitive to changes in the 'target market share' for the TBU. The surprising result was that most measures were not sensitive to changes in the market growth assumption, except for the financial measures, which showed some small sensitivity to changes in this parameter – but in the opposite direction to what was expected! This indicates that, with the current policy mix in the model, TBU was not coping well with growth.

The performance measures were not sensitive to small changes in the price and quality effects on market share, although the financial indicators were very sensitive to changes in the quality effect on price. However, there is considerable uncertainty in the estimation of these graphical relationships, and they will be subjected to more extensive sensitivity analysis in the scenario analysis section of this case.

● Operations sector parameters

The financial performance measures were generally highly sensitive to changes in nearly all the parameters in the operations sector. The operational performance measures were also sensitive to changes in most of these parameters.

● Human resources sector parameters

Surprisingly, plus or minus 10% changes to these parameters did not have any significant effect on the performance measures monitored, although there were some minor effects. However, we will investigate larger changes to these parameters and other structural changes to the HR policies in the policy section of this case.

● Finance sector parameters

The financial performance measures (NPV and the operating margin) were generally very sensitive to changes in TBU's costs, particularly the costs of materials, salaries, other overheads and contractors. However, although TBU management should investigate these costs very carefully, currently there are no feedback effects from the finance sector of the model back into the operations, marketing and human resource sectors. Feedback linkages can be investigated (e.g. the effects of advertising on marketing, bonuses to salary on staff productivity, etc.). These will not be investigated in this case. Here, this sector serves the purpose of a financial measurement of TBU's operating performance.

Case table 5.3   Summary of sensitivity tests and classification of input parameters

	Performance measures (1)				
	Marketing	**Operating**	**Human resources**	**Financial**	**Parameter classification (2)**
Market sector					
Industry price per job				***	External
Market growth rate					External
Target market share	*	*	*	**	Internal
Price effect on market share					External
Quality effect on market share					External
Quality effect on price				**	External
Operations sector					
Hours available per person		*	*	***	Both
Industry job completion time		*		***	External
Other delays		*		*	Both
Proportion of productive time		*	*	***	Both
Standard processing time per job		*	*	***	Both
Human resources sector					
Hiring delay				*	Both
Job arrival smoothing time				*	Internal
Staff replacement delay					Internal
Time in organisation					Both
Finance sector					
Average contractor job costs				**	External
Average salary				***	Both
Discount rate					Both
Equipment charge per person				*	External
Materials cost per unit				***	External
Other overheads				***	Both
Tax rate				*	External

(1) The detailed results from the sensitivity tests (plus 10% changes only) are provided in Case table 5.2. Relative job time is regarded as an operational performance measure; relative price ratio and market share are marketing measures; operations staff is treated as an operational and HR performance measure; and operating margin and net present value are regarded as financial measures. The key used to indicate how sensitive the performance measures are to plus or minus 10% changes to the input parameters or graphical relationships are:

*	=	sensitive	(5%–14%)
**	=	very sensitive	(15%–34%)
***	=	highly sensitive	(over 35%)

(2) Parameters are classified according to the extent to which they are subject to the control of TBU management:

internal	=	generally controlled by management
external	=	outside management's direct control
both	=	influenced both by management and by external factors.

Policy analysis

In the previous section, sensitivity tests were undertaken by varying each parameter and graphical relationship one at a time, by plus and minus 10%, and holding all the other parameters constant at their base case values. Hence there were 22 experiments, with the sensitivity tests for plus 10% changes summarised in Case table 5.2. To give an idea of the complexity involved in analysing a model of this size – if each parameter were varied with one other parameter, then there would be:

$$22 * 21 = 462 \text{ possible model experiments.}$$

However, if three parameters were varied together each time, then there would be:

$$22 * 21 * 20 = 9240 \text{ possible model experiments!}$$

This does not include possible combinations also involving structural changes to the model. Hence we need a 'systematic' way of structuring experiments in this model. This is what we are proposing here. Firstly, we need to remind ourselves of the purpose of this modelling work. As discussed in the introduction (p. 210), this systems thinking and modelling intervention is concerned with the following strategic issues identified by TBU's management:

1 how to stop the decline in TBU's market share;
2 how to stop TBU's average job time increasing relative to its competitors';
3 how to stop the falling average real prices received per job.

These issues provide the focus for the policy/strategic analysis in this case. However, it is convenient at this point to remind ourselves about how we define policy and strategy in terms of a systems thinking and modelling intervention.

> *Policy* refers to single or localised changes to the policy parameters in the model or structural changes to the policy relationships.
>
> *Strategy* refers to multiple changes to policy parameters and structures to achieve the strategic objectives set by management.

Causal loop analysis

In the earlier analysis of the CLD for this case (see Case figure 5.3), we came to the conclusion that a key element in resolving these strategic issues is to speed up the overall job completion time. We shall focus our attention on designing policies and strategies to achieve this. We have already identified the sensitive parameters in the previous section.

Policy parameter analysis

From the analysis of the 22 parameters and graphical relationships (summarised in Case table 5.3), we notice that management has total control of only three of these parameters. However, management has some influence over another nine parameters, although for this influence to be felt, there may have to be some corresponding changes in other parts of the system (e.g. by introducing new linkages and structure to the model). A further ten parameters are external ones, that is, outside TBU management's control, and we shall subject these parameters to further analysis in the scenario analysis section of this case, where we will test the robustness of our proposed redesigned policies and strategies to a range of alternative futures.

Structural changes to policies

We shall undertake a number of structural changes to the policies in the base case. These include redesigning the 'job arrivals' rate; restructuring elements of the hiring policy, and introducing behavioural linkages between the level of work intensity and the average time that staff members stay in the organisation.

● Policy experiment 1: (redesigned 'job arrivals' rate)

In the base case the job arrival rate was connected directly to the variable 'potential market' (see Case figure 5.5). However, what this indicated was that new jobs were still being accepted while the backlog queue was getting larger and larger. In this policy experiment we decided to restrict the arrival of new jobs, so that the backlog is controlled at a desired level. The desired level would depend on the cover required; in this case we agreed that one month's cover (i.e. work in backlog) would be acceptable. We also included information about the average job starts into this redesigned policy to smooth out arrivals to the current capacity to start new jobs. The stock flow diagram for this policy is provided in Case figure 5.15 on the following page, and the new equations are also provided below.

New equations for job arrivals rate:

Job_arrivals = Min(Potential_market, gap_in_desired_backlog/Time_to_correct_backlog +ave_job_starts) {jobs / month}

gap_in_desired_backlog = Desired_jobs_backlog-Jobs_in_backlog {jobs}

Desired_jobs_backlog = Potential_market*backlog_cover {jobs}

backlog_cover = 1 {months}

Time_to_correct_backlog = 2 {months}

ave_job_starts = SMTH3(Job_starts,3) {jobs/month}

The model behaviour for main variables for this policy experiment are provided in Case figure 5.16, and the final values (in month 60 of the simulation run) for a range of performance measures are summarised in Case table 5.5 on p. 245. Although TBU's market share has dropped to about 20% compared with 23% in the base case, TBU's overall performance has improved with higher real prices and faster job completion times than in the base case. However, the performance of TBU is still below the industry average, and the final gross margin of 4.4% is still relatively low for this industry.

Case figure 5.15   Stock flow diagram for the redesigned job arrivals rate

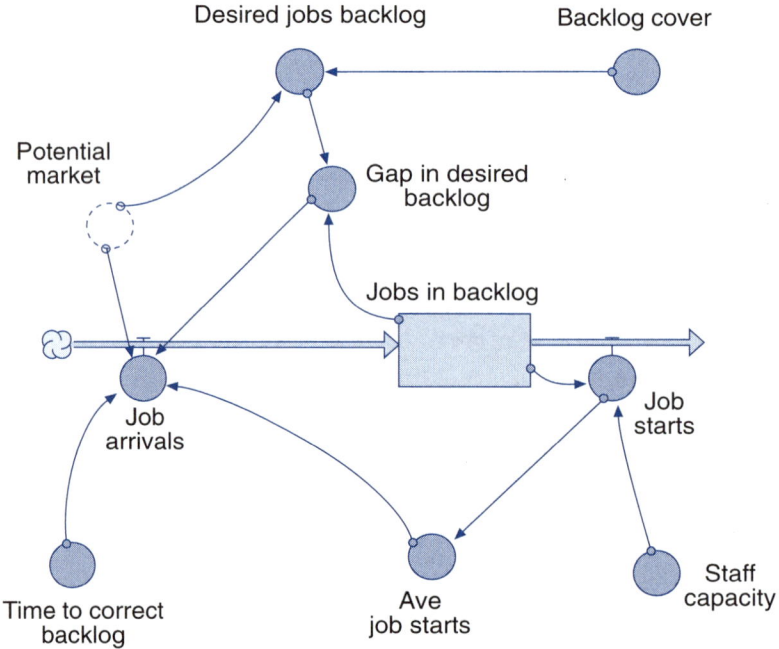

Case figure 5.16   Model behaviour for policy experiment 1 (redesigned job arrival rate)

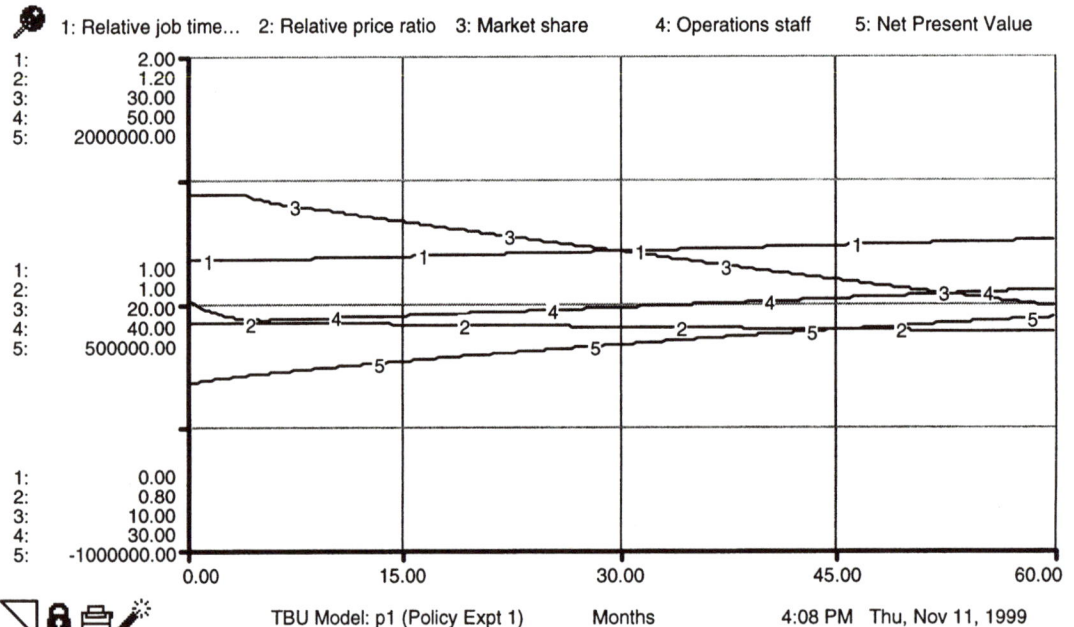

1: Relative job time...   2: Relative price ratio   3: Market share   4: Operations staff   5: Net Present Value

1:	2.00
2:	1.20
3:	30.00
4:	50.00
5:	2000000.00

1:	1.00
2:	1.00
3:	20.00
4:	40.00
5:	500000.00

1:	0.00
2:	0.80
3:	10.00
4:	30.00
5:	-1000000.00

TBU Model: p1 (Policy Expt 1)   Months   4:08 PM   Thu, Nov 11, 1999

● Policy experiment 2: (redesigned hiring policy)

In the previous policy experiment, we altered the relationships between 'job arrivals' and the 'potential market'. The redesigned 'job arrivals' policy effectively restricted the acceptance of new job orders based on current capacity. However, in the base case the hiring decision was based on a comparison of desired staff numbers with actual operating staff. The desired staff numbers were based on the smoothed job arrival rate. Clearly this would limit growth in the business in the longer term, so in this policy experiment we decided to base the desired staff numbers on the smoothed potential job arrivals (called 'potential market' in the model). The redesigned equations are:

Desired_Ops_staff = Ave_potential_job_arrivals/Productivity_per_person {persons}

Ave_potential_job_arrivals = SMTH3(Potential_market, potential_market_smoothing_time) {jobs / month}

potential_market_smoothing_time = 4 {months}

However, if we run the model with just this change to the base case, we get exactly the same results as in the base case, because 'job arrivals' equals 'potential market' in the base case. So for this experiment we combine the changes suggested above for the 'desired operations staff' with the redesigned 'job arrivals' rate in policy experiment 1. The graphical results of the main variables are shown in Case figure 5.17, and the end values (month 60) for a range of performance measures are provided in Case table 5.5 on p. 245. As can be seen, there are further improvements to the base case, and the relative job completion time does not deteriorate any further over the simulation run. All the performance measures show a considerable improvement and the gross margin has now climbed to a more respectable 7.5% by the end of the five-year planning horizon.

Case figure 5.17 Model behaviour for policy experiment 2 (redesigned hiring policy)

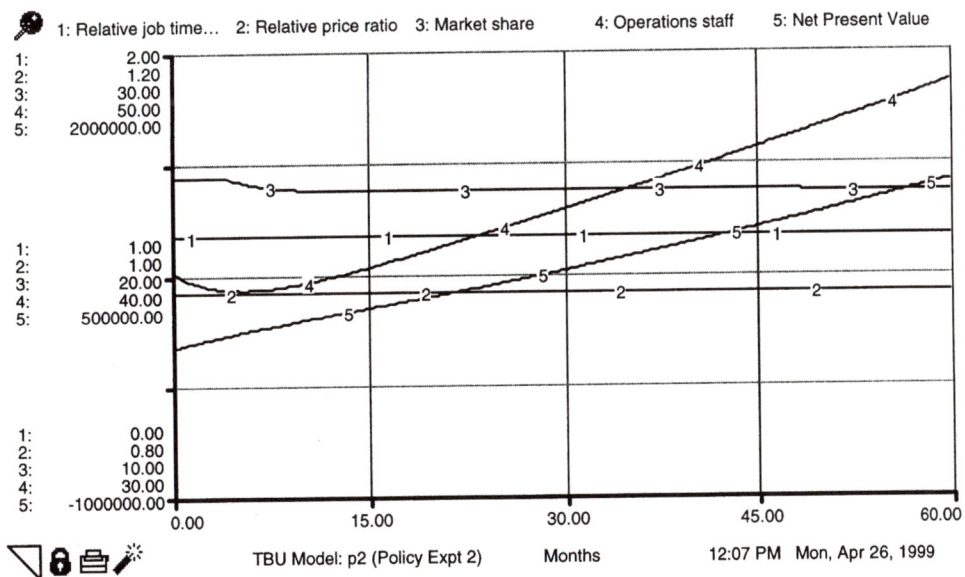

● Policy experiment 3: (restructured response to work intensity)

In this experiment we consider the effects of establishing a behavioural (soft) link between the level of 'work intensity' and staff members' decision to leave the organisation voluntarily (the variable 'time in organisation' in the model). We assume that the greater percentage of time that staff members have to spend on revenue-generating work for TBU, without additional compensation or bonus payments, will result in a reduction of morale and that staff will leave the organisation earlier. The greater percentage of time spent on direct revenue-generating work means that staff members will have less time for professional development, training, and other indirect work-related activities. This relationship is illustrated in Case figure 5.18.

Case figure 5.18   Input relationship between 'work intensity' and 'time in organisation'

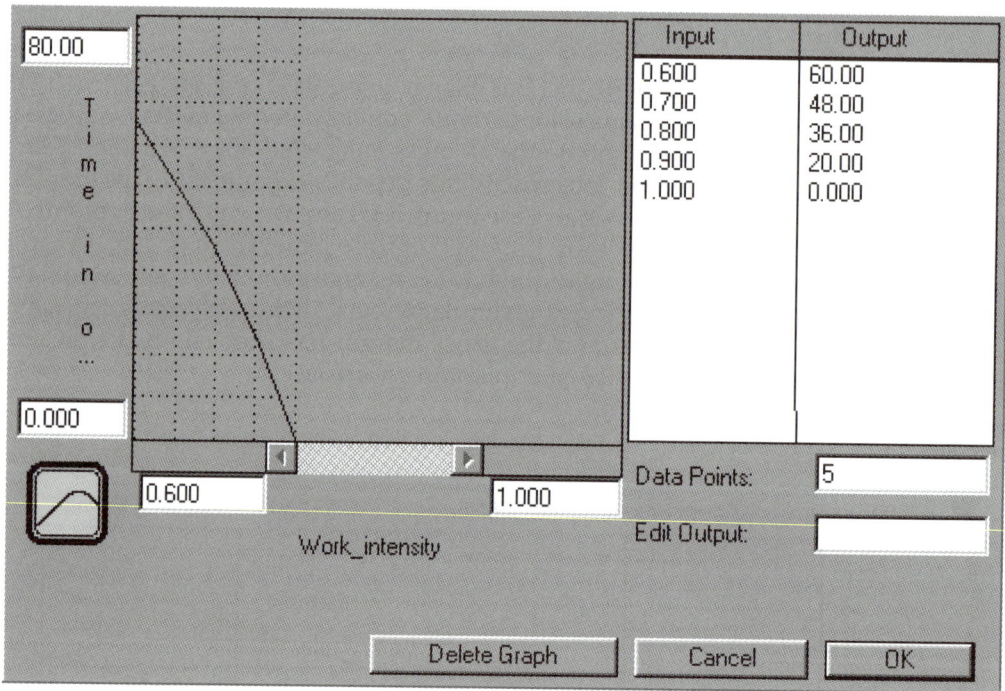

We also make 'work intensity' a graphical relationship, with TIME (i.e. the simulation parameter) as the independent variable. In this policy experiment we set 'work intensity' equal to 90% (or 0.9 if expressed as a decimal fraction) for the entire simulation run, as illustrated in Case figure 5.19.

In this experiment, we keep all the other parameter values and relationships the same as they were in the base case. The behaviour of the main variables is shown in Case figure 5.20, and the final values of the performance measures are provided in Case table 5.5. The main results for this policy experiment are similar to those of the base case, except that there are five fewer staff members at the end of the planning period (five years), and that the gross margin and NPV are considerably higher. However, we do observe one

Case figure 5.19   Input values for 'work intensity' as a function of 'TIME'

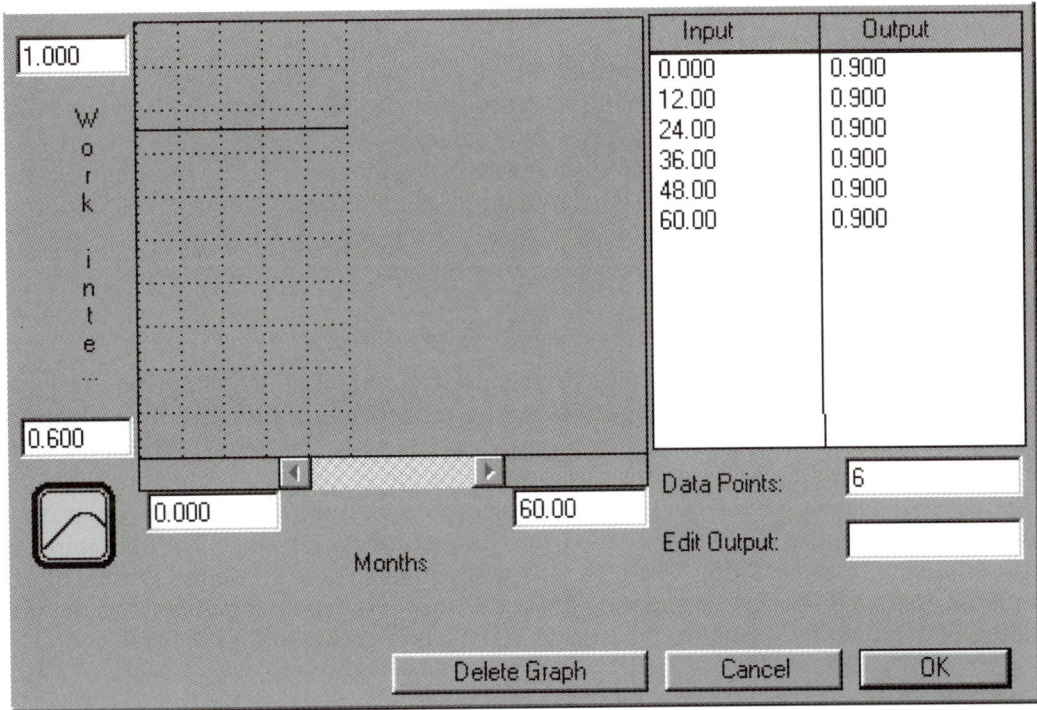

Input	Output
0.000	0.900
12.00	0.900
24.00	0.900
36.00	0.900
48.00	0.900
60.00	0.900

1.000

Work inte...

0.600

0.000   60.00

Months

Data Points: 6

Edit Output:

Delete Graph   Cancel   OK

Case figure 5.20   Model behaviour for policy experiment 3 (work intensity = 90%)

1: Relative job time...   2: Relative price ratio   3: Market share   4: Operations staff   5: Net Present Value

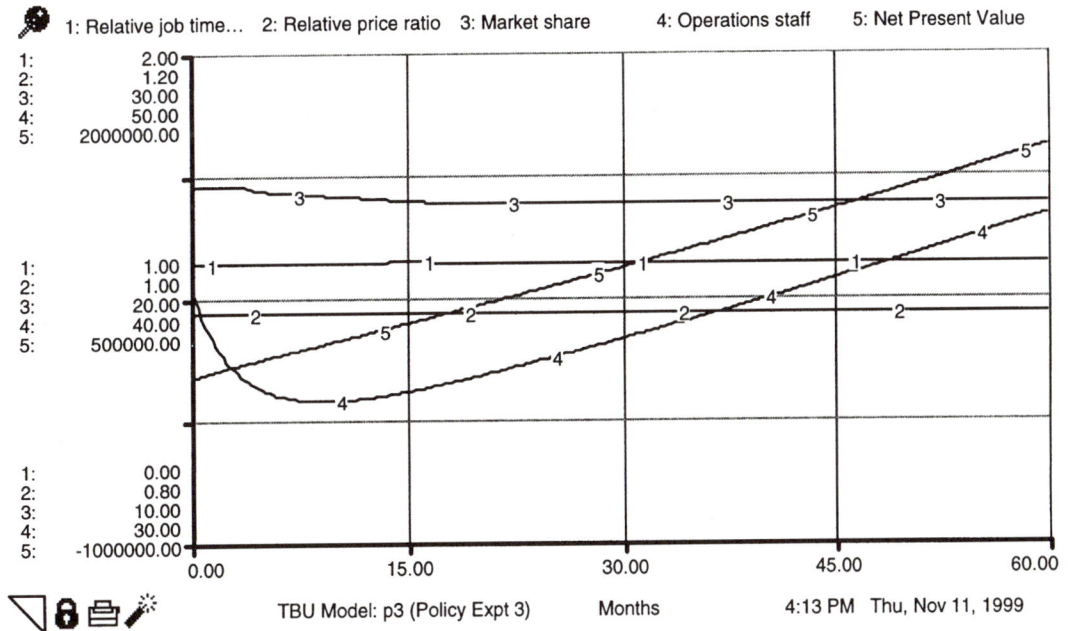

1:	2.00
2:	1.20
3:	30.00
4:	50.00
5:	2000000.00

1:	1.00
2:	1.00
3:	20.00
4:	40.00
5:	500000.00

1:	0.00
2:	0.80
3:	10.00
4:	30.00
5:	-1000000.00

0.00   15.00   30.00   45.00   60.00

TBU Model: p3 (Policy Expt 3)   Months   4:13 PM   Thu, Nov 11, 1999

important difference – the average time staff spend in the organisation has now plummeted to 20 months, compared with 36 months in the base case. This also draws attention to one of our original assumptions with this model, namely that there would be an ample supply of qualified staff to fill positions in TBU as such positions become vacant. In view of the HR polices outlined in this experiment, it is very questionable whether skilled staff would be prepared to work for TBU at the prevailing salary level.

We are now ready to consider some alternative strategies for TBU, by bringing together some of the policies outlined here with different combinations of some of the important policy parameters.

Strategy development

Strategies in a system dynamics study are regarded as combinations of policies designed to address strategic issues and objectives set by management. Based on the sensitivity tests and the design of policies in the preceding sections, we developed three alternative strategies for evaluation. These are summarised in the strategy development matrix in Case table 5.4. Names were given to these strategies to make them immediately recognisable by TBU management. They were called the 'base strategy' (strategy 1); 'tightening up ops' (strategy 2); and 'market boost' (strategy 3). Each of these strategies will be briefly outlined, followed by a graph showing the behaviour of the main variables, and the final values of the main performance measures will be summarised in Case table 5.5.

Case table 5.4   Strategy development matrix for TBU

Policy parameters under management control	Strategy 1 'base strategy'	Strategy 2 'tightening up ops'	Strategy 3 'market boost'
Target market share	25% each year	25% each year	25% initially, rising to 30% beginning of year 2, and returning to 25% from year 3
Other delays	1.25 mths	1 mth	1 mth
Work intensity	80% each year	82% each year	82% initially, rising to 85% beginning of year 2, and returning to 82% from year 3
Standard processing time per job	80 hrs	78 hrs	78 hrs
Hiring delay	3 mths	2.5 mths	2.5 mths
Staff replacement delay	4 mths	3 mths	3 mths
Average salary per month	$3750	$3960 (about + 5%)	$4100 (about + 10%)

Strategy 1 ('base strategy')

This strategy incorporates the structural changes to the policies outlined in the previous section, that is, the redesigned job arrivals rate, the redesigned hiring policy, and the behavioural response to increased work intensity by staff members. However, the parameter values in these restructured policies are assumed to be the same as in the base case, hence we called this strategy the 'base strategy'. The results indicate that the relative job times and relative prices remain the same over the simulation run, but that the market share and financial performance measures all show highly improved performances for TBU.

Case figure 5.21   Model behaviour for strategy 1 (base strategy)

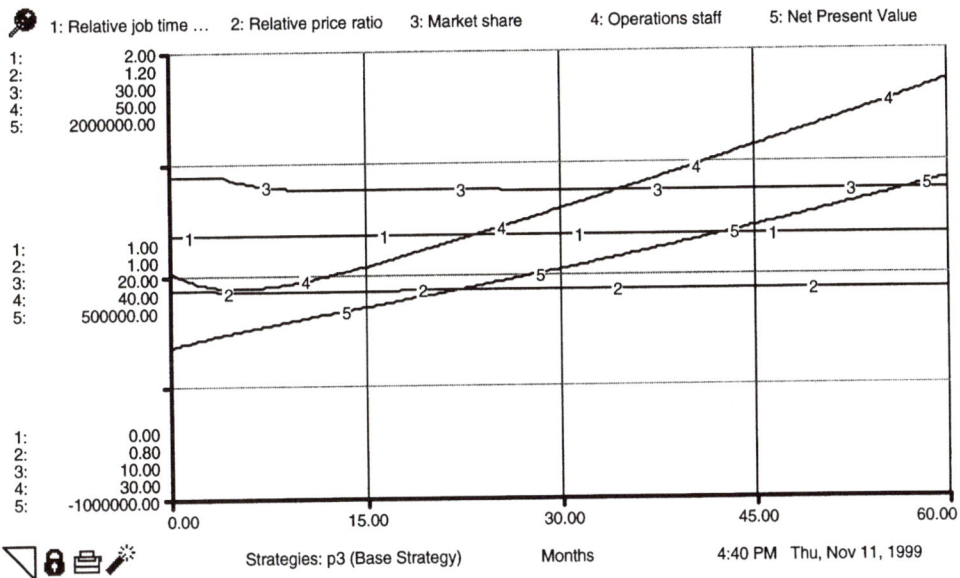

Strategy 2 ('tightening up ops')

This strategy also included the redesigned job arrivals rate, hiring policies and staff members' behavioural reactions to increased work pressure by management. In addition, this strategy included a general 'tightening up of operations'. This was done by shortening by 1/4 of a month the supply and regulatory delays in processing jobs, increasing the time staff members are actively employed on revenue-earning work by 2% throughout the simulation run, reducing the average time to process a job by two hours per job, reducing the hiring and staff replacement delays, and increasing the average salary per worker by about 5%.

The overall effect of this strategy was to improve the relative time to complete jobs by about 10% over the 5-year planning period, to improve relative prices compared with those of the base case, and to increase the gross margin to nearly 9% by the end of the period. This strategy generated the highest returns over the simulation run (measured in terms of net present value and gross margin).

Case figure 5.22   Model behaviour for strategy 2 (tightening up ops)

1: Relative job time ...   2: Relative price ratio   3: Market share   4: Operations staff   5: Net Present Value

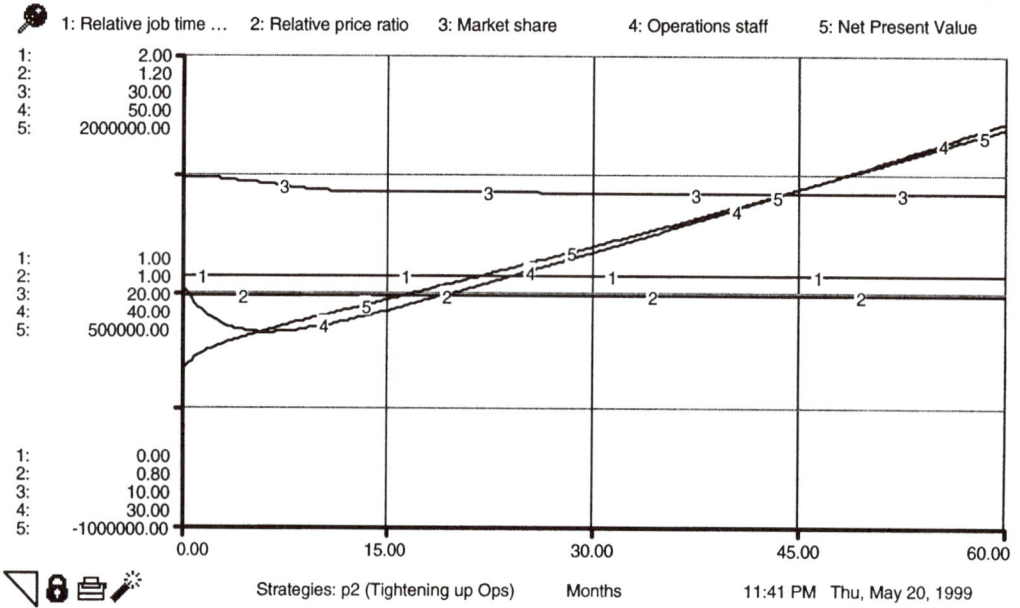

1:	2.00
2:	1.20
3:	30.00
4:	50.00
5:	2000000.00

1:	1.00
2:	1.00
3:	20.00
4:	40.00
5:	500000.00

1:	0.00
2:	0.80
3:	10.00
4:	30.00
5:	-1000000.00

Strategies: p2 (Tightening up Ops)   Months   11:41 PM Thu, May 20, 1999

Strategy 3 ('market boost')

Case figure 5.23   Model behaviour for strategy 3 (market boost)

1: Relative job time ...   2: Relative price ratio   3: Market share   4: Operations staff   5: Net Present Value

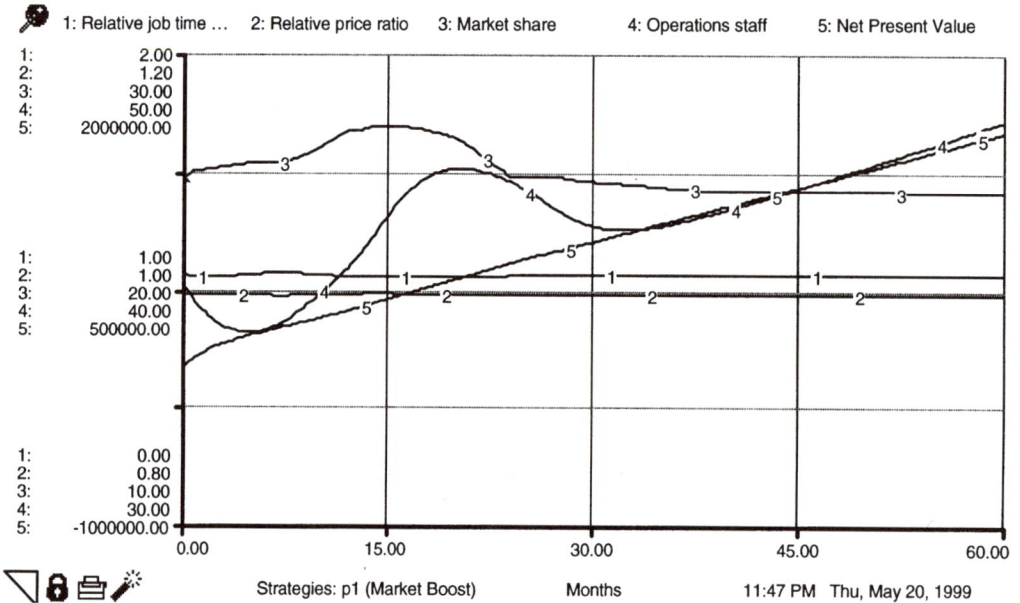

1:	2.00
2:	1.20
3:	30.00
4:	50.00
5:	2000000.00

1:	1.00
2:	1.00
3:	20.00
4:	40.00
5:	500000.00

1:	0.00
2:	0.80
3:	10.00
4:	30.00
5:	-1000000.00

Strategies: p1 (Market Boost)   Months   11:47 PM Thu, May 20, 1999

This strategy was very similar to strategy 2, except that we assumed there would be an effort to 'boost the market' for TBU's services at the end of the first year. This involved an increase in the target market share to 30% by the beginning of the second year, increasing it from 25% in year 1, and returning to that level by the end of the second year. We also assumed that the percentage of time staff members spent on revenue-earning work would show a similar pattern, to keep up with the extra work generated.

The results of this experiment are similar overall to those obtained in strategy 2, except that the gross margin and NPV are slightly lower over the simulation period, due mainly to the 5% extra salary costs assumed per staff member, to keep them in the organisation. The average time staff stays with TBU drops about 10% over the 5-year period, due mainly to the extra work intensity expected of staff.

Case table 5.5   Summarised results for the policy and strategy experiments

Model Experiment	Relative job time ratio	Relative price ratio	Market share (%)	Operations staff (no.)	Gross margin (%)	Net present value ($000)	Time in TBU (mths)
Initial values (month 0) Base case	1.17	0.98	24.4	40	5.0	0	36
Final values (month 60) Base case	1.55	0.94	22.8	46	3.1	728	36
Policy expt 1	1.25	0.98	19.8	41	4.4	846	36
Policy expt 2	1.17	0.98	23.7	49	7.5	1118	36
Policy expt 3	1.51	0.95	23.0	41	7.0	1490	20
Strategy 1	1.17	0.98	23.7	49	7.5	1118	36
Strategy 2	1.05	0.99	24.1	47	8.9	1531	32.8
Strategy 3	1.05	0.99	24.1	47	8.0	1496	32.8

Scenario analysis

In this section we present a range of scenarios for the TBU strategy case and then test the redesigned strategies against these alternative futures (i.e. scenarios). The approach we use is based on the method outlined by Schoemaker (1995) and discussed in Chapter 5 (and summarised in Table 5.1 on p. 85). Initially we indicate the scope of the major uncertainties that could have an impact on the TBU, then we present two 'forced' scenarios. These form the basis for the 'learning' scenarios, which we analyse with the dynamic simulation model to test the robustness of our redesigned strategies.

Uncertainties

There are a large number of uncertainties that could have an impact on the future of the TBU. These include the factors summarised in Case table 5.6.

Case table 5.6   Factors potentially affecting the future of TBU

Market factors
- Market – stagnation and decline, slow growth, rapid growth
- Competitors – major new competitors, some competitors departing
- Technological changes in market – nature of telecommunications greatly different, remains the same
- Prices – remain constant in real terms, declining

Operations factors
- Operations – big changes in delays (logistic, workers, regulatory authorities, etc.) – improvements and deterioration in relationships causing increased or decreased delays.
- Technological changes in equipment used – no change, substantial changes
- Equipment – continue leasing from market, purchase own equipment

Human relations factors
- Skilled labour availability – short supply (takes longer to hire), oversupply (short hire delay)
- Labour relations – greatly improved (staff stay longer, higher productivity), deterioration over time
- Labour compensation packages – linked to productivity changes, linked to oversupply/ undersupply of labour in market

Finance factors
- Costs – big changes in contractor costs, or materials costs, or other overhead costs
- Discount rate – changes in cost of loan money or equity capital
- Tax rate – increase or decreases in taxes

However, to undertake scenario analysis, we cannot consider every possible change that may take place in the future. Instead, we need to identify the changes that are likely to happen, or could have the biggest impact on the organisation (i.e. the TBU). Also we need to consider the variables, parameters and factors that are most uncertain, or are most important to the organisation.

⬛ Forced scenarios

Having identified a range of uncertainties and factors that could have an impact on the TBU, the project team then developed the forced scenarios which are summarised in Case table 5.7. The base case was taken as the 'surprise-free' scenario, and all the negative external parameter changes were 'dumped' into the 'pessimistic' scenario and all the positive external changes to the parameters were 'dumped' into the optimistic scenario.

The 'surprise-free' scenario is the one based on the existing model parameters that TBU management expected would continue into the future (i.e. the 'business as usual' scenario). These forced scenarios then needed to be checked for internal consistency and some extra research was necessary to determine realistic boundary values for the parameters and graphical relationships, so that 'learning' scenarios could be developed.

Case table 5.7   Forced scenarios for the TBU strategy case

	Major influence	Forced scenarios	
		Pessimistic	Optimistic
Market sector			
Industry price per job	External	-15%	+10%
Market growth rate	External	0%	+10%
Target market share	Internal	Decline to 20%	Increase to 30%
Price effect on market share	External	Deteriorate by 20%	Improve by 10%
Quality effect on market share	External	Deteriorate by 25%	Improve by 10%
Quality effect on price	External	Deteriorate by 20%	Improve by 10%
Operations sector			
Industry job completion time	External	-15%	+10%
Other delays	Both	+25%	-20%
Human resources sector			
Hiring delay	Both	+25%	-25%
Time in organisation	Both	-25%	+25%
Finance sector			
Average contractor job costs	External	+10%	-10%
Average salary	Both	+5%	-5%
Discount rate	Both	13%	7%
Equipment charge per person	External	+15%	-15%
Materials cost per unit	External	+10%	-10%
Other overheads	Both	+10%	-10%
Tax rate	External	40%	25%

We discussed these forced scenarios with TBU management and realised that there were some inconsistencies and some assumptions that were most unlikely to occur, or would affect the whole industry so the TBU would be no better off. This lead to the development of the 'learning scenarios' against which the new redesigned policies and strategies could be tested.

Learning scenarios

A number of the combinations included under the positive and pessimistic scenarios were not logically consistent. For example, the assumption that costs would decrease by between 10 and 20%, while the market is growing at 10% p.a., is probably not consistent with economic logic. An increase in demand for the final product or service is likely to result in an increase in the demand for the factor inputs and cause costs to rise rather than fall, unless there are some other compensating changes.

Similarly, TBU management was of the opinion that it was unlikely there would be any significant changes in the tax rate over the next five years, and most of the costs were expected to remain at about the same level. Some of the ranges for the parameter changes shown in the forced scenarios were also considered rather extreme.

Finally we generated some 'learning scenarios' for testing our strategies for TBU. These are summarised in Case table 5.8. We considered three scenarios: base case (i.e. 'business as usual'); 'bleak outlook' (a combination of 'consistent' negative parameters in the external environment); and a 'rosy picture' scenario (based on a feasible combination of positive factors that could occur in the external environment).

Case table 5.8   Learning scenarios for the TBU strategy case[9]

External parameter or behavioural relationship	Base case scenario	'Bleak outlook' scenario	'Rosy picture' scenario
Industry price per job	$10 000	$9500	$10 300
Market growth rate	5% p.a.	2% p.a.	8% p.a.
Price effect on market share	1.5/1.25/1/0.6/0.1	1.2/1.1/1/0.4/0.05	1.6/1.3/1/0.7/0.2
Quality effect on market share	1.2/1.1/1/0.9/0.8	1.1/1.05/1/0.8/0.6	1.3/1.15/1/0.95/0.9
Quality effect on price	1.1/1.05/1/0.95/0.9	1.05/1.025/1/0.8/0.6	1.2/1.1/1/0.975/0.95
Industry job completion time	2.5 mths	2.2 mths	2.8 mths
Time in organisation[10] (mths)	60/48/36/20/0	45/36/27/15/0	75/60/45/25/0

We inputted each of these scenarios into the model using the control panel features of the *ithink* computer simulation software, and tested each strategy against the scenarios. The results of these scenario tests are presented in Case table 5.9.

Case table 5.9 Selected results of the 'learning' scenario tests

Strategy	Base case scenario	'Bleak outlook' scenario	'Rosy picture' scenario
Relative job time ratio			
1 'Base case'	1.17	1.33	1.04
2 'Tightening up ops'	1.05	1.20	0.94
3 'Market boost'	1.05	1.20	0.94
Relative price ratio			
1 'Base case'	0.98	0.87	1.00
2 'Tightening up ops'	0.99	0.92	1.01
3 'Market boost'	0.99	0.92	1.01
Market share (%)			
1 'Base case'	23.7	22.1	23.8
2 'Tightening up ops'	24.1	23.1	24.2
3 'Market boost'	24.1	23.1	24.2
Net present value ($m)			
1 'Base case'	1.12	0	2.35
2 'Tightening up ops'	1.53	0.30	2.87
3 'Market boost'	1.50	0.20	2.88

This analysis indicates that strategy 2 (tightening up ops) and strategy 3 (market boost) are equally robust, when the alternative plausible future scenarios are taken into consideration. Both strategies perform about the same and they are better than the base case strategy under each of the performance measures, i.e. lower relative job times; higher relative price ratio; and greater market share. However, strategy 2 has a slightly higher net present value (NPV) for the base case and bleak outlook scenarios, whereas Strategy 3 performs slightly better from a financial point of view for the rosy picture scenario. Overall, strategies 2 and 3 do help TBU's management address the strategic issues that were outlined at the beginning of this case:

- how to stop the decline in TBU's market share;
- how to stop TBU's average job time increasing relative to that of their competitors;
- how to stop the falling average real prices received per job.

The systems thinking and strategic modelling approach outlined in this case provided considerable insights and learning for the whole TBU project team, including the managers from the TBU and the strategy support staff from the head office holding company. Subsequent to this analysis, the management of the TBU requested additional work – developing the model to consider these issues in more depth, as well as other strategic issues that the TBU was facing.

Technical appendix: Equations for the TBU strategy model

Finance sector

Cash(t) = Cash(t – dt) + (Revenues – Cash_outlflow) * dt

INIT Cash = 0 {$}

DOCUMENT: Cash accumulated during the simulation run (planning horizon). Note that it is assumed that there are no interest payments on overdraft balances or interest receipts on cash held, since the purpose of this case is to analyse the operational performance of the business unit, not the funds management performance of the finance manager.

INFLOWS:

Revenues = Job_completions*Price_per_job {$/month}

DOCUMENT: The revenues collected each month based on the jobs completed multiplied by the average price per job. It is assumed that all revenues are received in cash when the jobs are completed.

OUTFLOWS:

Cash_outlflow = Operating_costs+Taxes {$/month}

DOCUMENT: The total cash outflow each month is the sum of the operating costs plus taxes paid.

Ave_contractor_job_costs = 900 {$/job}

DOCUMENT: These are costs which are incurred by sub-contractors in delivering services. They are estimated on the basis of the 'average' job.

Ave_salary = 3750 {$/person/month}

DOCUMENT: Average monthly employment cost of a front-level staff member directly involved with processing jobs (based on an annual cost of $45 000).

Contractor_costs = Ave_contractor_job_costs*Job_completions {$/month}

DOCUMENT: The total cost of work sub-contracted each month.

Discount_rate = 0.10 {fraction/year}

DOCUMENT: The real weighted average cost of capital for the organisation. The annual discount rate is expressed as a decimal fraction, e.g. 10% is expressed as 0.10.

Equipment_charge_per_person = 500 {$/person/month}

DOCUMENT: The equipment required for processing jobs is assumed not to be owned by the business unit, instead it is assumed to be rented and available to meet the business unit's need. This cost is assumed to be variable, and expressed as a charge per direct staff persons involved in processing jobs.

Equipment_rentals = Operations_staff*Equipment_charge_per_person {$/month}

DOCUMENT: The total costs of equipment rented by the business unit each month.

Gross_margin = (Revenues-Operating_costs)/Revenues*100 {%}

DOCUMENT: Gross margin = revenue less operating costs as a percentage of revenue from jobs. This is an indicator of the financial performance of the business unit.

Labour_costs = Ave_salary * Operations_staff {$/month}

DOCUMENT: The total labour costs per month for operations staff involved in processing jobs.

Materials_cost_per_unit = 3800 {$/job}

DOCUMENT: Estimate of the costs of material inputs per job.

Material_costs = Materials_cost_per_unit*Job_starts {$/month}

DOCUMENT: The total material input costs per month.

Net_cash_flow = Revenues-Cash_outlflow {$/month}

DOCUMENT: Total revenues less costs and taxes per month (not including financial charges). This is the after tax net cash flow (cash surplus or deficit) generated by the business unit each month.

Net_Present_Value = NPV(Net_cash_flow, Discount_rate/12,0) {$/month}

DOCUMENT: The cumulated net present value of the net cash flow after taxes generated by the business unit, discounted by the weighted cost of capital for the organisation. This figure does not include financial charges or income, and is equivalent to the discounted sum of the monthly economic value added by the business unit. The annual discount rate is divided by 12 to give the monthly equivalent rate.

Operating_costs =
Contractor_costs+Equipment_rentals+Labour_costs+Material_costs+Other_overheads {$/month}

DOCUMENT: The total monthly costs related to the business unit's job processing business.

Other_overheads = 108250 {$/month}

DOCUMENT: Base monthly value for overheads, office and building rentals, support staff and other operating costs after deducting direct labour, materials and contractors costs. This monthly figure an be adjusted for other overhead changes, such as advertising.

Taxes = MAX(0, Tax_rate*(Revenues-Operating_costs)) {$/month}

DOCUMENT: The MAX functions ensures that taxes only get paid if operating net cash flow is positive. Taxes are assumed to be paid on a monthly basis, when the revenues are received and costs paid.

Tax_rate = 0.33 {fraction}

DOCUMENT: Assuming a marginal tax rate of 33c in the dollar, expressed as a decimal fraction.

Human resources sector

Operations_staff(t) = Operations_staff(t – dt) + (Staff_hiring – Staff_leaving) * dt

INIT Operations_staff = 40 {persons}

DOCUMENT: Operations staff numbers involved in processing jobs, i.e. in planning, designing and undertaking the installation and repair of telecommunications connections, etc.

INFLOWS:

Staff_hiring = Gap_in_staff_numbers/Hiring_delay+Staff_replacements {persons/month}

DOCUMENT: The number of people hired or fired each month, including replacements of staff leaving as a result of attrition. This variable is modelled as a biflow, i.e. a negative quantity indicates that staff are being fired.

OUTFLOWS:

Staff_leaving = Operations_staff/Time_in_organisation {people/month}

DOCUMENT: The natural rate of people voluntarily leaving the organisation each month.

Ave_job_arrivals = SMTH3(Job_arrivals, Job_arrivals_smoothing_time) {jobs/month}

DOCUMENT: The job arrivals rate averaged out over a few months (i.e. by the job arrivals smoothing time).

Desired_Ops_staff = Ave_job_arrivals/Productivity_per_person {persons}

DOCUMENT: The desired number of operations processing staff based on the average workload and the productivity per person.

Gap_in_staff_numbers = Desired_Ops_staff-Operations_staff {persons}

DOCUMENT: The difference between the desired and actual number of direct processing staff.

Hiring_delay = 3 {months}

DOCUMENT: Time in months to recruit new staff or to fire existing staff.

Job_arrivals_smoothing_time = 4 {months}

DOCUMENT: The averaging time selected to smooth out job arrivals.

Staff_replacements = SMTH3(Staff_leaving, Staff_replacements_delay) {persons/month}

DOCUMENT: Staff replacements are based on the average of the last few months' voluntary attrition rate. The averaging time is set by the replacements delay.

Staff_replacements_delay = 4 {months}

DOCUMENT: The averaging (delay) time selected to replace staff leaving by attrition.

Time_in_organisation = 36 {months}

DOCUMENT: The average time an employee stays with the organisation before leaving, without being fired. {months}

Market sector

Total_market(t) = Total_market(t – dt) + (Change_in_market_size) * dt

INIT Total_market = 240 {jobs/month}

DOCUMENT: Total number of jobs in the market per month, related to the planning, designing and undertaking the installation and repair of telecommunications connections, etc.

INFLOWS:

Change_in_market_size = Total_market*Market_growth_rate/12 {jobs/month/month}

Industry_price_per_job = 10000 {$/job}

DOCUMENT: The standard industry price per job is $10 000, but the business unit was only receiving an average price below this at the beginning of the simulation run.

Market_growth_rate =.05 {fraction/year}

DOCUMENT: Assumed to depend on the economy, substitutes, technology change, etc. Annual growth rate is expressed as a decimal fraction, e.g. 5% is expressed as 0.05.

Market_share = Job_arrivals/Total_market*100 {%}

DOCUMENT: This is the actual market share gained by the TBU. It is measured as the ratio of job arrivals to the total market size, expressed as a percentage.

Potential_market = Total_market*Potential_Market_share/100 {jobs/month}

DOCUMENT: The total number of jobs per month that the business unit could bid for = total market size less share where 'customer needs are not addressed' or customers are 'captive to other vendors' or those customers that 'do not buy from us'.

Potential_Market_share = min(100, Target_market_share*Quality_effect_on_market_share*Price_effect_on_market_share) {%}

DOCUMENT: The business unit's potential market share is the minimum of 1 (100%) or the business unit's target market share adjusted for the price and quality effects.

Price_per_job = Industry_price_per_job*Quality_effect_on_price {$/job}

DOCUMENT: Actual price per job received by the business unit for an 'average' job.

Relative_price_ratio = Price_per_job/Industry_price_per_job {dimensionless}

DOCUMENT: The ratio of the business unit's average price per job to the standard industry average price per job.

Price_effect_on_market_share = GRAPH(Relative_price_ratio)

(0.00, 1.50), (0.5, 1.25), (1.00, 1.00), (1.50, 0.6), (2.00, 0.1)

DOCUMENT: This is based on the price elasticity of demand or the sensitivity of the quantity of a service/product desired by the market depending on the price relative to competitors' prices after adjustments have been made for relative quality, etc. For example, a lower price relative to competitors' (i.e. the industry average) will result in an increase in market share and a higher price, relative to competitors', will result in a reduction in market share. {dimensionless}

Quality_effect_on_market_share = GRAPH(Relative_job_time_ratio)

(0.00, 1.20), (0.5, 1.10), (1.00, 1.00), (1.50, 0.9), (2.00, 0.8)

DOCUMENT: The effect of the organisation's quality relative to competitors' on market share. Here the relative job completion time is regarded as the indicator of quality. The faster the jobs are completed by the organisation relative to the industry, the greater the market share. {dimensionless}

Quality_effect_on_price = GRAPH(Relative_job_time_ratio)

(0.00, 1.10), (0.5, 1.05), (1.00, 1.00), (1.50, 0.95), (2.00, 0.9)

DOCUMENT: The effect of the organisation's quality relative to competitors on price. Here the relative job completion time is regarded as the indicator of quality. A faster job completion relative to industry indicates that the organisation can charge a higher price. {dimensionless}

Target_market_share = GRAPH(TIME)

(0.00, 25.0), (12.0, 25.0), (24.0, 25.0), (36.0, 25.0), (48.0, 25.0), (60.0, 25.0)

DOCUMENT: The 'target market share' is the percentage of the total market that the organisation can expect to gain under 'normal' circumstances (i.e. if operating with the same quality and prices as the 'industry average'. Percentages are inputted into the graph for the beginning of each 12-month period. This graph provides the facility to examine the impact of exogenous changes on market share. For example, by either taking over a major competitor's business, or moving into a new market (either in New Zealand or overseas). {%}

Operations sector

Jobs_in_backlog(t) = Jobs_in_backlog(t – dt) + (Job_arrivals – Job_starts) * dt

INIT Jobs_in_backlog = 60 {jobs}

DOCUMENT: Orders for 'average' jobs from the market already accepted by the business unit.

INFLOWS:

Job_arrivals = Potential_market {jobs/month}

DOCUMENT: Job arrivals per month are assumed to be equivalent to the business unit's market size.

OUTFLOWS:

Job_starts = MIN(Staff_capacity,Jobs_in_backlog) {jobs/month}

DOCUMENT: The number of jobs started each month is the lower of the staff capacity or the number of jobs in the backlog awaiting commencement.

Jobs_in_process(t) = Jobs_in_process(t – dt) + (Job_starts – Job_completions) * dt

INIT Jobs_in_process = 115 {jobs}

INFLOWS:

Job_starts = MIN(Staff_capacity,Jobs_in_backlog) {jobs/month}

DOCUMENT: The number of jobs started each month is the lower of the staff capacity or the number of jobs in the backlog awaiting commencement.

OUTFLOWS:

Job_completions = Jobs_in_process/(Ave_process_time+Other_delays) {jobs/month}

DOCUMENT: Job completions depend on the number of jobs being processed and the total processing time plus other delays, including regualtory and supply delays, and staff stoppages, etc. An increase in delays will slow down the rate of job completions and vice versa.

Ave_backlog_time = Jobs_in_backlog/Job_starts {months}

DOCUMENT: The average time the jobs are held up in the backlog before they are started.

Ave_completion_time = Ave_process_time+Other_delays+Ave_backlog_time {months}

DOCUMENT: Average time from arrival to completion of jobs by the organisation.

Ave_process_time = 1/Productivity_per_person {months}

DOCUMENT: The actual time that operations staff spend working on an 'average' job.

Hours_available_per_person = 150 {hours/person/month}

DOCUMENT: The average hours available per person per month, assuming each person works on average 37.5 hours per week for 48 weeks per year = 1800 hours p.a. (assuming four weeks of annual holiday per year, including statutory holidays).

Industry_job_completion_time = 2.5 {months/job}

DOCUMENT: This is the expected time to complete a job under normal industry conditions. This is measured in months per job.

Other_delays = 1.25 {months}

DOCUMENT: Internal decision and process delays in process. This includes material and logistics delays, unplanned stoppages, and regulatory delays. Regulatory delays, for example, are due to approvals required by local authorities, delays required by the Resource Management Act and other regulations. (In the base case, regulatory delays are assumed to be about three weeks or 0.75 months and the other delays are assumed to be about two weeks or 0.5 months.)

Productive_hours_per_person = Work_intensity*Hours_available_per_person {hours/person/month}

DOCUMENT: The average number of hours per month spent per person on productive revenue-generating work.

Productivity_per_person = Productive_hours_per_person/Standard_processing_time_per_job {jobs/month}

DOCUMENT: The average output per person per month measured in terms of jobs per month.

Relative_job_time_ratio = Ave_completion_time/Industry_job_completion_time {dimensionless}

DOCUMENT: The ratio of the organisation's average time to complete a job relative to the standard industry time is used as a surrogate quality index. A value of less than 1 indicates that the organisation is more efficient than the industry average and a value over 1 indicates that the organisation is operating at a less efficient level.

Staff_capacity = Productivity_per_person*Operations_staff {jobs/month}

DOCUMENT: Effective direct staff available to start jobs.

Standard_processing_time_per_job = 80 {hours/job}

DOCUMENT: Estimate of the actual time an operations staff member needs to spend working on the 'average' job to fully complete it.

Work_intensity = 0.8 {fraction}

DOCUMENT: The work intensity is defined as the average proportion of staff time engaged in productive revenue-earning work, expressed as a decimal fraction.

Notes

1 This case is adapted from a consultancy project outlined in Cavana and Hughes (1995).
2 The *ithink* Analyst software was used to develop the model in this case, outlined in Richmond and Petersen, 1997.
3 Research by Professor John Sterman at the Massachusetts Institute of Technology in the USA has shown that most people are only capable of analysing the implications of two or three feedback loops at the most before they start making incorrect assumptions about the dynamic behaviour generated by the loops. See Sterman, 1989 and Paich and Sterman, 1993.

4 For example, it is assumed that if TBU's price is lower than that of its competitors, this will increase TBU's market share, but if TBU's quality is perceived to be lower than that of its competitors, this will decrease TBU's market share.

5 For illustrative purposes we have used a 10% after tax weighted average cost of capital as the discount rate. This is slightly higher than the average rate Bevan Wallace considers appropriate for corporates in New Zealand: 'We therefore consider that the typical post-corporate tax discount rate for the pre-financing operating returns reflecting average business risk alone should be around 9%' (Wallace, 1999).

6 Coyle uses terminology that differs slightly from ours. For example, Coyle refers to 'influence diagrams', not 'causal loop diagrams', and uses the symbols '+' and '-', instead of 's' and 'o' on the links in these diagrams.

7 See Richmond and Peterson (1997) for details of 'pulse' and 'step' functions.

8 Only the results of the 10% increase in parameter and graphical values are shown in Case table 5.2. The sensitivity results for a 10% decrease were very similar in magnitude (absolute value), but in the other direction.

9 Refer to the technical appendix to this case for the model equations for these parameter and behaviour relationships in this table. An interpretation of the graphical functions is provided in the technical appendix to Chapter 4.

10 This is the graphical relationship shown in Case figure 5.18 and discussed under 'Policy experiment 3' on p. 240.

REFERENCES

Cavana, R.Y. and Hughes, R.D. (1995) 'Strategic Modelling for Competitive Advantage', *Proceedings of the 1995 International System Dynamics Conference*. Gakushuin University, Tokyo, Japan. July 30 – Aug 4, Vol II: 408–417.

Coyle, R.G. (1996) *System Dynamics Modelling: A Practical Approach*. Chapman and Hall, London.

Forrester, J.W. and Senge, P.M. (1980) Tests for building confidence in system dynamics models. *TIMS Studies in the Management Sciences* 14: 209–228.

Paich, M. and Sterman, J.D. (1993) Boom, bust, and failures to learn in experimental markets. *Management Science* 39(12): 1439–1458.

Richmond, B. and Peterson, S. (1997) *An Introduction to Systems Thinking*. High Performance Systems, Hanover.

Schoemaker, P.J.H. (1995) Scenario planning: a tool for strategic thinking. *Sloan Management Review*, Winter.

Sterman, J.D. (1989) Modeling managerial behaviour: misperceptions of feedback in a dynamic decision making experiment. *Management Science* 35(3): 321–339.

Wallace, B. (1999) Integrating Strategy and Finance – the financial analysts toolkit. Business Information in Action Conference, Auckland, 15–17 March.

Index